GENERAL SIR ARTHUR CURRIE:
A MILITARY BIOGRAPHY

Canadian War Museum
Historical Publication No. 22

A.M.J. HYATT

General Sir Arthur Currie:
A Military Biography

UNIVERSITY OF TORONTO PRESS
IN COLLABORATION WITH
CANADIAN WAR MUSEUM
CANADIAN MUSEUM OF CIVILIZATION
NATIONAL MUSEUMS OF CANADA

ISBN 0-8020-2603-6

Canadian Cataloguing in Publication Data

Hyatt, A.M.J., 1934–
  General Sir Arthur Currie
  (Historical publication / Canadian War Museum; no. 22)
  Includes bibliographical references and index.
  ISBN 0-8020-2603-6
  1. Currie, Arthur, Sir, 1875–1933. 2. Generals –
  Canada – Biography. 3. Canada. Canadian Army –
  Biography. 4. World War, 1914–1918 – Biography.
  I. Canadian War Museum. II. Title. III. Series:
  Historical publication (Canadian War Museum); no. 22.
  FC556.C8H93 1987   940.4′144′0924   C87-094734-6
  F1034.C8H93 1987

University of Toronto Press
Toronto Buffalo London
in collaboration with
Canadian War Museum
Canadian Museum of Civilization
National Museums of Canada
Printed in Canada

In the writing of this book the inferences drawn and the opinions expressed are those of the author himself, and the National Museums of Canada are in no way responsible for his presentation of the facts as stated.

The two photographs of Currie as a young man are used courtesy of Lucy C.M. Lewis; the rest are from the Public Archives of Canada.

This book has been published with the help of grants from the Social Science Federation of Canada, using funds provided by the Social Sciences and Humanities Research Council of Canada, and from the University of Western Ontario.

This book is dedicated to my teachers. In formal education, at all levels, I was lucky enough to have had at least one outstanding teacher. To the following I shall always be grateful.

Mr Glen Mitchell	Dr D.M. Schurman
Dr Richard A. Preston	Professor S.R. Mealing
Dr E. Cappadocia	Dr Theodore Ropp

My general education has benefited most from the persistent efforts of the best critic I have ever known, Barbara Hyatt.

Contents

viii Contents

Preface

I began to study Arthur Currie nearly two decades ago. At that time I quickly came to the conclusion that Currie was 'an unrecognized hero.' He was hardly mentioned in textbooks on Canadian history and was frequently misidentified. Happily this is no longer the case. The wide circulation of G.W.L. Nicholson's *Canadian Expeditionary Force*, the publication of books by J.A. Swettenham, Herbert Wood, Don Goodspeed, Jack Granatstein, and Desmond Morton has added enormously to our understanding of Canada's role in the First World War. Daniel G. Dancocks's biography of Arthur Currie provides a popular portrait of the general. Returning to Currie after a break of several years and after the appearance of these works, my view has changed. He is no longer unknown and is certainly not unrecognized. It now is also apparent to me that if he was a 'hero,' he was also a person with a fair share of human frailty. Sometimes stiff and awkward, Currie could also be petulant and vain. He obviously never enjoyed mass popularity with the soldiers he commanded, although he never lost their respect. In spite of the welcome and substantial writing that has appeared, there has been no detailed analysis of Currie's military capacity, which was his main contribution to Canadian history. What follows is an attempt to describe Currie as a soldier and to compare him with other soldiers.

Many years ago G.F.G. Stanley wrote *Canada's Soldiers* and through his brilliant subtitle, *The Military History of an Unmilitary People*, provided a fundamental insight into Canadian attitudes towards all things military. Currie's story, it could be argued, provides the pattern for an unmilitary general: he was a prewar and postwar civilian who loved the army and came to hate war. He instinctively developed the characteristics of a dedicated professional soldier without ever becoming one.

In writing about Currie I have learned a great deal from fellow historians. Writing may be a solitary endeavour, but scholarship is a collective process.

Without the work of Robert Craig Brown and Desmond Morton, my own attempt to understand Currie could not have been completed. Morton, more than anyone else, has made it possible for me to evaluate not only the political background of the Canadian Expeditionary Force, but the militia background of the nineteenth century. I owe him and many others an enormous debt. Theodore Ropp, Richard A. Preston, and C.P. Stacey have helped me over many years in my struggle to understand war and history. Ronald Haycock taught me much about Sam Hughes. Dr W.A.B. Douglas and his predecessors and their staffs at the Directorate of History in Ottawa have provided invaluable help, as have the staff at the Public Archives of Canada. Mr William Constable interrupted a busy schedule to produce the maps in this volume. I am extremely grateful to Mr Herb Ariss for allowing me to use his splendid pastel drawing of Currie. My colleagues at the University of Western Ontario have helped me with good advice over many years. I am particularly indebted to Professor Peter Neary and Professor George Metcalf. The errors and inconsistencies that remain in this account I have created myself.

Canadian War Museum historical publications

19 *1944: The Canadians in Normandy*, by Reginald H. Roy. Macmillan of Canada, Toronto, 1984. French edition available.

20 *Redcoats and Patriotes: The Rebellions in Lower Canada, 1837–38*, by Elinor Kyte Senior. Canada's Wings, Stittsville, Ontario, 1985. French edition available.

21 *Sam Hughes: The Public Career of a Controversial Canadian, 1885–1916*, by Ronald G. Haycock. Wilfrid Laurier University Press, Waterloo, 1986.

For further information on these titles, please write to the Canadian War Museum, Canadian Museum of Civilization, National Museums of Canada, Ottawa, Ontario K1A 0M8

Arthur Curry: a schoolboy in Strathroy

Currie as a captain in the 5th Regiment, Canadian Garrison Artillery

A young soldier observed: 'He always looked too heavy for his horse.'

Directing a practice attack near the Canadian front, June 1917

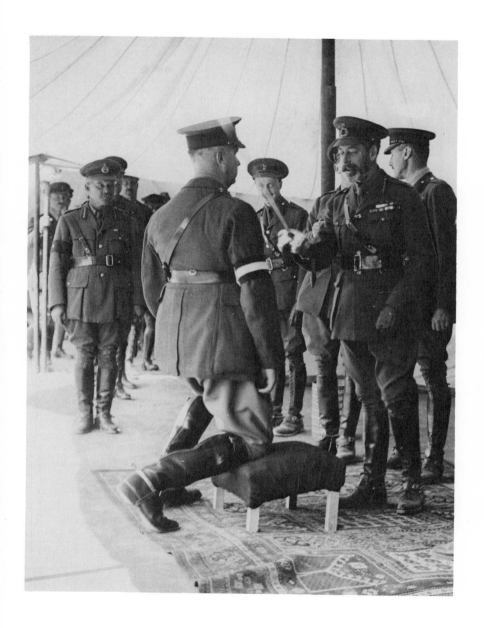

Currie receiving a knighthood, June 1917

Field Marshal Sir Douglas Haig with Lieutenant-General Sir Arthur Currie

Major-General Sir H.F. Mercer, Lieutenant-General Sir Arthur Currie, General Horne, and General Sir Julian Byng, February 1918

HRH The Prince of Wales with Generals Currie, Morrison, and Watson, 27 October 1918

13th Brigade, Canadian Field Artillery marches past General Currie, December 1918

Pastel drawing of Lieutenant-General Sir Arthur Currie by H.J. Ariss

GENERAL SIR ARTHUR CURRIE:
A MILITARY BIOGRAPHY

1

Before the war

In 1933, only a few days before he contracted a fatal case of pneumonia, Sir Arthur Currie reflected on the experience of 1914–18. 'I wish,' he wrote, 'I had the power to make all Canadians see clearly one day of the gas battle in April 1915, or of the Passchendaele Battle of 1917.' The reason he longed for such an opportunity is quite clear in the context of his manuscript. Anyone, he assumed, who could share the experience of Ypres or Passchendaele would never advocate another war. Anyone who truly understood the nature of battle would never propose its repetition. Even as he wrote, Currie was aware of the naïveté of his argument. The memory of war days, even for him, had been 'dulled' by the 'lapse of sixteen years,' so that 'today people are saying quite glibly, and, I believe, quite truthfully, that some nations of the world are again preparing for war.'[1]

The extent to which a man's last jottings reveal his true convictions about events that occurred years before, is a point disputed endlessly by scholars. But there is at least some evidence in Currie's final reflections to indicate that the First World War – at least the experience on the battlefield – for him was final proof of the horror and futility of war. There is also reason to suggest from the statement quoted above that the former Canadian Corps commander realized that however horrible and futile had been the experience of his generation, it was unlikely that future generations would escape the experience. The conclusion seemed to fill him with despair.

Currie had been an extraordinarily successful field commander in a war that did not produce a great many successful generals. Perhaps, to put it more accurately, the most prominent generals of the war were at the time figures of contention, and they have remained controversial in the historical literature. Currie's experience is particularly fascinating, since he entered the war as an 'amateur' soldier in the army of a small 'colonial' power. In the Canadian army before the First World War, politics, influence, and patronage were more likely than ability to bring advancement. There were distinguished exceptions to this general rule, but initially Currie was no exception. In 1914 he owed his appointment in the Canadian Expeditionary Force (CEF) to the fact that Garnet Hughes, his friend and subordinate in the 50th Regiment of the Canadian Militia, was the son of the minister of militia and defence, Sam Hughes. Currie was also well qualified compared with many others who received senior positions, but he was singled out by Sam Hughes. As the war proceeded, his 'influence' declined as he rose in rank and responsibility. At the end of the war Sam Hughes denounced Currie's leadership in parliament. Although supported by the minister at the start of the war, Currie was at the same time in dire personal difficulties. An incipient scandal hovered which would spell disgrace if it became public: on the verge of bankruptcy, he used the funds provided by the Department of Militia for the 50th Regiment to pay personal debts. Although he eventually returned the money, Currie made little effort to do so for the next three years. One might assume that for someone to succeed under such conditions, he must possess a flamboyance, a charisma, that would overcome the disadvantage by sheer strength of personal leadership. Currie did not have such flair. He was not a heroic leader. In many ways, as a consequence, his story is more fascinating.

War, the most complicated and destructive of all human activity, will always provide a niche for the charismatic leader. However, as war has changed, so have the prerequisites of military leadership. Napoleon Bonaparte has often been described as the last of the great captains: the last man in history able to dominate an entire battle, campaign, or war by the strength of his character, personality, and military brilliance. The truth of the argument derives from the changing nature of war rather than from a decline in human ability. After Napoleon, weapons became more efficiently destructive, armies became larger, and the art of commanding became correspondingly more difficult. As war became progressively complex, the role that any one general could play diminished. In proportion to an entire war, the general's personal influence on events inevitably declined. At the beginning of the First World War there seemed to be little recognition of this change in the popular press. Generals in 1914 were acclaimed as saviours, often before they had directed a single action. It is a natural human reaction to look for a saviour in time of peril, and thus it may be unfair to judge military commanders according to the standards of journalists at the beginning of the war. Certainly when the war ended, there was a pronounced change in the credits given to generals. The steady slaughter of the years 1914–18 in Europe demonstrated that the generals were only men, and their talents often were mediocre. In the Second World War the public probably expected less from military commanders, who, sensitive to the criticism levelled against their predecessors in the First World War, were satisfied at the beginning to be less than martial heroes.

It is difficult to think of an episode in history wherein the defects of high commanders have been examined more minutely than the First World War. Much of the opprobrium of historians and commentators is well deserved, but blanket criticism inevitably obscures genuine merit as much as does hero worship. There are examples in the First World War of fine generalship, by men who recognized the changes that had taken place in the nature of war and who discovered new methods of overcoming the obstacles imposed by such change. Not the least important of such men was Lieutenant-General Sir Arthur Currie, Canadian Corps commander. Currie was not a heroic leader, *sans peur et sans reproche*, but he provided what was needed to minimize the death and destruction of the young Canadians under his control. Surely this is an achievement of which any modern commander could be proud.

Information concerning Currie's early life is sparse and its content is trivial compared with that available for the war years. An intensive search after his death failed to uncover 'letters from the family, close friends or kindred sources.'[2] Consequently, it is very difficult – almost impossible for his early life – to know with precision how he reacted to events. His friend, admirer, and first biographer, Colonel Hugh M. Urquhart, has suggested that he was a man 'made by crises.'[3] Urquhart's judgment seems fair, though he deliberately obscured Currie's greatest prewar crisis, which was revealed only by the patient detective work of two Toronto historians some forty-five years after Currie's death.[4] In many ways Currie's life was a series of struggles – against poor health, bankruptcy, overwhelming debt, possible criminal charges, and, above all, struggle to achieve success in the most devastating war that history had so far known, without sacrificing the lives of those under his command.

Arthur William Curry – he changed the spelling of his name at the age of twenty-two – was born on 5 December 1875 on a farm in Adelaide township outside the village of Strathroy in rural southwestern Ontario.[5] The farm had been cleared by his paternal grandparents, Irish refugees from sectarian division, who had arrived in Canada in 1838. They were the first family members to change both surname and religion. Later, Arthur would adopt the Anglicanism which his grandmother had rejected for Methodism.

Arthur, the third of seven children, was considered 'sickly' as a boy. Probably as a result he was kept in school longer than his brothers and sisters. Evidently his parents hoped he would take up the study of law or medicine, a hope nourished by the considerable promise he showed in Strathroy Collegiate. However, the death of his father in 1891 ended such costly ambitions, and young Currie decided to train as a teacher. Possibly the end of his legal or medical prospects and the shock of his father's death weakened his incentive; for he graduated from the model, or teacher training, school with a third-class certificate which entitled one to teach but was no guarantee of a teaching position. Unable to find a job, Currie decided to return to collegiate to try for honours standing, which would give him entrance to university. Nineteen years old in 1894, he was a tall – over six feet – normal adolescent, no doubt prey to all the anxieties and frustrations of his age. His record at collegiate was good, and it seemed that he would gain his honours standing. However, quite suddenly, only a month before graduation, Currie withdrew from school. The reason for this precipitate action is not clear, although Colonel Hugh M. Urquhart suggests that the decision was possibly the result of adolescent pique following a quarrel with one of his teachers.

Whatever the reason, Arthur's decision to leave school and home at the age of nineteen was the first extraordinary event of his career. His background was ordinary; his early life had been normal; his education was extended for a farm boy; his prospects were unexceptional. His sudden departure from school to embark on a long journey was probably the first major step of his adult life.

Arthur headed for the home of his maternal great-aunt in Victoria, then a bustling provincial capital with a population approaching 20,000. Soon after his arrival, he enrolled in teacher training school, since his Ontario qualifications were not recognized in British Columbia. His first six years in British Columbia followed a more or less predictable pattern: graduation from teacher's college; a teaching position in Sydney (a village about twenty miles north of Victoria); finally, a better teaching post in Victoria. From the evidence available, it would seem that Currie was a good teacher – at any rate his principal thought so.

In 1897, the year that the Canadian prime minister, Wilfrid Laurier, fell temporarily in love with the British Empire and accepted a knighthood, Arthur Currie joined the Canadian militia (the BC Brigade, Canadian Garrison Artillery, to be precise) as a gunner (artillery, private). At least one historian, Professor Underhill, has argued that the militia in Canada was not 'taken very seriously by the country at large and hardly even by itself.'[6] However, Currie took the militia very seriously indeed. He had no military background, no member of his family had ever been associated with the military in Canada. Militia training in 1897, moreover, lagged significantly behind the most up-to-date military developments. None the less, for an ambitious young man anxious to improve his standing in the community, joining the militia was a sensible step. Membership in the local regiment provided social and economic contacts that would be useful for advancement in the community.

In 1900 Currie took a second step which probably seemed even more significant at the time. He decided to forgo the respectability and security of the teaching profession for the much riskier but more lucrative rewards of a business career. Currie joined a local insurance agency, Matson and Coles, and there he began to accumulate capital and friends. The most important friend was J.S.H. Matson, owner of the agency. Sam Matson had many business interests, and he increasingly looked on Currie as a protégé. When Matson in 1909 decided to concentrate his energy on publishing the newspaper that his family owned, the Victoria *Daily Colonist*, Currie took over the insurance agency. Sam Matson would remain a firm friend of Currie's, and must have been pleased when the younger man became provincial manager for one of the companies that the agency had represented.

Currie's business flourished, and he continued to rise in the militia. Having served in each of the non-commissioned ranks, he was offered a commission in December 1901. By May 1906 he had become a major and second-in-command of the 5th Regiment. More importantly, he had met and married the woman to whom he was devoted for the rest of his life, Lucy Sophia Chaworth-Muster, the daughter of an emigrant from Nottingham. His life thus acquired a new centre of gravity which Currie always guarded fiercely from publicity. Later, at a time when his personal finances were in total disarray, he wrote to Matson, 'my wife knows nothing of this nor shall she ever know.'[7] Mrs Currie remained in the background of Arthur's career, but she provided a core of domestic affection and security.

Domestic stability was an important asset to Currie during the early, exciting years in British Columbia. As the historian of the province put it, 'one could feel a new spirit of optimism' in the province. In Victoria property values began to rise, 'social life was gayer than it had been for some time.'[8] Immigrants continued to pour into the province, while reports of new mineral discoveries and railway construction contributed to the general air of elation. By 1908 boom conditions prevailed, as the population and prospects of the province continued to grow. In Victoria the 'sound of hammering could be heard everywhere ... as wealthy residents built ... the graceful and comfortable "Maclure houses" which incorporated so many of the architectural ideas of Frank Lloyd Wright.'[9] In this heady atmosphere Arthur Currie expanded his outside interests as well as his business operations. He was an active freemason and became a member of the Victoria Young Men's Liberal Association. He spent even more time with the militia.

In 1908 Currie entered a real estate partnership that was to become a milestone in his career. As senior partner in the firm of Currie & Power, it seemed possible to reach an undreamed of level of affluence. Here was a business that promised enormous returns, and there seemed to be little risk, since the provincial government of Richard McBride encouraged the boom in real estate. Profit seemed plentiful. The steady routine and minute detail of insurance must have seemed dull in comparison, the slow advance in commissions paltry compared with the profits derived from land. Before long Currie became involved in speculative buying, and apparently he urged his friends to do likewise.

Subsequently, friends claimed that, like many others, he 'threw reason to the winds,' and his investments considerably exceeded his modest resources.[10]

Currie's association with the militia, however, became increasingly intimate in the years before the outbreak of the First World War, while his attention to business grew more perfunctory. Membership in a militia regiment, as Desmond Morton demonstrates convincingly, was a many-faceted undertaking involving more than military training and the social prestige of membership. It was a costly business, particularly for officers. The pay they received for service was handed directly to the regimental fund, as was a healthy annual subscription. Uniforms and all the accoutrements of the officers' mess had to be paid for by the officers themselves.[11] To be commanding officer of a militia unit was particularly expensive, since the co was expected to be a man of considerable means, who could raise money for regimental purposes and, if necessary, personally subsidize the often substantial expenses the regiment incurred.

When Currie took over command of the 5th Regiment of Artillery in 1909, there seemed to be little reason for concern. His financial prospects seemed excellent, and his regiment soon became an outstanding example to others. For four of the five years he was commanding officer, the 5th won the Governor-General's Cup for Efficiency, in competition with all other artillery units in Canada. The regimental band became one of the most sought after attractions at any local festivity. Rank and file of the 5th Regiment discovered that virtually every parade was observed by the keen eye of their commander. The ordinary volunteer, it has been estimated, devoted an average of two hours per week to his training during the winter months.[12] Currie, according to Colonel Urquhart, 'was at the armoury nearly one hundred and fifty nights out of three hundred and sixty-five.'[13] This represented an expenditure of time and money that he could ill afford as time went on.

In 1913 real estate in British Columbia slumped badly. By summer the general recession in Canada had hit investors in the province and elsewhere very hard. Currie was no exception. When the real estate market virtually collapsed, he was substantially over-extended. Luckily his term as commanding officer of the 5th Regiment finished in August 1913, and it appeared that he would be free of the time and financial burdens imposed by the position. The state of the property market certainly suggested that financial retrenchment was a prudent course. Instead, Currie was intrigued by the suggestion that he take over command of a new Highland regiment (the 50th) that was to form part of the expanded militia organization advocated by the minister of militia and defence in Robert Borden's new Conservative government.

The minister, Sam Hughes, was an extraordinary man, and he already had played a role in Currie's career. Hughes had been given the militia portfolio when

Borden's Conservatives came to power, and in some ways he seemed an ideal selection. Hughes was a party stalwart with considerable Orange lodge support from central Ontario and a man with a passionate, if somewhat unconventional, interest in military affairs. When his offer of a regiment for service in the Boer War had been refused, Hughes went to Africa as a civilian, free-lance writer at his own expense. After the war he became the chief Conservative defence critic in parliament and attended the Imperial Conference in London in 1911 as part of the Canadian delegation. To the prime minister, Hughes appeared to have 'marked ability and sound judgement in many respects.' Somewhat eccentric, Hughes was occasionally embarrasing to the government. For example, in August 1912 he made a public speech in Vancouver in which he claimed that 'war is closer than you dream; the great peril is from Germany.'[14] When asked in parliament if he had indeed made such a statement, and if so, on whose authority, Hughes replied that the press report was not 'in all respects literally accurate,' but that the minister of militia needed no permission to make a statement and he was 'alone responsible for what he had uttered on that occasion.'[15] None the less, in Borden's view Hughes possessed 'astonishing' energy and did his best to increase the size and efficiency of Canadian military forces.[16] He was a 'tireless advocate of the principle that colonies should assist the Mother Country in time of War.'[17]

Arthur Currie first met Sam Hughes in Victoria in 1912. Shortly thereafter the two men came into conflict in circumstances that might have been disastrous for Currie's future but proved to have the opposite effect. Without Currie's knowledge, arrangements had been made for the band of the 5th Regiment to play for a local group associated with the Conservative party. Since such arrangements were contrary to standing orders, on discovering the situation, Currie cancelled the parade. The local organization appealed directly to Hughes, who ordered Currie to let the band play. He refused. At their next meeting Hughes insisted that Currie was guilty of insubordination, to which Currie replied that the real issue was 'did he or did he not command his regiment?'[18] Temporarily taken aback, in his quixotic fashion Hughes was pleased by such a direct stand. The incident was petty, but it brought Currie to Hughes's attention in a favourable way; for the next four years the minister of militia remained fond of Currie.

Hughes had a special interest in the newly established 50th Regiment, since his son, Garnet, was a junior major. However, the new regiment had problems. The originally designated commander failed to qualify for the post, and it appeared that the new Highland regiment was an organization without a head. Currie, retired from command of the 5th Regiment at the age of thirty-eight, well known and popular in Victoria, was a natural candidate. At first Currie declined the position. As Professor Morton has noted, he 'knew perfectly well what was involved. When a regiment proposed to wear the elaborate, costly Highland regalia of kilts and plaids and feather bonnets, the financial responsibiltiy [of the commanding officer] would be enormous.'[19] Moreover, the 50th Regiment had substantial plans for the future. It was to have a pipe band of sixteen and a brass band of twenty-four ranks in addition to the elaborate dress of the Gordon Highlanders.[20] Currie's financial position was an obvious reason for his hesitation in taking on the position of commanding officer, so his eventual acquiesence is puzzling. Without doubt he was pressed to take the position by his friends. But almost certainly the deciding factor was the offer by William H. Coy, a local business leader, to give the regiment $35,000 as a foundation grant. In return Coy was to become honorary colonel of the regiment. Currie and others believed that Coy, as honorary colonel, would undertake the financial responsibility normally assumed by the commanding officer. It seemed an ideal solution.

The *Daily Colonist* devoted an editorial to Coy when his gift to the 50th was announced. His generosity was praised and his indulgence asked concerning the publicity, since, according to the editorial, he was a diffident as well as a public-spirited individual, who preferred to avoid the limelight.[21] The glow of a splendid beginning lasted for some time. Three months after the announcement, when Sam Hughes visited Victoria, he referred publicly to the splendid spirit shown by Colonel Coy whose 'liberality' gave 'pleasure and encouragement' to the entire Ministry of Militia and Defence.[22] Coy, who had been born in New Brunswick, had lived in Calgary, Edmonton, and Saskatoon. He had worked for the CPR and in the United States. Recently settled in Victoria, he seemed to be the ideal answer to the regiment's financial dilemma – a perfect honorary colonel and benefactor. Even the provincial premier, Sir Richard McBride, praised Coy's gesture in parliament, and his commendation was echoed by civil and military leaders.[23]

Confident about the future, the new regiment immediately ordered uniforms and other highland regalia from a firm of Scottish outfitters, Moore, Taggart and Company, whose representative appeared in Victoria in December 1913.[24] As commanding officer, Currie guaranteed payment to Moore, Taggart for all kit ordered by individual officers.[25] He also signed the order for uniforms for the band and other ranks. It appears that there was an understanding that the regimental uniforms would be paid for by Colonel Coy. Indeed the outfitter's representative later confirmed that this was his understanding, and Coy also agreed that this was his intention at the time.[26] However, the commanding officer remained legally responsible. The agreement with Moore, Taggart was that half of the total bill would be paid on delivery and the balance within thirty days.

Between the time the order was placed for the uniforms and their delivery, despite the declining real estate market, Currie invested a substantial sum in at least two land deals with Colonel Coy as a partner. This suggests that initially he had enough confidence in the honorary colonel at least to engage in business with him. But confidence soon gave way to chagrin. In September 1914 Currie confided to his old mentor, Sam Matson, that he had discounted one of his private arrangements to Coy, because Coy 'told me that unless I did he would not pay for the uniforms when they came in.'[27] As time went on, apparently, Coy became increasingly difficult. 'He has been as sulky as a man could be. We all had to toady to him always to get him to do anything. For weeks he would not come near us. Would get offended if we were not always running after him and seemed to want no one but himself in the limelight.'[28] There were good reasons to be upset with Coy – the chief one, of course, was his refusal to put up the $35,000 that he had promised the regimental fund. It should also be said that by September 1914 Currie was probably so vehement about the honorary colonel in good part because his own behaviour could not bear close scrutiny.

From the beginning Coy had insisted that the regimental account be held at the Bank of Nova Scotia – where he personally banked. As the government did not issue uniforms directly to the 50th, it paid the regiment a subsidy for each man outfitted at regimental expense. Apparently, the senior officers in the regiment decided not to place this government subsidy into the regimental account, since they feared Coy would not make good on his pledge if he knew that the regiment had money available. Instead, the government cheques were placed in Currie's account at the Bank of Montreal. Such a practice, probably for other reasons, had many precedents elsewhere in the country, but it was surely unwise. At the very least it would make accountability difficult; a worst it would raise the suspicion of conflict of interest, if not fraud.

Throughout the spring of 1914, as rumours of war increased and the real estate market continued its calamitous decline, Currie's financial situation deteriorated. His properties became virtually unsaleable. When the uniforms arrived in May, the first instalment to Moore, Taggart was promptly paid, in part with money that Coy advanced and in part by the first government subsidy which was transferred from Currie's account. When a second and final cheque for $10,833.34 arrived from the Department of Milita and Defence, like its predecessor it was placed in Currie's personal account. It would have covered the balance owing to Moore, Taggart, even if Coy failed to make good on his promise.

When the British ultimatum to Germany expired on 4 August 1914, Canada was automatically at war. Currie, because of his personal situation, did not instantly volunteer. How could a man with his obligations simply walk away from them, regardless of how tempting the proposition might seem? As plans for Canadian participation in the war developed, Currie received an offer directly from the minister of militia for command of the British Columbia Military District. Such a position promised neither escape from his financial difficulties nor the excitement of command in battle, and Currie declined. Shortly afterwards, however, he received a second offer which could not be refused so easily. Currie was promised command of one of the provisional brigades in the Canadian Expeditionary Force then forming at Valcartier Camp in Quebec. His dilemma was acute. War meant there would be no break in the dismal prospects for real estate. He still had a wife, two children, and large debts. On the other hand, the war itself could be an avenue of escape. The appointment as a brigade commander was a tremendous opportunity, one of the most desirable appointments possible. Currie asked for time to settle his affairs. Garnet Hughes, Currie's junior major in the 50th and son of the minister of militia, subsequently suggested that at this time Currie turned to Coy for financial help, and that Coy agreed to assist in return for a heavily discounted note; Currie himself suggests that he discounted an agreement with Coy much earlier.[29] Regardless of when Currie made such an arrangement, it is clear that he believed Coy contributed to his difficulties by failing to put up the money promised to the 50th Regiment. It is also apparent that Currie could not raise the money to ·clear all his personal obligations. Finally, with the brigade appointment in the balance, Currie took the money from the second uniform subsidy, $10,833.34, which was still in his account, and used it to pay his personal debts. He then accepted the offer of command of a brigade and left Victoria almost immediately for Valcartier Camp, where the expeditionary force was concentrating.

Before the Canadian Expeditionary Force left Canada, Currie's successor in command of the 50th Regiment, Major Cecil Roberts applied to Arthur Currie for the transfer of the government allowance back to the regiment. Currie then begged his old friend Sam Matson to intervene on his behalf and ask for time to repay the money. 'Bobby Roberts,' he wrote to Matson, 'has wired me to hand the whole amount over to him and, Sam I cannot hand it all over. Some of it went to pay some of the accounts mentioned to you before leaving Victoria.'[30] Whether this was the case, or whether, as Professors Brown and Morton suggest, 'not just a part but virtually all of the 31 July cheques had been devoured by Currie's financial needs,' it is undisputed 'that almost three years would pass before Currie took any practical steps to settle his debt to the regiment.'[31] In his appeal to Matson, Currie demonstrated that he still held property and could return the regimental money when the property was sold. In the meantime, he suggested, if Coy made good on his promise, the outfitters could be paid off. Coy, according to Currie, wanted to use the government grant 'to pay for the uniforms by pretending he cannot pay for them just now.' If the matter became public, Currie had no illusions about the course of action that would follow: 'I would have to go back to Victoria.' Nor did he have any doubts about his final obligation. 'If I am killed,' he told Matson, 'I have left a letter in Victoria authorizing that out of my estate the first charge will be this $10,833.34.'[32]

He wanted time, however, and he begged Matson to get it for him.[33] The hard fact is that Currie took money that was not his and used it to pay personal debts so that he could go overseas. It is also true that for the next three years Currie appeared to do nothing beyond his appeal to Matson in September 1914 to settle his obligations, though, as we shall see, during this time he was fully engaged with other matters. Professors Brown and Morton suggest that taking the regimental funds was 'the act of a desperate man.' Perhaps it was. It was an unfortunate act which could have resulted in Currie's recall and disgrace and even in legal redress against him. Currie's situation, in fact, is an illustration of one of the besetting sins in Canada's prewar militia system. Officers in the militia were frequently unable to separate public and private matters. The Denison family, in Brown and Morton's words, 'virtually owned the Governor General's Body Guard through much of its existence,'[34] and there were many other examples of the rich mixing public and private affairs in the Canadian militia. The sins of others, of course, are no excuse for Currie's mistakes. He should not have taken the money, and he should never have deposited the government cheques in his private account. Nor does it lessen his culpability to point out that he never attempted to disavow his debt or to hide its trail. None the less, if his appeal to Matson appears to be less than fulsome, it was made for honourable reasons. 'Sam I am going to make good here and I do not want to be recalled ... You'll be proud of me yet if I get the chance and so will the regiment and the province. All I want is the chance.'[35]

For the moment, the continuing story of Currie's finances need not concern us. It is enough to note that he began his career in the Canadian Expeditionary Force distracted by a considerable personal difficulty. And for all his experience in the militia, Arthur Currie was hardly equipped to become a brigade commander in an expeditionary force. His biographer remarked: 'The amateur soldier who had never handled more than four hundred ranks in peace time was [in 1914] in command of four thousand in time of war.' The specific military knowledge, in a technical or tactical sense, that Currie had acquired in the militia was probably of little use to him. The 5th Regiment, for example, until 1907 had been equipped with muzzle-loading guns. Currie was not well prepared for war – virtually no Canadian was – but in relative terms he was probably an 'outstanding choice as a brigadier-general.' Such, at any rate, was the judgment of Canada's most loved soldier in a later war, General A.G.L. McNaughton.[36] Considering the inexperience of other Canadian officers, Currie's long militia service, his command experience, and his training in militia staff course, McNaughton was probably right. Currie had attended the militia staff course in the winter of 1914. The purpose of this course was to give Canadian militia officers an introduction to staff procedures and methods. Instruction was either by British officers on loan to Canada or by Canadian regular officers who had graduated from the British staff college at Camberley. In addition to staff procedures, the students were given lectures in 'tactics, topography and military administration,' and in the practical aspects of the course they had an opportunity to test the theory in a variety of tactical and administrative exercises.[37] Currie was one of 125 prewar militia officers to graduate from the course by the outbreak of war.[38] Nearly all the graduates served in the forces in some capacity during the war, the majority going overseas with the expeditionary force. Six of these men served as commanders of either infantry divisions or divisional artilleries, and many more commanded brigades or battalions and served in various staff positions over the war years.

Perhaps the most prudent judgment would be that Currie was as well prepared in terms of training as anyone else who joined up in 1914, indeed better prepared than most. But he left for war under greater strain than many officers. His stay at Valcartier Camp would provide new challenges and new strains but no release from his immediate personal problems.

2

Preparation for war

On 7 August 1914, three days after the British ultimatum to Germany expired, the Canadian government's offer to send an expeditionary force to Europe was accepted. The strength of the contingent was established by order-in-council at 25,000, roughly the size of one division.[1] Since 1910 there had been a continuing, if sporadic, effort to produce a mobilization plan for just such a force. Although this scheme had deficiencies, in the judgment of Canada's official historian, Colonel G.W.L. Nicholson, the plan would have worked. Nicholson argued that the scheme supplied 'a considered plan for the provision of troops on a fair ratio throughout the Dominion for a Contingent of the same strength as that subsequently mobilized in 1914.'[2]

But the plan was never tested. Sam Hughes ignored the existing plan and centralized control of mobilization in his own hands. Hughes described the process that took place as 'different from anything that had ever happened before,' which was perhaps the most accurate of his many statements about mobilization. 'There was,' he added, 'a call to arms like the fiery cross passing through the Highlands of Scotland or the mountains of Ireland in former days.'[3] If this was indeed the case, then Currie and a great many others probably misread the call. Probably the most accurate description of Canadian mobilization at Valcartier is 'confused.'

Much of the difficulty at Valcartier resulted from the fact that many of those involved were not familiar with standard military organization. That the minister of militia freely and frequently changed standard organization added to the confusion. It would be tedious and bewildering to follow in detail the structural changes in Currie's command, but two examples are instructive. First, the composition and command of the infantry brigades altered several times and were not settled until almost the end of September. Second, at the bottom of the scale, the number of companies in an infantry battalion continued to fluctuate even after the Canadians arrived in England. Six times the War Office in Britain changed the number from four to eight and back to four, demonstrating that not all the confusion was attributable to Canada.[4]

Ranks and formations may seem unnecessarily complex at first, but some notion of the structure of the Canadian Expeditionary Force (CEF) is essential if Currie's role is to be understood. If we concentrate on the CEF as it eventually went into battle and recognize that virtually all military formations are part of a pyramidal structure, the problem is considerably easier. Currie's command, an infantry brigade, was commanded by a brigadier-general and consisted, in round numbers, of 130 officers, 4,000 men, and 275 horses. Unlike the next higher formation, a division, the brigade had no permanently attached artillery units. It was the largest purely infantry formation, though at times artillery, medical, engineer, and other units could be temporarily attached to it. In the brigade were four infantry battalions. Each battalion was commanded by a lieutenant-colonel and contained approximately 1,000 men. The battalion was divided into four companies, each commanded normally by a captain or a major, and the companies were divided into four platoons, each led by a lieutenant. At brigade headquarters the brigadier was assisted by a brigade major, his chief staff officer, and four other junior staff officers as well as by a small staff of clerks and orderlies. Much of Currie's energy at Valcartier was directed towards establishing this structure and learning to operate within it.

Because of his relatively high rank, Currie's experience at Valcartier was not typical of the average volunteer, but even as a brigadier he experienced his share of confusion and frustration. In the uniform of the colonel of the 50th Regiment, Currie arrived at the camp on 1 September 1914 with the fatigue of a five-day train trip clinging to him. That morning camp orders had indicated that Currie was to command the 1st Provisional (Western) Brigade; but they had neglected to indicate the location of that formation or the nature of its staff and facilities. Luckily Currie met Garnet Hughes on arrival and the minister's son generously shared his tent with the brigade commander that night. Next morning, 2 September, new orders showed Currie as commander of the 2nd Provisional (Western) Brigade composed of the 5th, 6th, 7th, and 8th Battalions. He still had no headquarters, but knowing which troops he would command, he could now move to the area where his battalions were located. For the next six days he shared accommodation with the 8th Battalion, temporarily commanded (subsequently this was confirmed) by Major L.J. Lipsett, a British regular officer who had been Currie's instructor on the militia staff course.[5] Brigade headquarters became one-half of a folding table in the 8th Battalion command tent at which usually sat the entire staff of what would eventually become the 2nd Canadian Infantry Brigade: Lieutenant-Colonel A.W. Currie. If the brigade commander was absent, one could always leave a message at the other half of the table, with the pay sergeant of the 8th Battalion.

Still, things could have been worse: Currie's rank and status were reflected by his possession of a stretcher cot – 'a great luxury in Valcartier' – and a tent shared with one of the company commanders of the 8th Battalion. Not everyone was so lucky.[6]

Disorder was to be expected of any enterprise on the scale of the Canadian mobilization, but the turmoil at Valcartier was fantastic. The supply of equipment of all kinds, including stretcher cots, is a case in point. At most of the imperial conferences before 1914 the principle that arms and equipment should be standardized throughout the empire had been repeatedly advanced by the British and as frequently endorsed by Canadian representatives. Yet it was the inability or unwillingness of British suppliers to meet colonial requirements that had led in part to the production of substitute equipment in the colonies, for instance, the Ross rifle. The long, complicated, and notorious story of the Ross has been fully recorded in the Canadian official history but must be outlined here; for Currie became involved in the controversy that the use of this weapon provoked.

In the nineteenth century the government arsenal at Quebec had begun manufacturing small-arms ammunition in 1882, but the Canadian militia had been equipped with rifles purchased in Britain, often of obsolete patterns. During the Boer War the Canadian minister of militia and defence, Sir Frederick Borden, made repeated attempts to order rifles of up-to-date pattern from Britain. He had no success. The Canadian government, therefore, decided to manufacture its own rifles.[7] That policy might have contributed substantially to empire defence by widening the source of supply had the rifle so manufactured been of the standard British pattern. However, the rifle adopted was the Ross, not the Lee-Enfield. While the Ross rifle used sucessfully on occasion in competitions, its deficiencies were well documented as early as 1901. Sam Hughes, however, was one of the Ross's most enthusiastic advocates and saw to it that Canadian soldiers in 1914 were equipped with the rifle. On numerous tragic occasions the Ross would prove unsatisfactory in combat. Although it was ostensibly the same calibre as the British weapon (.303 inches), it would not fire standard British ammunition without jamming. Despite many modifications it was eventually withdrawn from Canadian soldiers, but not until 1916.[8]

In the summer of 1914 the Ross rifle was only one example of the unsatisfactory state of Canadian military equipment. In regard to other supplies, despite the efforts at standardization that had been made, the stockpiles of all types of equipment on hand were found to be 'totally inadequate' to supply the mobilized Canadian forces.[9] Lack of equipment gave rise to frantic improvisation to outfit the troops before they sailed for England. Equally frantic efforts were then necessary to re-equip them with standard British equipment before they embarked for France. Canadian boots, described by a soldier-diarist as having 'a veneer of leather on the sole, beneath which was a kind of gum or glue, the uppers were made of very soft porous leather which became soaked with the slightest rain,' were unserviceable.[10] Canadian motor vehicles had to be replaced because there were no spare parts for them. Wagons, horse harness, bicycles, and water carts – practically all the equipment issued so hastily in Valcartier – subsequently were replaced, despite violent objections by Sam Hughes. Particularly maddening to Hughes was the British rejection of the Ross rifle and another item that he had also personally introduced, the MacAdam shovel.[11]

Hughes deserves particular mention, since it was he, more than deficient equipment of faulty liaison with Britain, that disrupted orderly mobilization in Canada. Sir Robert Borden's testimony to Hughes's energy and enthusiasm has been noted. After the war Borden felt compelled to point out that Hughes's 'temperament was so peculiar and his actions and language so unusual on many occasions that one was inclined to doubt his usefulness as a minister.' Borden noted that about half of the time Hughes was 'an able, reasonable and useful colleague,' but for the other half he was either 'extremely excitable, impatient of control and almost impossible to work with,' or, more seriously, 'so eccentric as to justify the conclusion that his mind was unbalanced.'[12] There seems no doubt that the latter mood became increasingly frequent after August 1914. That he was able to accomplish as much as he did (by 8 September a modern camp had been built at Valcartier, and some 32,665 men had been concentrated) is testimony to his enthusiasm and boundless energy. The subsequent chaos is a measure of his deficiencies.

The first volunteers had arrived in Camp Valcartier in mid-August, several days before Arthur Currie, and they continued to arrive until 8 September.[13] But no fixed organization existed for the men. Camp orders of 17 August stated that the expeditionary force would be 'organized as closely as possible on the lines indicated in [British] Expeditionary Force War Establishments, 1914,' but a series of new orders quickly strained the usual definition of 'closely as possible.' Currie arrived in the midst of bewildering ongoing organizational changes. The first comprehensive camp structure had been issued on 10 August. It was countermanded on the 22 August, amended on 1 September, changed again on 2 September, and once more on 25 September.[14] Artillery, engineer, and signal units, though experiencing their share of difficulties with inadequate or missing equipment, were mobilized with rather less confusion because they received less personal attention from the minister. From time to time Hughes authorized the formation of entirely new units: some, like a motor machine gun unit, were to prove useful; others were ephemeral such as 'The Canadian Army Hydrological Corps and Advisors on Sanitation.' The precise, if circumspect, prose of Colonel A.F. Duguid's official history gives a fair picture of Hughes's position: 'The Minister of Militia was omnipresent. His visits to the camp were frequent and he exercised the closest and most direct control over matters of administration and training; in respect to appointments of officers he was the final authority, though for the junior positions he was willing, in most cases, to accept the recommendations of unit commanders. To representatives of the press he gave nightly interviews and stated his opinions freely and forcibly.'[15]

On the question of officers' appointments two things should be said in Hughes's defence, even though the minister was notorious for making sudden, last-minute, completely personal decisions about appointments. First, his predecessor as minister of militia, Sir Frederick Borden, had also left the question of appointments an open matter until a few days before the Canadian contingent had sailed to the Boer War. Secondly, whatever else can be said about Hughes, his choices for command of the infantry brigades in Valcartier seemed sound. The other two selections were Colonel R.E.W. Turner of Quebec City and Lieutenant-Colonel Malcolm S. Mercer of Toronto. Turner had seen active service as a junior officer in the Boer War and had been awarded a Victoria Cross and a Distinguished Service Order for his gallant conduct. In 1914 he was forty-three years old, serving on the 'Reserve of Officers,' a former president of the Canadian Cavalry Association, and operating a family wholesale grocery business. Oldest of the acting brigadiers at fifty-five, Mercer was a lawyer and had been commissioned in the Queen's Own Rifles of Canada in 1885, the same year he graduated from the University of Toronto. A fourth provisional brigade was subsequently disbanded and was temporarily given to Lieutenant-Colonel J.E. Cohoe, who also had had long service in the militia. Only Cohoe was not subsequently promoted. Currie, Turner, and Mercer all later served as division commanders, and Mercer was killed in action in 1916. Three of the four men, Currie, Mercer, and Cohoe, had graduated from the militia staff course mentioned above which provided the most advanced staff training normally available to a militia officer.[16]

Given the inadequate state of prewar preparation in Canada, some, indeed considerable, disorder inevitably would have accompanied the process of mobilization. But there was no doubt that the procedures adopted by Hughes were responsible for many of the difficulties. His personal interference and constant vacillation did much to obstruct the organization of the first contingent.

Training of all ranks at Valcartier was based on a pamphlet issued by the Department of Militia and Defence that outlined procedure for training to be followed in militia summer camps. The situation at Valcartier was obviously different. Colonel A.F. Duguid, himself a participant in the 1914 mobilization and later its historian noting this difference, observed that 'the force assembled at Valcartier ... had ... no comparable organization to a militia unit training in the summer: the composition, location and command of C.E.F. units were repeatedly changed; officers and N.C.O.'s being temporary and provisional were on probation, until a few days before departure. One provisional battalion had four lieutenant-colonels, another none, and so with the lower ranks; new appointments, promotions, replacements, transfers and reductions were of bewildering frequency in the hectic, alternating process of shaking up and shaking down.'[17] Sam Hughes boasted that, on leaving Valcartier, the men of the first contingent were 'trained to handle a rifle as no men had ever handled it before.'[18] Since the minimum training requirement for infantry was fifty rounds fired at various ranges and not all the infantrymen at Valcartier completed this requirement, the accuracy of his statement may be questioned. (It may also have been literally true in a sense not intended.) A battalion commander in the first contingent subsequently observed that 'it was fondly imagined that any Canadian who could shoot straight and who had a week's training could take his place in the ranks and would be just as good as a [regular] soldier.'[19]

Meanwhile, the men of the first contingent were busy: tents and field kitchens were erected, moved, and re-erected; supplies were issued, withdrawn, and re-issued; men were paraded for attestation, medical examinations, anti-typhoid vaccinations (which were voluntary), and reviews for the governor-general or Colonel Hughes; officers and civilians authorized as horse buyers scoured the country and purchased 8,150 animals which had to be cared for; men went on twenty-four hour passes to Quebec City; military police searched for hidden stores of whiskey; transports were hired to carry the force to Europe; men sweated and shivered, hurried and waited, cursed and joked; and, in the midst of the chaos, training for war began.[20]

Currie, too, was busy. Organizational changes naturally compounded the paperwork that is an inevitable part of military life. For a time, the burden of such detail in the 2nd Brigade fell on Currie alone. Although he was responsible for the welfare and training of four battalions of infantry, each approximately 1,000 men strong, he did not receive his full complement of staff officers until shortly before the brigade sailed for England. A brigadier who commanded untrained troops without the aid of a staff could easily impair efficiency by intervening with the orders or plans of his battalion commanders. Currie recognized this danger. Realizing that men must first be trained on the lowest level, he wisely refrained from interfering with the battalions. Long conferences and even longer hours at his desk filled the days and most of the evenings. But he did what he could to cut red tape for his men. He tried to be present when one of his battalions was drawing stores, so that, if possible, he could speed the routine of the quartermaster. Whenever possible he watched his men at their rifle practice, an exercise that he, as a past-president of the British Columbia Rifle Association, thoroughly understood. He reluctantly planned the participation of elements of his brigade in the reviews arranged for various dignitaries. Above all he studied his officers, trying to form a fair estimation of how they would function under more rigorous conditions than those that mobilization provided.[21]

Part of the difficulty at Valcartier was that the existing militia organization was virtually abandoned, and an entirely new structure was superimposed. For example, Currie's old 50th Regiment, instead of becoming the nucleus of a battalion in the expeditionary force, became a part of the 16th Battalion in the 3rd Brigade. All battalions in the CEF were to be identified by a number, though there remained a rough territorial alignment in the brigades. The 1st Brigade was composed almost entirely of men from Ontario militia units, and Currie's 2nd Brigade was composed mainly of westerners.[22] In this situation men and officers were unfamiliar with each other as well as with the new structure. It was therefore particularly important for officers at all levels to learn their new commands as quickly as possible. Currie liked what he saw in the 2nd Brigade.

Writing to his old friend Sam Matson, Currie indicated that his men were young and fit, 'averaging from 28 to 35, hardy men from the plains of the North West, the interior of B.C. and the Coast Cities.' They will fight, he predicted, 'like Billy be damned.'[23] His four battalion commanders also seemed like excellent prospects. Lieutenant-Colonel George S. Tuxford's 5th Battalion came, for the most part, from militia cavalry regiments, and Tuxford himself was impressive. Athletic and slim, Tuxford was forty-four years old; he had immigrated to Canada from England at the age of eighteen and eventually would command a division in France. The 6th Battalion was composed mainly of men from Manitoba and Saskatchewan, who were also from militia cavalry. Their commander, Lieutenant-Colonel J.G. Rattray, was an experienced militia officer from Manitoba. The 7th Battalion was eventually commanded by Lieutenant-Colonel Colonel W.F.R. Hart-McHarg, who would later be killed near St Julien. The second-in-command of the 7th was Major Victor Odlum, who not only took over from Hart-McHarg but went on to command the 11th Infantry Brigade. Perhaps the most experienced soldier in the entire 2nd Brigade was the commander of Currie's 8th Battalion, Lieutenant-Colonel L.J. Lipsett. A British regular officer, one of twenty-nine serving in Canada in 1914 and one of four British officers who joined the CEF,[24] Lipsett had been Currie's instructor on the militia staff course, and Currie constantly relied on his expertise. Lipsett was noted for his insistence on sharing the experience of his men.[25] Later he would command the 3rd Canadian Division, and his passion for knowing what was happening at the front would cost him his life during the last stages of the war. On balance, then, Currie was well pleased with his battalion commanders and the officers in his headquarters. 'I have surrounded myself with a splendid staff,' he told Sam Matson, and noted at the same time that 'the Artillery say we are easily the best brigade' in the camp.[26]

Although Currie was satisfied with his men and officers, other experiences in

Valcartier were not always so pleasing. There was, for example, his relationship with Sam Hughes. Currie was well aware that he owed his position to Hughes and equally aware that this connection would be resented by some of his subordinates. He had a certain sympathy for Hughes, noting that his life must have been a 'misery for days on end,' since as every 'squirt of a politician in the country and especially those in the camp' tried to get Hughes to assure them of a position.[27] Currie's problem was to maintain his independence of the minister without losing his position on the one hand, and on the other trying to gain the confidence of his subordinates without compromising his integrity. He was determined to walk this narrow line, and the available evidence indicates that he was successful. He left Canada in command of the 2nd Infantry Brigade with the full support of the minister, but he had not compromised himself. He had deliberately kept away from Hughes as much as possible. He had carefully rehearsed his men for participation in parades or reviews so that they avoided the instant displeasure that a mistake made during these ceremonies easily aroused in the volatile Hughes. In addressing his officers, some of whom were undoubtedly suspicious of him, Currie dwelt on the trials that would confront them later, rather than on the difficulties that they presently suffered. A diarist, critical of the whole process of mobilization under Hughes, and especially stung when 'highly qualified' officers had 'men of lesser experience ... placed over their heads,' found that his concern was much relieved by a lecture that Currie gave to officers of the 2nd Brigade.[28] Evidently, Currie was able to turn the thoughts of the disgruntled to more important matters. This was no small feat, because he was not always so impressive in first encounters. Currie was intelligent, thoughtful, and rather shy, qualities that become effective over time. Colonel Urquhart makes much of his sense of humour, describing him as having before the First World War the disposition of a 'happy-go-lucky overgrown boy.'[29] Currie's letters are marked by occasional touches of wit, but seldom by ebullient humour. Photographs of him smiling are rare indeed. His correspondence reveals a sober rather than an effervescent personality, a thoughtful rather than a brilliant mind, a man with a straightforward rather than a devious approach. Like Sir Douglas Haig, later commander-in-chief of the British forces, Currie was no stylist, but he wrote quite as clearly as Haig, and he was not afflicted by the latter's astonishing inability to express himself verbally. In discussion Currie could be persuasive. Occasionally in argument he demonstrated a fluent command of the scabrous side of military vocabulary.[30]

Directness characterized Currie's methods of command as much as it did his personal relationships. This directness, sometimes exaggerated by his shyness, often on first acquaintance made him appear blunt and severe. His physical appearance also was disadvantageous. He was a big man, over six feet tall and well over 200 pounds. His size, which might have been impressive, made him conspicuous and awkward rather than big and dignified. He had a pear-shaped figure topped with a narrow head which looked even narrower because of his long, lugubrious jowls. According to a young soldier serving in the ranks, 'he always looked too heavy for his horse.'[31] His uniform seemed uncomfortable for him, the tunic habitually bunching over the top of his Sam Browne belt, which, because of his large bottom half, appeared to encircle his chest rather than his waist. His forage cap was perched ludicrously on his head. In soldierly bearing, Currie was at the other extreme from Sir Douglas Haig. Whatever else may be said of him, Haig looked a soldier, an impeccable military portrait. Furthermore, he liked his officers to have a 'soldierly deportment.'[32] Currie did not qualify.

Yet, as has been suggested above, Currie made a good impression on his officers during their short stay at Valcartier. Postwar memoirs of prewar events are often misleading, but in this case they confirm contemporary testimony. The Duke of Connaught, a frequent visitor to Valcartier in those earlier days, later recorded that he had been 'convinced he [Currie] would be a very suitable man to command a brigade.'[33] Sir Robert Borden also recalled that he had been impressed by the way Currie responded to an address that Borden gave to the 2nd Brigade. Currie spoke 'with apt expression and a thorough appreciation of the duty that lay in front of him and his men.'[34]

One wonders just how that duty seemed to these men. What were the thoughts of the young Canadians as they prepared for a war for which they had little foreknowledge and no responsibility? Not a man in the brigade, from Currie to the youngest orderly, had been compelled to join up. Why had they done so, and what did they anticipate? Such questions fascinate and bedevil the historian; there can be no single answer, and to speak for 4,000 men is impossible. Among the young Canadians assembled at Valcartier, however, a few sentiments were widely shared.

In the first place, none of them had foreseen the war; indeed it had come as a surprise to most people the world over. After the first shock they had responded with great enthusiasm. This exuberance is difficult for a more cynical and experienced generation to understand, since it resulted partly from a conception of war that is now very rare. Most men then believed that the war would be short and glorious. Indeed the greatest punishment that could be awarded to an offending volunteer at Valcartier or on Salisbury Plain in those early days was to send him home, to leave him out.[35] For their unrealistic conception of war Canadians could hardly be blamed. The most recent examples of European warfare, the Austro-Prussian and Franco-Prussian wars, had been short. Europeans were on the whole similarly misguided. Indeed the townsfolk of Ontario who thought that 'martial music, brass helmets, waving plumes, clinking spurs, and scarlet tunics, together with splendid cavalry charges and easy victories ... symbolized soldiers and war,'[36] were far less parochial than might be imagined.

They, and the majority of soldiers in Valcartier, shared a widely held – possibly even a relatively sophisticated – view of the nature of war. An idealization of war combined with late Victorian romanticism and, at least among the English-speaking, a utopian view of 'empire' and 'mother country,' fashioned the attitudes of many in Valcartier. Currie later reflected that the men of the first Canadian contingent left Canada 'with no very definite opinion as to the causes of the war, its probable length or its results. They knew only that the Mother Country was in danger and they felt that their place was by her side.'[37] An anonymous barrack-room philosopher later wrote that he had 'asked many men why they were in the army,' and found 'they could give no good reason except that it was the thing to do.' Which was, he reflects, 'the base of our lives. We do what we think is best at the time.'[38] The soldiers left Valcartier with their misconceptions intact and their hopes still bright. For Currie, reflection on the future was prevented by the immediate problems confronting his brigade. In less than a month they would embark. Once again this manoeuvre with all its difficulties was personally supervised by the minister of militia. After several postponements, it began on 27 September 1914. Only two days before, Hughes's impatience with fixed procedures had led him to remove control of the operation from the director of supply and transport in Ottawa and reject the plan that he had prepared.[39] The last ship took on its troops on 1 October. Although the entire process of loading was completed in four days, (except for left-overs consisting of 863 horses and a few men and vehicles),[40] the untangling at disembarkation in England required nine days.[41]

In recounting the very short period that Currie spent at Valcartier Camp, I have given considerable attention to the actions of the minister of militia; for it was he who had been responsible for Currie's appointment and who controlled the activities of every Canadian at the camp. The mobilization of the first Canadian contingent was unique. When later contingents from Canada arrived in Europe, many of the aberrations that Hughes had created in the first contingent were avoided. The Canadian army increasingly came to resemble the territorial force envisaged by Lord Haldane and the prewar British Army reformers. When, for example, Canada decided to raise a second division, the system of mobilization was radically amended. Men were enrolled in units in the military districts and remained there until immediately before embarkation.[42] In short, a modified form of the original plan, which Hughes had rejected for the first contingent, was used.

In Britain there was also difficulty in implementing the mobilization plan. The British plan was largely the work of Douglas Haig, who, with the enthusiastic backing of Lord Haldane, virtually created the territorial force. When Kitchener became secretary of state for War, he rejected the territorials mainly because he abhorred their 'amateur spirit.' He was determined that his new armies should 'spring out of the ground as regulars, enlisted for the duration of the war, cut to the standard professional pattern, and conditioned from the outset to the urgent needs of his personal military machine.'[43] In Canada Hughes was just as prejudiced, but in his case it was against professionalism in soldiers. So in Britain mobilization was modified by a civilian minister who had been a professional soldier and who rejected a brilliant plan conceived by another professional soldier for raising an army by utilizing the part-time soldiers of the nation. In the first dominion chaos resulted when a civilian minister who had been an amateur soldier rejected a sensible plan created by a professional soldier. Mobilization for war is an enormous enterprise and last-minute modifications are as likely to complicate as simplify the process whoever makes them. But for those involved, including the commander of the 2nd Canadian Infantry Brigade, there was little time for such reflection.

At Valcartier Camp most of the senior officers in the contingent, including Currie, occupied positions of command that were abnormal, even bizarre. They commanded units but exercised no authority, since major decisions could be taken only by the minister. They trained their men, but they could not exercise their units as a whole, because the soldiers were so inexperienced that the lowest level of training had to be mastered before battalions or brigades could be assembled. To be sure, senior officers filled important positions in a pyramidal command structure, but all blocks in the pyramid were 'provisional,' and the keystone was missing. No overall commander was present, except the ubiquitous Sam, who, after all, was a member of the Canadian government, not the force commander. Not all or even most of these difficulties disappeared with the journey down the St Lawrence. For Currie and other senior officers, however, the voyage to England was a welcome respite from the chaos of Valcartier. When it ended, they would meet their new commander.

Sir Robert Borden believed that Hughes wanted to become commander of the force while maintaining his position as minister of militia.[44] Colonel Duguid argued that Hughes intended to command only the artillery component of the contingent.[45] In any event, Borden would not allow Hughes to take on any additional responsibility while still a minister, and Hughes was unwilling to give up his militia portfolio. Thus, when the British War Office inquired about the appointment of a force commander, Hughes undertook direct negotiations on the matter with Lord Kitchener. Although he indicated that Kitchener's choice would be satisfactory, Hughes expressed a preference for Major-General E.A.H. Alderson, who was finally selected as commander of the Canadian Division. Fifty-five years old, a graduate of staff college, and a veteran of the Boer War and several other campaigns, Alderson had a 'high reputation as a leader of irregular troops.'[46] He would soon discover the difficulties of leading an 'irregular' division, formed by an 'irregular' minister of militia.

The force that arrived at Plymouth on 14 October 1914 had not been organized, equipped, or trained as a standard British division. Much of the time of the new commander would be devoted to reorganizing his force to a closer approximation of the standard. The task was not made easier by Sam Hughes's presence. Immediately after the CEF left Canada, Hughes travelled to New York, boarded a fast liner, and arrived in England before the Canadian soldiers. He did so in 'an unofficial capacity for a holiday,' according to Sir Robert Borden, but with the intention of briefing General Alderson on 'officer[s] and other important matters.'[47] For Currie and other senior officers of the contingent General Alderson provided a welcome buffer from the minister's attention. At all levels serious military training was essential. With or without Sam Hughes it was a sobering, formidable task.

No one took the job more seriously than Currie. 'I believe I'm getting on well,' he confided after a time to his mother. He was working very hard; and his judgment was tentative and cautious. 'It is a great responsibility,' he added, 'and although I try not to do so I cannot help worrying.'[48] And well he might worry. As one of the soldiers in the contingent later recorded, the rank and file were 'still civilians in uniform.'[49] There was so much to do, so little time, and events transpired so rapidly. Valcartier had seemed busy, but in Europe everything happened with frightening speed. For Currie the pattern of events during the first weeks of the war must have appeared remarkable. He stepped ashore in England on 18 October, two months after the German First Army had driven the Belgian forces into Antwerp and eight days after that city had fallen. Before his acceptance of the provisional appointment in the CEF, the British Expeditionary Force had slipped quietly into France, had met the Germans at Mons, and had begun the disheartening withdrawal that was to end at the Marne. While Currie travelled from Vancouver to Valcartier, Hindenberg and Ludendorff were victorious at Tannenburg. Currie's second day in Valcartier Camp, 2 September 1914, was marked by the exodus of the French government from Paris lest the Germans invest the capital. When Currie led part of his brigade in review past the Governor-General, the Duke of Connaught, on 6 September, the battle of the Marne was in its third day. Simultaneously with a second review for the Duke on 14 September, a messenger secretly informed General Helmuth Moltke, chief of the Prussian general staff, that he was to be replaced as effective commander of the German armies on the Western Front by General Erich Falkenhayn. By the time Currie arrived at Salisbury Plain, where the Canadians were to train in England, the so-called 'race to the sea' had ended; trench lines were established across the length of France, and the First Battle of Ypres had begun. Even before Currie was through training his brigade in England, war of movement had finished on the Western Front, except for a very short period in 1918.

Although it was not yet apparent to Currie, this kaleidoscopic rush of events was to favour the Canadians. Very few military experts were prepared for trench warfare. To be sure, a few people had foreseen such a development: Ivan Bloch, a civilian, had predicted that war soon would produce 'slaughter on so terrible a scale as to render it impossible to get troops to push the battle to a decisive issue.'[50] A few dedicated professional soldiers were also studying the problems of fire power, but there were no easy solutions.[51] The Canadians were woefully unprepared for any kind of war, but no more so for trench warfare than any other troops. To put it another way, because they knew so little, the Canadians had relatively little to forget. J.F.C. Fuller, one of the co-authors of the Blitzkreig technique so effectively exploited by the Germans during the Second World War, has observed that 'nothing is more dangerous in war than to rely upon peace training; for in modern times, when war is declared, training has always been proved out of date.'[52] This danger, at least, the Canadians avoided. One should not push such an argument too far; but it does seem likely that the nature of the war they would fight in some ways made up for their lack of training. One hastens to add that this lack of training was painfully apparent to contemporary observers. Fuller himself, after watching the Canadians disembark, could not resist commenting that Canadian soldiers 'would be good enough after six months' training:, providing that Canadian 'officers could be all shot.'[53]

The trouble was that there were not six months for training, and shooting was reserved for the enemy. Currie did everything possible to conserve time. He avoided leaving the camp unless it was absolutely essential, and he often must have known bitter frustration when training schedules were cut for non-instructional, if necessary, reasons. Time was lost, for example, while the final organizational structure of the Canadian Division was settled. Particularly bothersome were the large numbers of surplus senior officers who had accompanied the contingent, by the authority of Sam Hughes. Uncertainty over the basic structure of an infantry battalion, whether it should have four or eight companies, was a problem that affected training and occupied officers in what must have seemed unnecessary wrangling. This issue, after six changes of thought by the War Office, was finally resolved in January.[54] The laborious job of withdrawing unsatisfactory equipment and issuing new kit was a lengthy one. Meanwhile, of course, Currie had to establish his own methods of control and communication with his battalions on the one hand and from his headquarters to division on the other.

He seemed to possess considerable talent for reconciling conflicting views and getting the most out of his fellow officers. British officers attached to the Canadian staff were usually impressed by the tact and efficiency of the big Canadian. Major Gordon-Hall, a member of General Alderson's staff, noted the way Currie 'listened to the other side of the matter under discussion: [without] ... blindly and violently pushing his own interests.'[55] With time at a premium such patience was invariably admired. Probably it was the fastest way to weld team spirit, which was Currie's main preoccupation on Salisbury Plain. He constantly studied his officers, learning how to exploit their strengths and minimize their deficiencies.

Patience and tact, however, were as impotent as rage in dealing with the factor that caused the Canadians the greatest difficulty. When Currie's headquarters arrived at its allotted area on the Plain it was raining. It rained intermittently for three days while the men struggled to erect shelters and provide warmth. On 21 October it began to rain in earnest. The brigade commander himself was repeatedly soaked to the skin as high winds accompanied the rain and flattened the Canadian canvas with monotonous regularity.[56] Currie's brigade spent a total of 123 days on Salisbury Plain in the area known as West Down South. On eighty-nine of these days nearly thirteen inches of rain fell, sufficient under the best of circumstances to disrupt a training program.[57] Before long low temperatures and frost added to the general discomfort. Under these conditions, 'the thin turf ... which covered a few inches of poor soil overlaying impervious chalk' quickly became waterlogged and the slightest traffic churned the ground into a veritable quagmire.[58] In an attempt to provide more adequate protection from the elements, the men of the 2nd Brigade built huts for themselves, but shortly after moving into overcrowded and poorly ventilated huts, some contracted influenza and meningitis.[59]

Even in the perversity of the elements, however, there was some luck for the Canadians. The loss of training time due to inclement weather was serious, as were the resulting discomfort and sickness. But these same conditions created an atmosphere that was a foretaste of the future. The 1st Canadian Division was destined to spend most of the next three years in the mud trenches of Flanders. As preparation for such an experience, learning to cope with water and discomfort was more important than all the bayonet and close order drill in the world. The 123 days on Salisbury Plain introduced the Canadians to a 'semi-aquatic' life. Moreover, thanks partly to Currie's organizational talent, some rather useful training was accomplished. Battalion commanders were encouraged to work out their own schemes. Since range facilities were limited, practice shooting was carried out daily with dummy cartridges. Currie was particularly concerned that his men should keep physically fit in such conditions, and he personally accompanied each of his battalions on long route marches: on 5 November he covered a twelve-mile course in four hours during a driving rain storm. Just before Christmas, the first of three away from his family, the brigade commander took part in a skeleton divisional exercise which he later pondered carefully.[60]

For the men of the 2nd Brigade – indeed for all Canadians – life was brightened immeasurably by General Alderson's decision that wet canteens should be opened. Hitherto, by order of Sam Hughes, the Canadian soldiers had been barred from purchasing any alcoholic beverages in an army canteen. This action led to appalling bouts of drunkenness when there was unsupervised access to public houses or bars. The ability to buy a beer at the canteen, it seemed, not only relieved the monotony of the weather but also, the opinion of temperance organizations at home notwithstanding, reduced crime. As one of Currie's officers put it: 'The wet canteen is a Godsend and drinking has been reduced to a minimum. A man who is free to buy a mug of beer a couple of times a day does not try to keep a bottle of whisky in his tent. Drunkenness has been practically stamped out and offences of all sorts have tended to steadily decrease. General Alderson is to be thanked for this.'[61]

To Currie, however, neither this welcome relief nor his promotion to full colonel (so far he had done the work of a brigadier-general with the rank of lieutenant-colonel) compensated for a final rearrangement of his brigade. Until January 1915 the 2nd Brigade had consisted of the 5th, 6th, 7th, and 8th battalions. But in January, just as Currie was beginning to have the 'feel' of his command, the 6th was withdrawn. This was the result of a final rearrangement of the Canadian Division which transformed the 4th Brigade into a reinforcement depot for the division. Currie's 6th Battalion, composed in the main of men and officers from the Fort Garry Horse, was to become a reinforcement depot for the Canadian cavalry. On learning of these plans, Currie requested that the 6th be replaced by the 11th Battalion, which was composed of men from four Saskatchewan and one Manitoba regiments. Instead, the 11th became a reinforcement unit for the 2nd Brigade, and Currie was given the 10th Battalion, composed of men from the Calgary Rifles and the Winnipeg Light Infantry.[62] A change of such magnitude so close to the beginning of operations against the enemy was extremely serious. None the less, on Wednesday 10 February the 2nd Brigade marched aboard the *City of Dunkirk* and crossed the channel to France with the 10th Battalion in place of the 6th.[63] Luckily, the new battalion was commanded by Lieutenant-Colonel R.L. Boyle, an experienced officer who had graduated from the militia staff course and who helped to minimize the disruption caused by the substitution of his battalion.

After Salisbury Plain Currie and his companions in the 2nd Brigade can hardly have felt like Rupert Brooke's swimmers 'into cleanness leaping,' but they were still innocents. However, school days were over. The happy, frustrating, seemingly endless novitiate was finished. Many who had feared the war would end before they got to the front would soon begin to insist 'the first seven years are the worst.'[64] Currie, who had begun his military apprenticeship in leisurely fashion in 1897, who had witnessed so many things and covered so much ground in the last months, still had to hear his first shot fired in anger – but he did not have much longer to wait.

3

Brigade commander

For the headquarters contingent of the 2nd Brigade the last stages of the trip to the front were perhaps the most unforgettable of the entire journey. The holds of the channel steamer *City of Dunkirk* were crammed with stores and men, the decks packed with horses. For the normally short trip from Avonmouth to St Nazaire such crowding was justifiable, particularly when channel shipping was so overloaded. However, gales stretched a trip of hours into two full days, and Currie noted in his diary that so many men became sick that it was impossible to mount a proper guard over the animals on deck. Throughout this hectic passage Currie himself remained fit. But his apparently strong stomach was no proof against travel on French trains; it took forty-three hours for the 2nd Brigade to reach the British front by rail, travelling via Abbéville, Calais, and Hazebrouck, and by the time of his arrival Currie was thoroughly sick. Vomiting and diarrhoea, then simply diagnosed as 'grippe,' kept him weak for six days.[1]

From the 21 to 28 February the 2nd Brigade was attached to the British 4th Division, part of the III Corps of General Smith-Dorrien's Second Army. This period of attachment was designed to familiarize the Canadians with trench routine. A divisional order stated that 'each Canadian [is] to be associated with a thoroughly well trained soldier who ... [will] teach him all he knows under the Section, Platoon, and Company Commanders.'[2] After this brief introduction, the 2nd Brigade was scheduled to go to rest billets, but on 26 February Currie was informed that his brigade would take over a section of 'live trenches.' Three days later it occupied a portion of the 7th British Division front.[3]

In 1915 French strategy called for a blow against the Germans in the north as quickly as possible. The British commander-in-chief, Sir John French, had agreed to join this offensive and also to help his ally by taking over a section of the French front as soon as reinforcements arrived. The British field marshal anticipated reinforcement by the 29th British as well as the Canadian Division. When the

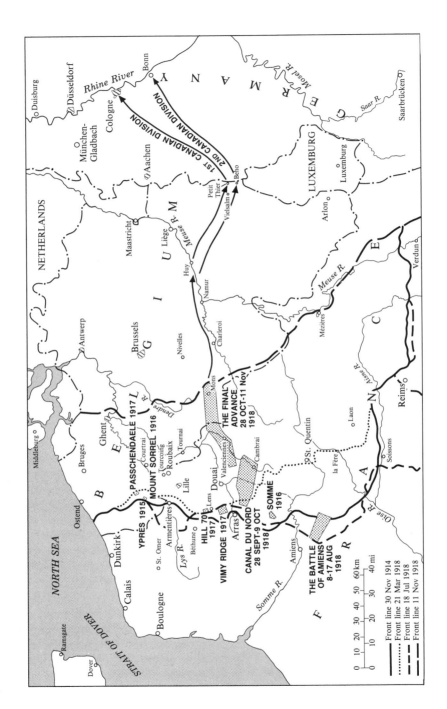

CEF operations: France and Belgium, 1915–18

former was diverted to Gallipoli, he was forced to choose between taking over some of the French line and joining the attack. He chose the latter course. Meanwhile, exasperated by Sir John's delay, Joffre had cancelled the French attack in the north. The British thrust thus became an independent operation. Details of the battle of Neuve Chapelle which ensued need not concern us here since Currie's brigade was not directly involved. The Canadian Division was on the British left. Its only task was to provide fire demonstrations along the front and, in the event of success, to follow up the British.[4]

Yet the battle had a latent significance that should not be overlooked. The British troops began the attack at 7:30 a.m. on 10 March, and within twenty minutes a breach of almost a mile was made in the German line. After the initial objective was taken about 10 a.m., the troops stopped and waited for further orders. Owing to broken communication lines, these did not arrive until almost dusk. Utilizing this delay, the Germans rushed up reinforcements, so that the new British attacks were quickly halted. Colonel Nicholson has claimed that Neuve Chapelle 'disastrously' demonstrated 'the disadvantages of rigid control from a high level.'[5] Although the initial attack had proved successful and had taken the enemy completely by surprise, delay in relaying orders and the refusal or inability of the troops on the ground to act on their own initiative without orders, were regrettable. Still more deplorable, however, was the absurd belief held by Sir John French and apparently concurred with by the commander of the First Army, Sir Douglas Haig, that having surprised the enemy on the morning of 10 March and having given him the afternoon to re-establish his line, the British could then achieve surprise on the morning of 11 March. On the evening of 10 March, when French sent congratulations to the officers and men of the First Army who had participated in the attack, his message contained the following sentence: 'The enemy has been completely surprised and I trust that tomorrow the effect of today's fighting will result in still greater success.'[6]

Attacks were ordered for the next day and again on 12 March. There were 'reports of sweeping British gains,' but these 'subsequently proved unfounded.'[7] Nevertheless the Canadian official history concludes: 'The realization that neither the Germans nor their defences were invulnerable contributed much to the morale of the Allied soldiers. The B.E.F. was now held in greater respect, both by the enemy ... and the French High Command, who would no longer relegate the British role to taking over additional frontage so as to relieve French troops for offensive action.'[8] From the present vantage point in time, however, it seems that the most pertinent feature of the Battle of Neuve Chapelle was the tenacity with which British generals persisted in the attempt to break through the enemy line after surprise had been lost. For those who had to do the fighting this inflexibility often had fatal consequences. As R.H. Mottram was to put it: 'We did not grasp, not being professional students of tactics, that in losing the surprise of the first few weeks, both sides lost the war.'[9] The tragedy was that professional soldiers sometimes seemed equally ignorant.

Giving fire support at Neuve Chapelle provided the first opportunity for the Canadians to use the tools of their deadly new trade; and those tools proved less than satisfactory. The Ross rifle had given a considerable amount of difficulty during training, but at Neuve Chapelle the men found it even more troublesome. The bayonet tended to fall off the rifle if the latter fired while the bayonet was fixed. Even worse, after sustained or rapid fire the bolt in the rifle would jam so that the breach could not be opened, Despite the fact that he knew such a report would not be welcomed by the minister of militia, a long-time champion of the Ross rifle, Currie reported these deficiencies after the battle. Currie also urged General Alderson, to whom his report was directed, to conduct the 'most rigid investigation' of the performance of the Ross rifle, since 'serious interference with rapid firing may prove fatal on occasions.'[10] Later this comment was to seem prophetic.

Shortly after Neuve Chapelle the Canadian Division was withdrawn from the front line for a short period of rest. On 1 April, while still resting, the Canadians came under command of Lieutenant-General Sir Herbert Plumer's v Corps. In his *History of Warfare* Field Marshal Viscount Montgomery of Alamein called Plumer a 'soldier's soldier.'[11] The Canadians would come to know him well. Plumer was then in command of British troops in the Ypres salient – an ugly bulge in the trench line around the city of Ypres – towards which the Canadians began to move on 5 April. The bulge was approximately ten miles across and about five miles deep, with Ypres more or less at its focal point. The city itself was in the centre of a shallow basin, and from the front lines on the rim of the basin the enemy's view of allied movements was excellent. The basin was bisected from north to south by the Yser canal and laced with small streams and roads that connected the tiny villages dotting the landscape. In April the British extended their front to man approximately two-thirds of the salient. The Canadian Division was placed on the extreme northern end of the British line, adjacent to the 45th Algerian Division.[12]

The Western Front, in Cyril Falls's words, had already 'coagulated' by the end of 1914; that is, the trench lines had been extended from Switzerland to the North Sea.[13] But in many places the trenches were for a long time very primitive. In few areas were they in a more haphazard condition than on the front that the Canadian Division took over from the 11th French Division in April 1915. The nature of this area and the shock that it produced when first encountered are clearly evident in the report of an engineer captain sent to inspect the trenches that Currie's brigade was to occupy. After noting that the trenches were not connected effectively for easy defence, that most of them lacked the protection of a parados, and that where breastworks existed they could easily be pierced by a bullet, the report continued: 'The water level is about 2 feet down below the surface of the ground with numerous shell holes and also a section of the trench behind partially filled with water ... in front ... are numerous dead bodies in a decomposed state laying on the surface of the ground, also in the trench itself ... there are numerous bodies buried at a very shallow depth making it impossible ... at many places to excavate at all. There is also human excreta littered all over the place ... [In conclusion] things were in a *deplorable state* from the standpoint of defence, safety and sanitation, and large quantities of disinfectant should be sent into the trenches immediately for liberal use.'[14]

The French had been able to hold these lines mainly because they kept a minimum number of troops in forward positions and relied on their excellent field guns to quell enemy attacks. The British, on the other hand, usually kept as many troops in the front line as possible with orders to 'hold the front trenches at all costs and in the event of any trench being lost, to counter-attack at once.'[15] Ironically, the traditional faith of the British in their defensive ability had produced less sophisticated defensive tactics than those of the French, whose traditional faith in the offensive had produced Plan XVII (the 1914 French war plan), one of the bloodiest blunders in history. The Canadians noted that although conditions in the salient were appalling, French casualties had been light, partly, perhaps, because of the 'state of semi-truce which obtained in some French sections when active operations were not in progress.'[16] But Currie's men were inclined to take no chances. They followed the French practice of restricting movement in the trenches during daylight hours and then refrained from giving away their position by futile firing on enemy aircraft.

Such were the conditions that confronted the 2nd Canadian Brigade when it occupied the Ypres salient. The fighting in which it was about to figure importantly is called officially the 'Battles of Ypres 1915,' and the Battles Nomenclature Committee subdivided the action into four separate battles.[17] Unofficially, it is usually known as 'Second Ypres' or as the 'First Gas Attack.' This action was the most important in which Currie, promoted to brigadier-general on 4 March 1915, participated as a brigade commander. By the end of March the German high command had decided to adopt a defensive attitude in the west until Russia had been beaten in the east. To cover preparation for an all-out offensive in the east, the remaining troops on the Western Front were to keep the Allies busy in every way possible, including 'attacks in so far as the modest numbers remaining there permitted.'[18] The attacks on the Ypres salient in April 1915 formed a part of this general strategy, and they were to introduce a new weapon – poison gas. In fact this was not the first occasion on which gas had been used, but the previous results had been disappointing, and the Germans still considered the weapon to be largely experimental.[19]

The Allied Forces were warned of an impending attack with gas, but there has been considerable debate as to whether the warning was passed down to the troops in the front line. Liddell Hart argues that the warning was given to divisional commanders but that 'no precautions against gas were suggested or ordered.'[20] A more recent critic claims that warnings were circulated only in the Artois area, several miles from Ypres.[21] Hart indicates that suspicion of enemy attack was lulled by a 'lack of any sign that the Germans were concentrating reserves,' and 'this lack of signs was due, not to special precautions, but the lack of such reserves.' In fact, word that a gas attack was to be expected was circulated to every battalion commander in the Canadian Division;[22] and as early as 15 April Currie recorded in his diary that an attack was 'expected at night to be preceded by the sending of poisonous gases to our lines.'[23] Colonel Duguid maintains that though there may have been no German reserves, there were, nevertheless, many indications of forthcoming attack opposite the Canadian and French troops in the salient, including 'pipes of some sort ... being installed in the enemy's parapet.'[24] In other words, Currie's brigade was thoroughly warned of the impending attack, but few preparations were made to meet it other than those already under way – namely, doing everything possible to strengthen the trenches taken over from the French. The men were not told specifically what to expect, simply because no one knew what to expect. If British generals had not taken the warnings as seriously as they might have done, they had not completely ignored them. By the same token Canadian soldiers did not take more definite steps to prepare for this attack because they were already doing everything they could.

The first phase of the German attack – the Battle of Gravenstafel Ridge – can be quickly summarized. Within the Ypres salient there was a total of six Allied divisions, while surrounding it were seven divisions and two independent brigades of the German Fourth Army.[25] Currie's men were placed in the line on the right of the Canadian front: to their right was the 28th British Division, on their left the 3rd Canadian Brigade under Brigadier-General R.E.W. Turner. That day, 22 April, proceeded as many another in the line: it was bright and the Germans intermittently shelled roads and bridges north and east of Ypres. About 5 p.m. the bombardment suddenly intensified and the Germans opened the valves on cylinders of chlorine gas buried along the northern edge of the salient. A greenish yellow cloud began to float slowly in a southwesterly direction enveloping elements of the 45th Algerian Division on the Canadian left flank. The Canadians were warned of the menace to their flank by the sound of small arms and the firing of French field guns. Soon the French colonial troops went streaming back, coughing and choking. What followed, according to the British official historian, was a 'soldiers' battle fought by brigadiers, regimental officers, and other ranks.'[26] The Germans rushed through the breach in the French line, while the Canadians desperately attempted to throw back a line along their left flank to seal the gap. Artillery fire had broken most telephone lines to the rear, and, not surprisingly, such information as did filter back was badly garbled. Turner, the commander of the 3rd Canadian Brigade, unwittingly was partly responsible for the confusion. He mistakenly reported that his left wing had withdrawn from the front to the reserve (or GHQ) line. In fact it still held the front.[27] When Currie learned that the 3rd Brigade on his left appeared to be in trouble, without waiting for orders he immediately sent the 10th Battalion to its assistance. He sensed that the most important area in the coming battle would be on Gravenstafel Ridge, known as locality 'C,' and he concentrated the 7th Battalion in this area.[28]

Gradually the situation became clear. Troops of the 3rd Brigade had not fallen back to the GHQ line, but a breach of some 8,000 yards long had been made in the Allied line to the left of the Canadian division. Disaster was averted not so much by the heroic efforts of the Canadians to guard this flank as by the fact that the German advance stopped. Instead of pouring through the gap in the Allied line and seizing the entire salient, the German troops were content to take a neat but generous portion of it. About 8 p.m. General Alderson was asked to co-operate with the French in an attempt to force the Germans to withdraw. He agreed to mount an attack with the 3rd Brigade.[29] Turner's men thus assaulted Kitcheners Wood, a small copse that the Germans had overrun. They managed to clear most of it by about midnight. The French attack, however, had failed to materialize, and the 3rd Brigade was forced to pull back from its exposed positions. British, French, and Canadian soldiers were thrown in wherever possible, and by first light on 23 April a ragged front had been established. Somehow during the night the German perimeter had been rimmed and the gap was closed. Arrangements were made for a second counter-attack on 23 April, again with French co-operation. It was mounted about 4:30 p.m., but it failed with substantial cost of life.[30]

The situation of the 2nd and 3rd Canadian Brigades on the morning of 24 April was critical indeed. The sizeable chunk of the salient that the Germans had taken on 22 and 23 April meant that the Canadians, instead of holding the centre of a gradual bulge, were now at the point of a fairly sharp angle. Further attacks, if not directly against them, must certainly threaten the Canadian lines of communication. The night of 23–24 April was thus a turmoil of preparation – bringing up ammunition, improving trench lines, repairing telephone wires, and evacuating wounded. At 4 a.m. on 24 April these preparations were interrupted, and the second phase of the fight, the battle of St Julien, opened with another gas attack. This time Currie's brigade was directly involved since the gas was released along a 1,200 yard front that bridged the boundary between the 2nd and 3rd Brigades.

For three days the situation in the salient was marked by slow German inroads, by confusion among the Allied forces which bordered on chaos, by individual and group actions of incredible bravery, and by indescribable horror. Nowhere was the 'fog of war' thicker than at Currie's headquarters. Throughout the successive attacks that followed his command was in the centre of the fighting.

Currie had received reassuring reports from his battalions in the line just before midnight of 23–24 April. Since he was enormously tired and also because there had been no aggressive action on his front for several hours, the brigadier lay down just after midnight to rest at his advance headquarters near the village of Fortuin.[31] Sleep was difficult, and barely three hours later he was up again, checking the latest situation reports. By 4 a.m. it was growing lighter. Hope began to grow that there would be no new attack. This fantasy was killed by the ring of a field telephone and the report of another gas release. The gas cloud, following the drift of the wind, partly enveloped the 8th, Currie's left battalion, where the men had been issued with makeshift respirators. It also completely covered the right battalion of the 3rd Brigade. The respirators worn by the men of the 8th Battalion were nothing but wet cotton bandoliers tied over the mouth and nose;[32] but they seemed to help, since the men of the 8th were able to repel the German infantry attack that followed the gas. On their left the battalions of the 3rd Brigade were not so successful; this was their second exposure to gas. Very quickly the Germans achieved a break of some 700 yards in the line of the 3rd Brigade, leaving the left flank of Currie's force ominously open. By 4:30 a.m. he was aware of this extreme danger on his left, and he quickly moved the reserves he could muster to that flank.[33] His task was made no easier by the sharp German artillery fire that accompanied the infantry attack. This barrage played havoc with telephone wires from brigade to the battalions and made communication by written messages carried by runners slow and uncertain.[34] As the situation became more critical and messages from his battalion commanders diminished, partly because of the difficulty with communications, partly because they were literally fighting for their lives, Currie asked for help from the British 85th Brigade on his right.[35] He received no encouragement there, but he was informed shortly afterwards that two battalions of the York and Durham Brigade were moving into his area to help as necessary. The gas by the time it reached Currie at brigade headquarters was no longer sufficienctly concentrated to be lethal, but 'it made the nose and eyes run and ... heads ache';[36] and brigade headquarters was under almost continuous artillery bombardment. Indeed, about 7 a.m. Currie's headquarters with all his kit was destroyed when a shell ignited the old building in which his command post was located. The brigadier quickly moved to the headquarters of the 2nd Artillery Brigade almost half a mile away and used the communication network established there for his own messages.[37]

By the time his move was accomplished, almost an hour and a half had elapsed since he had received the promise of reinforcements. Recognizing that time was critically important, since it was almost 10 a.m., Currie sent an officer from his staff to find the York and Durhams and lead them forward to the gap between the 2nd and 3rd Canadian Brigades.[38] Within an hour the messenger returned to say there was no sign of the promised help. He was immediately sent out again with instructions to await their arrival.

Meanwhile the situation on the left of the 2nd Canadian Brigade had become steadily worse. A series of messages from Colonel Lipsett indicated that the Germans had begun to move around the end of the 8th Battalion and were threatening to surround it. Shortly afterwards this bad news was substantiated by a message from Brigadier Turner of the 3rd Brigade, who confirmed the existence of a gap between his men and Currie's left. From the conversation with Turner, Currie obtained the impression that the 3rd Brigade was pulling back. This would leave his men even more exposed.[39] Throughout the morning Currie had sent every help that he could to the 8th Battalion, but now his reserves were exhausted and everything depended on the arrival of the British reinforcements. Currie could do no more than warn his men and the neighbouring 85th Brigade on his right that the 2nd might have to pull back.

About 11:35 there was better news. The divisional commander had ordered the 3rd Brigade to counter-attack rather than withdraw. Almost simultaneously Currie learned from Colonel Lipsett that the German advance around his battalion appeared to have slowed. Moments later, just before noon, Currie's orderly officer returned for the second time from his search for the York and Durham reinforcements. This time he reported that one of the promised battalions had arrived in the area near Wieltje, but that it would go no further forward. Apparently, the officer in charge of the battalion had been instructed to reinforce both the 2nd and 3rd Brigades, and he would not move further forward until more detailed instructions on the disposition of his troops arrived from his divisional headquarters.

Currie recognized that the moment for decisive action was close at hand. His own left was still in a critical position, so critical that he still contemplated a withdrawal, but the 3rd Brigade had been ordered to counter-attack in the gap of the Canadian line. Also the German advance seemed to be stopping, and there were Allied reserves in the support line near Wieltje. If only the 3rd could attack at once, if only those waiting reserves could be brought into the line quickly to help the counter-attack, the situation might be saved. It was almost noon on 24 April when Arthur Currie came to an important decision. Currie determined to leave his command post, return to the GHQ or support line, and personally bring back the reinforcements, hoping that 'they might move for me when unlikely to move for officers of lesser rank.'[40]

Before leaving, he contacted Colonel Lipsett, telling him of his plan and giving Lipsett provisional instructions to carry out a withdrawal if necessary. Currie later wrote that Lipsett 'felt that he might have to retire, but he did not wish to do so without an order.' Currie thus gave him authority to retire if necessary but told Lipsett that he was not to use it 'unless forced by circumstances.' 'As he was the man on the spot,' wrote Currie, 'I left it to his judgement, and Lipsett and myself had a clear understanding.'[41] With this understanding arranged, Currie immediately left his forward headquarters on foot for Wieltje, approximately a mile and a half to the rear. The journey was not an easy one. He was subjected to continous artillery fire from the enemy, and the roads were pocked with shell holes and littered with fallen trees. Currie found the York and Durhams at the GHQ line and talked with their brigadier who, however, refused to move his troops forward without orders from division.[42] Currie at this point learned that he was only a short distance from the temporary headquarters of the British 27th Divison, whose commander, Major-General T. D'O. Snow, that morning had been placed in command of all troops in corps reserve. Currie proceeded quickly to Snow's headquarters, less than a mile away, and again the route was under fire. He was once more refused help. Before leaving, he sent a complete report of his movements to General Alderson.[43] Then he retraced his steps to his command post.

Unknown to their commander, and also unknown to General Alderson, the men of the 2nd Brigade had maintained their front almost intact thanks to the welcome support of five British battalions that had begun moving into the gap on their left while Currie was making his report from the headquarters of General Snow. However, Currie thought that his efforts to secure help had been fruitless. He was anxious to get back to his command post and re-establish control of his men, a task likely to be as difficult as anything he had undertaken so far that day, because enemy shelling along the way seemed heavier than ever. On his way back to the front Currie encountered a number of men who had lost contact with their units and had drifted to the rear. He collected them as he proceeded and brought them forward with him. On arriving at his command post near Fortuin, Currie discovered that his staff had been forced to move once again, this time back to rear headquarters near Wieltje. After confirming the locations of his forward battalions and seeing that the strangers he had collected were sent forward, he again began the dangerous journey to the rear to Wieltje, where he finally found his staff. He brought himself up to date on the situation as quickly as possible and sent a further report on his brigade to divisional headquarters.[44]

By the time Currie's report was completed it was after 11 p.m. He had begun the day twenty hours earlier, refreshed only by a fitful sleep of less than three hours. Since that time he had been constantly alert and under considerable strain. If we plot his movements on a map, which makes no allowances for bends or twists in paths or roads or the endless detours necessitated by constant shelling, it can be seen that he walked over six miles during the day. For most of that period worry and frustration, to say nothing of danger, had been his constant companions. The situation still seemed dangerous, but there appeared little more that he could do. Thus, shortly before midnight, he dropped into an exhausted sleep.

Throughout the day the overall position of the 2nd Canadian Brigade had been hazardous to say the least, but Currie, or in his absence his brigade major, Lieutenant-Colonel Kemmis-Betty,[45] had maintained a clear picture of the location of the 2nd Brigade forward units and an equally clear appreciation of their danger. This was not always the case in the other components of the Canadian Division, or at General Alderson's headquarters. Indeed after the gap in the Canadian line to the left of Currie's troops had been closed by the fortuitous appearance of the British battalions, Brigadier-General Turner, unaware of the nature of the situation, ordered part of the British troops to withdraw. At dusk the gap was beginning to open once again.[46] Units had become hopelessly jumbled in most of the Ypres salient. In an effort to restore order as well as stop the re-opening of the gap between the 2nd and 3rd Brigades, General Alderson sent his chief staff officer forward in the early hours of 25 April with 'full powers to take whatever action he might find necessary.'[47] This officer, Lieutenant-Colonel Gordon-Hall, like his chief a British officer serving with the Canadians, had summoned all the Canadian brigade commanders to a meeting at the headquarters of the 2nd Brigade. Gordon-Hall arrived at Currie's headquarters between 2 and 3 a.m. on the morning of 25 April. He found Currie 'worn out and in a dead sleep'; but none of the other commanders had arrived. He woke Currie and later described the scene which followed:

I ... asked for details of the situation on the 2nd and adjacent brigade fronts, and was given them so fully that by the time the other brigadiers arrived a plan had been decided upon.

I could not help being struck by Currie's attitude. He knew that the 5th and 8th Battalions still held and that the remnants of the 7th and 10th were near by, but as to what had happened to the latter units he did not know further than that they had gone to the assistance of the other brigadiers. He might have asked many questions ... but he raised no difficulties. He collected his staff, walked out into the night to get in touch with Lipsett and fill in, as far as he could, the gap between Lipsett's left and the General Headquarters Line.[48]

There were in fact almost 300 men from the 7th and 10th Battalions who had become separated from their units and had collected near Currie's headquarters. Currie gathered these soldiers together and took them forward to reinforce his extreme left flank. To be better in touch with the situation Currie decided to go with the men and make a personal reconnaissance of his front. Once there he established his command post at the 5th Battalion headquarters.

In many respects 25 April was a repeat of 24 April. It was just as harrowing, and no less bloody for the men of the 2nd Brigade than the previous day had been. For Currie the chief difference was that he spent the entire day in the front line with the 5th Battalion. It became obvious in the early morning that unless other troops could push the Germans back on the left of the 2nd Brigade, it would be impossible for Currie's men to hang on to their original positions. The British 10th Brigade was pushed forward from reserve to achieve this objective; but in spite of heroic efforts, the counter-attack failed. Early in the afternoon Currie was forced to order a withdrawal from the exposed positions. Withdrawal in daylight, however, would have been more dangerous than remaining forward, so the movement was to begin at dusk. Throughout the long afternoon Currie had ample opportunity to observe the number of Canadians who had thrown away their jammed Ross rifles and picked up Lee-Enfields dropped by British casualties.'[49] All around him men were dying from an increasingly intense German bombardment. Colonel Nicholson later recorded that as they waited for the cover of darkness many of Currie's men were 'simply blown out of their trenches by artillery fire.'[50]

At nightfall the withdrawal began. Shortly after midnight most of the remaining soldiers of the 2nd Brigade were safely behind the GHQ line. Although the rest of the Canadian Division was relieved almost at once, the 2nd Brigade was ordered slightly forward once again, in support of the British 28th Division. It remained ready to move into the front but was harassed by artillery fire until after dark on 27 April, when it was finally placed in reserve and marched back to bivouack. On 6 May, after his brigade had reached its rest area, Currie for the first time in fifteen days was able to sleep through the night undisturbed.[51]

Of all the battles on the Western Front in 1915, the Battle of Ypres was unique in three respects. First, it was the only German offensive in the northwest and came within an ace of being successful. Second, it introduced a new and terrifying weapon, poison gas. At Ypres the Allied forces had no defence whatsoever against this weapon. Gradually a whole system, alarms, respirators, gas-proof dugouts and clothing, was developed, and gas became 'only another of the known horrors of war.'[52] At Ypres, however, Currie and his men had faced a psychologically and physically horrifying secret weapon. Finally, this battle was Currie's first tour in a major operation; to use a lugubrious military term, the 2nd Brigade was 'blooded' at Ypres. It had sustained 1,829 casualties between 22 April and 3 May.[53] His 10th Battalion, which had been under the orders of the 3rd Brigade for most of the operation, had been severely mauled. On 23 April 'two-thirds of the officers, all the company commanders and half of the men,' including Lieutenant-Colonel Boyle, the battalion commander, were lost during the attack on Kitcheners Wood.[54]

Despite these distinctive features, the battle that continued for some three weeks after Currie's little force had been withdrawn, was remarkably similar to other battles in 1915 in which the British or French took the offensive. In all of them superlatives can justifiably be used for the suffering and heroism ever present; yet repetition of the horrors of this fighting becomes monotonous. In tactics there was practically no variation, and, other than changing place names, a single description fits nearly all: 'After air reconnaisance of the ... enemy positions, artillery pounded their wire, machine gun nests, and trenches. After the barrage had been 'lifted to the rear ... the men went 'over the top' in waves about a hundred yards apart, with the men in each wave six to eight feet from each other ... . The attackers usually carried the first line and often the second before being halted by the enemy's reserves. In all of 1915 the British and French did not gain more than three miles at any one point.'[55]

Currie was promoted to brigadier-general on 13 September 1915. On 18 May 1915 the 2nd Brigade took over a section of line held by the 7th British Division near the Village of Festubert. Two days later Currie was ordered to attack in the evening and seize a point in the German front line designated on the map as 'K.5.' After careful reconnaissance Currie was unable to identify his objective. Shelling had destroyed most landmarks, and complicating the situation was the fact that the only available map of Festubert not only contained a number of errors but was printed with south at the top of the sheet.[56] Currie argued that the attack should be postponed to give more time for reconnaissance and preparations.[57] His request was denied, but the implication it contained, that without postponement the attack would fail, proved correct. Despite repeated attempts by the 2nd Brigade and urgent supplications from the army commander, K.5 was not taken until the morning of 24 May, when an attack for which there had been 'careful reconnaissance and detailed preparation,' proved successful.[58]

The last front line tour in which Currie's brigade played a role took place near the tiny village of Givenchy, where the 2nd Brigade took over a section of trenches. In June 1915 the battalions of the 2nd were under 60 per cent of establishment, and special tactical dispositions were arranged to link them in pairs in order to make up for the deficiency of numbers.[59] Fortunately the 2nd was not required to mount a major attack, and its tour at Givenchy was therefore not so costly as previous tours at the front. On the night of 22–23 June, the brigade was relieved and began marching north to join the III Corps of Second Army near Ploegsteert, some seventeen miles to the north. The entire Canadian Division remained in that area until mid-September 1915. A quiet time was essential to re-build the shattered Canadian ranks, and fortunately the summer of 1915 at Ploegsteert provided this. In the words of the Canadian official history: 'From late June to mid-September a strange tranquility persisted across the Canadian front. Apart from the activity of snipers on both sides and one small patrol clash in no man's land, the only hostilities were an occasional exchange of light shelling by the opposing artilleries, which in general confined their attention to registering targets.'[60]

The summer of 1915, however, was not an easy one for Currie. Many people have noted the curious effect that rest can produce after intense strain – in the dressing room the competitive athlete often gives way to tears following a victory or a defeat; the public speaker, once off the platform, seems tongue-tied; the surgeon, so steady during the operation, afterwards seems to fumble. Lord Moran in his analysis of the qualities that produce courage in war wrote that 'when you get into Division Rest, right back here under peace conditions, when you see the men full of life and fun, it is then the stupid cruelty of things eats into the mind.'[61] He noted that often men who have appeared cool and sure in action will become morose or unstrung in the period of rest following battle. The summer of 1915 was Currie's first opportunity to relax from the strain of a winter and spring in the trenches, to review in his own mind the decisions he had made in battle and to contemplate the possible effect of alternative decisions. Perhaps it was lucky that Currie was not a more introspective or imaginative person, for in that case the review inevitably would have been even more painful. If not self-analytical, Currie was nevertheless a sensitive man, and he could hardly avoid periods of near despair when casualty figues indicated the toll of a winter in the line. But, except in his prewar financial arrangements, he was a man of common sense, and common sense indicated that the best way to prevent losses in the future was to make good the losses of the past. Unprepared and understrength units always had more casualties than others. Thus, Currie became engaged in the process of assimilating into the ranks of the 2nd Brigade the reinforcement drafts that arrived during the summer. While he was spared for the moment making decisions that immediately affected the lives of those he commanded, the rest period presented other responsiblities. He had to meet and entertain a variety of visitors, often men of importance. During a short leave in July he went to London and there met and dined with the prime minister, the acting Canadian high commissioner in London, Sir George Perley, and the influential Sir Max Aitken (later Lord Beaverbrook). Sam Hughes was also in London and later visited Currie's brigade headquarters. As yet there was no open break between the two men, and Hughes congratulated Currie on the success of his brigade.[62]

During the spring of 1915 units of the second contingent of volunteers from Canada began arriving in England. Throughout the summer there was considerable speculation on who would be selected to command the new division. Most people assumed that once the 2nd Division was formed, the precedent established by the Australians would be followed, and a Canadian corps of two divisions would be established.[63] Although the War Office offered a selection from any of the unemployed generals in the British army,[64] the Canadian government eventually decided that the new division should be commanded by one of the serving Canadian brigadiers. Kitchener was inclined to accept the recommendation of Sir John French that Currie was the most able and the best choice of the Canadian brigadiers,[65] but Sam Hughes insisted on choosing the commanders of any new units. Hughes favoured the appointment of Richard Turner, and as usual he got his way. But he agreed that Currie should be given the 1st Division if and when a Canadian corps were formed under General Alderson.[66] Thus, after the formation of the Canadian Corps and Alderson's elevation to corps commander, Currie was given command of the 1st Division on 13 September 1915.

How successful was Currie as a brigadier-general? The answer is not simple, partly because of the paucity of resource material. Currie's diary in 1915 was more an intinerary and log of events than a record of his reflections, and little of his correspondence from this period has survived. The answer is complex mostly because of the shadowy role that a brigadier-general had to play in the First World War. Although it would not be difficult to write at greater length than has been done about the operations in which the Canadians participated, little more could be said of Currie's involvement or the nature of his contribution.

Strategy was not the concern of the infantry brigadier; he was involved solely with tactical employment of his brigade, and even here freedom of action was more restricted than one might imagine. When the brigade was employed offensively, as at Festubert, objectives were predetermined by a higher command. The brigade commander would then decide whether the assigned task required one, two, or more of the battalions under his command; usually even the outlines of artillery and other support were passed to him from higher formations and worked out in detail at the battalion level. When involved in a defensive battle, the brigadier's role was similar: his major tactical decisions concerned the disposition of his battalions (leaving, of course, battalion dispositions to battalion commanders) and the commitment of his brigade reserve. Obviously a good brigadier might do more than this – he would provide troops with that inestimable sense of security that comes only from the presence of a general officer sharing a dangerous position; he would not hesitate to oppose higher or lower commands if their actions appeared dangerous to his command. A good brigadier-general in short, would display certain requisite characteristics of good generalship on any level. Among other things these would include 'Insight on the battlefield, boldness, concentration and generally sophisticated following of the principles of war, all of which ... reflect an analysis of some continuing features of human behaviour in ... the conduct of war.'[67] But because the brigadier's objectives were limited and his resources defined by a superior commander, it is rather more difficult to judge generalship at the brigade level than in more senior ranks.

By these standards Currie stood out very favourably indeed. During training days in England he had done an admirable job under miserable conditions. He avoided excessive interference in the battalion commanders' affairs, yet took every opportunity to see the troops personally. There is no record of whether Currie inspected the trenches his brigade occupied at Ypres, but it is certain that he was thoroughly familiar with them by the time the Germans attacked. Moreover, in all subsequent operations there is evidence that he made a careful personal reconnaissance of the front before his brigade moved in.

Defensively, Currie again shows up very well. He was quick to appreciate the tactical advantages of the French methods of defence. Throughout the rest of his career in France he continued to insist that daytime activity meant heavy casualties and that large numbers of men in the front line trenches served no useful purpose. During the gas attack at Ypres Currie did not hesitate to commit his reserves, which explains the long stand made by his brigade. He displayed boldness in going back for more reinforcements when other means failed. Considering the gravity of the situation at Ypres, he maintained remarkable control over his brigade. Though the full story of other brigades has not been dealt with here, Currie, by comparison with other brigadier-generals, performed most creditably. In the 3rd Brigade on 24 April, for example, conditions were at least as difficult as in the 2nd Brigade. General Turner, who was never certain of the position of his front line, was unable to remedy the situation and sent a stream of conflicting location reports to divisional headquarters.[68] In contrast, when Currie's front threatened to break on 25 April, he moved his command post and his reserves to the threatened area and throughout the entire attack he frequently shared exposed positions with his soldiers. There is some evidence to indicate that Currie kept abreast of weapon performance. After the battle of Ypres his adverse report on the Ross rifle contributed to Sir John French's decision to withdraw the rifle from the Canadian Division.[69] During Ypres it was Currie's 8th Battalion, along with the 15th Battalion of the 3rd Brigade, that was subjected to the most severe gas attack on the morning of 24 April. The men of the 8th Battalion, however, had been provided with makeshift respirators which, though primitive, were better than nothing and probably contributed to the firm stand that was made.

Regarding offensive action, there is little to say about Brigadier-General Currie, simply because he was not engaged in any offensive to rival the gas attack in scale. We note that at Festubert he did not hesitate to make objections when he considered the attack on K.5 to be premature, and, according to Urquhart, Currie also protested against a later minor attack at Givenchy and 'got rapped over the knuckles for doing so.'[70]

Obviously the evidence for making sound judgment on Currie's capacity for commanding a brigade is not as conclusive as one would wish. Some of the

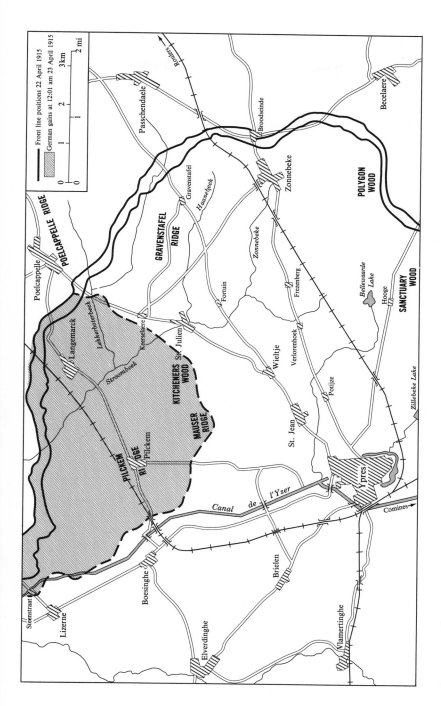

Area surrounding Ypres, 1915–17

Front line positions 22 April 1915
German gains at 12:01 am 23 April 1915

0   1   2   3km
0   1   2 mi

POELCAPPELLE RIDGE
Poelcappelle
Langemarck
Lekkerboterbeek
Keerselare
Stroombeek
St. Julien
KITCHENERS WOOD
MAUSER RIDGE
PILCKEM RIDGE
Pilckem
Steenstraat
Lizerne
Boesinghe
Canal de l'Yser
Elverdinghe
Brielen
Vlamertinghe
St. Jean
Wieltje
Verlorenhoek
Potijze
Ypres
Comines
Zillebeke Lake
SANCTUARY WOOD
Hooge
Bellewaarde Lake
Frezenberg
Zonnebeke
Fortuin
Haanebeek
Gravenstafel
GRAVENSTAFEL RIDGE
Zonnebeke
POLYGON WOOD
Becelaere
Broodseinde
Passchendaele
Roulers

evidence here presented might be used to qualify a favourable assessment of his conduct. One might, for example, suggest that the commander of the 8th Battalion deserved the credit for improvising respirators, but a search of the available records sheds no light on this possibility. It may also seem that Currie committed his reserve too soon at Ypres and that he ought not to have left his command post in a futile personal search for reinforcements. For such questions there are no final answers. But, given reasonable benefit of any doubt, it appears that Currie acquitted himself well.

4

Division commander

Field Marshal Viscount Montgomery of Alamein has argued that the difficulty in most military problems is the necessity 'to simplify, and to select from the mass of detail those things and only those things which are important.'[1] In September 1915 this was precisely Currie's problem. During the previous winter the Canadians were introduced to trench warfare and learned the cost of modern war. The price had been high, which meant that the comparatively light casualties in July and August, coming on top of the heavy winter losses, hurt more than the relatively low numbers for the summer months would suggest. Total casualties for the 2nd Canadian Infantry Brigade to the end of May 1915 had been approximately 75 per cent of its establishment,[2] which meant that assimilating reinforcements and rebuilding the battalions took priority over virtually all other tasks. Just as he was beginning to feel comfortable in command of the 2nd Brigade, Currie had been made responsible for an entire division. The change in scale was substantial – and he was confronted with a myriad of details and problems that were new and unfamiliar. The only answer was to simplify and concentrate on the most essential matters. The task was the most challenging he had ever faced, and he felt ill prepared for it.[3]

The 2nd Brigade had consisted of approximately 4,000 infantry soldiers. The division, by comparison, was a self-contained fighting formation that included its own ancillary fighting arms and services; in addition to three infantry brigades it comprised cavalry, artillery, engineers, medical services, a supply train, and many other smaller components. While larger formations, a corps or an army, could vary in size (a corps being two or more divisions, an army two or more corps) a division was a fixed quantity in terms of which a commander-in-chief normally reckoned his forces. In 1914–15 the division, in round numbers, consisted of 18,000 men, 76 field guns and howitzers, and 5,600 horses, as well as the means to feed, supply, and sustain them.[4] To assist in controlling this formation the divisional commander had a substantial staff. In the command of the 2nd Brigade, Currie had been accustomed to reaching most decisions on the spot and by himself, the only person in a position to offer advice being his brigade major. At division, he was surrounded with a coterie of administrative specialists to relieve him of the day-to-day maintenance of the division, and by expert artillery and engineer officers to advise him on the technical difficulties of their particular arms.[5] Not only was it necessary for the divisional commander to exercise personal command, but it was also essential that he run a happy team.

Fortunately for Currie, the autumn of 1915 was relatively quiet. In the abortive Battle of Loos, which resulted in the replacement of Sir John French by Sir Douglas Haig as commander-in-chief, the Canadians were given no significant role, and, apart from one or two minor raids, the troops of the 1st Division were not involved in any important fighting until the end of March 1916. This was fortunate for Currie in three respects. The heavy losses of early 1915 and the change in command meant that for some months his division would not be at peak efficiency. Secondly, he found all ranks of his division involved in a battle with the elements which sapped their energy and spirits. Only a year before, Salisbury Plain had seemed unbelievably inhospitable, but in 1915 'Flanders rain was like no other rain that had ever fallen on earth.' Trenches and shelters dissolved, cooking fires were almost impossible, disease rates rose alarmingly, and the consequent misery of the soldiers was intense.[6] Finally, problems of a partly personal nature occupied Currie's attention at this time and no doubt would have hampered his efficiency if the division had been engaged in action.

Apparently undiminishable, Currie's debts must have remained a waspish irritation. The debts, of course, were linked unbreakably to the cashed uniform cheque which he had made no move to redeem in spite of his substanial increase in salary. As a brigade commander he had earned approximately $4,380 per year. As a divisional commander his pay jumped to $8,760 per year.[7] Whether he did not repay the 50th Regiment because he was simply too busy, or because the problem no longer seemed important, or for some other reason, we do not know. However, it is clear that he took no steps to clear the slate. Like most soldiers, Currie missed his wife and family, and the joy of a thirteen-day reunion in England late in November was marred only by the expense the family's trip had involved. Notes in his diaries indicate a close bond between Currie and his family but give little insight into his relationships. He kept family affairs rigidly separated from his professional day-to-day routine. This was not the case, however, with his personal relationship with Sam Hughes.

Toward Hughes Currie had mixed feelings which became increasingly complicated in 1915. In a sense Currie had come into the CEF as Hughes's protege. He had served in the militia with Garnet Hughes, who had urged the acceptance of his father's offer of a brigade. Currie therefore felt a certain obligation towards the elder Hughes, and he expressed this sentiment in May 1915 in a personal letter to the minister: 'I am in more ways than one indebted to you,' he wrote, 'for the privilege of being connected with ... [the 2nd] Brigade since its mobilization ... . Let me express my deep and lasting gratitude to you for your kindness to me and for having given me this chance.'[8] But as Hughes's behaviour became increasingly erratic, the strain of this obligation became more difficult to bear. Any reciprocity of affection had been prejudiced when Currie, in April 1915, made an adverse report on the performance of the Ross rifle. In the autumn two other matters contributed further to the derogation of Currie in Hughes's estimation.

When the 2nd Canadian Division was formed and General Turner took command of it in August 1915, the need for experienced staff officers in various positions became apparent. With the formation of the Canadian Corps under General Alderson in mid-September, the need was elevated to an urgent demand. In December 1915 the 3rd Canadian Division was formed, basically from men and organizations already in England, and placed under command of General Mercer, previously commander of the 3rd Brigade. It was then even more apparent that there was a great need for experienced specialists on the staff of all Canadian fighting formations. There were simply not enough Canadian officers with the training and experience to fill these positions, and British officers, consequently, were placed in key staff jobs.

At each stage in the expansion of the Canadian forces, Sir[9] Sam Hughes strenuously insisted that staff positions should be filled by Canadians. Hughes had an early ally in Sir Max Aitken, later Lord Beaverbrook. Hughes appointed Aitken the Canadian 'Eyewitness,' a kind of glorified official war correspondent.[10] In this position Aitken held an office that, if poorly defined, suited him perfectly and gave him access to virtually all senior officers in the British forces. In November 1915 Sir Sam gave Aitken very specific instructions on the issue of British staff officers with the Canadian forces.

You will kindly protest most emphatically against staff and other positions ... being filled by British officers. We have soldiers fit for the highest positions. It is discreditable to have British officers run the Army Corps and Divisional positions. It would be insulting to have them brought into the Brigades. The men ... require no staff college theorists to direct them ... . There is altogether too much staff college paternalism and espionage abroad. If the feeling of returned soldiers were known, another Boston tea party might be looked for. Surely they can find positions for their pets among the British but I will not submit to our force being burdened with them. They were no strength whatever in any of the big fights, on the contrary in some instances they were a serious weakness to us. You may make this as clear as you wish. Better read this to Bonar Law.[11]

Currie was an advocate of the Canadian Corps, becoming a national formation, but he recognized that this was impossible without serious loss of efficiency. British officers could not be replaced by Canadians, in his estimation, unless the Canadians possessed the training and experience to do the job. When asked about the employment of British officers in his own division, he replied that those serving in the 1st Divison could not then be replaced by Canadians; for it was not a 'question of whether a man is a Canadian or otherwise, it is one of the best man for the job.'[12]

During the autumn of 1915 Currie confronted the known wishes of Sam Hughes in a second and unprecedented fashion. Garnet Hughes had been General Turner's chief staff officer in the 3rd Brigade during the gas attack at Ypres. When the 2nd Division was formed, he was given a staff position in that formation. In October 1915 Sir Sam directed that Garnet be again promoted and placed in command of one of the brigades of the 2nd Division. General Alderson, concerned about the inexperience of 2nd Division soldiers, wanted the senior officers of that division to have as much combat experience as possible. He therefore directed that Garnet should become a brigadier in the 1st rather than the 2nd Division.[13] Currie, however, was worried about his own formation. He, too, wanted experienced officers. When General Turner moved from the 3rd Brigade to the 2nd Division, he had been replaced by Brigadier R.G.E. Leckie. Leckie was a veteran of the Boer War and had come overseas as commanding officer of the 16th Battalion. Currie's own replacement in the 2nd Brigade was Lieutenant-Colonel Lipsett from the 8th Battalion upon whom he had learned to rely. When he learned that Mercer was leaving the command of the 1st Brigade, he wanted an experienced replacement. Although Currie liked Garnet Hughes personally, he argued that Hughes was not sufficiently experienced to command a brigade. Because of Currie's objection the appointment of Garnet Hughes was delayed for over a month. It was confirmed only when Currie was on leave in England.[14]

Currie's opposition to Garnet Hughes as a brigade commander could not be concealed from the minister, and to Currie's credit he made no attempt to hide it. Currie was not a schemer and seemed incapable of operating slyly. Typically, he attempted to clear the air by explaining his objections directly to Garnet Hughes. At that time an open breach between the two men was avoided, and on the surface at least there was no difficulty. Currie heard nothing from Hughes senior and the episode appeared to be closed. Soon, however, other causes of estrangement were to arise.

Refreshed from his leave and reassured after seeing his family, Currie plunged into the task of mastering his job. Without a major operation to supervise, he was able to concentrate on becoming thoroughly familiar with his new command. He began by picking the brains of corps staff officers, particularly those British officers who had had experience in divisional actions. For several months, according to General McNaughton, then a staff officer in the corps artillery, Currie spent hours each week in conversation with the corps staff, demanding solutions for one theoretical problem after another.[15] He took every opportunity to know his subordinate officers well. Currie's diary indicates that a day rarely passed without his slipping away from his headquarters to visit units and study the officers working there.

Periodically Currie also tried to see the rank and file under his command, but his relationship with the troops was usually formal. On Christmas Day 1915 he was on his feet for almost twelve hours walking from one unit to another in the trenches; but he did not possess the capacity to inspire as Montgomery did during the Second World War. Surviving veterans of the ranks usually believe Currie was a good general but have no strong affection for him. To the men in the ranks he often seemed pompous. Superficially at least, Currie resembled the British commander-in-chief, Sir Douglas Haig, in his inability to be impressive before a large group. The difference between them was that Currie was reserved because he was shy; he did not possess the stiff dignity that often inhibited Haig. This point is perhaps best illustrated by two anecdotes told about Haig and Currie. Haig used to conduct his formal inspections of troops in complete silence: 'There is a story told that one of his staff suggested it would create a good impression if he would occasionally stop and speak to one or two men. He took the advice and asked one man; 'Where did you start this war?' The astonished soldier replied: 'I didn't start this war, sir; I think the Kaiser did.''[16] Haig never tried again. Currie, on the other hand, reacted with good humour when challenged from below. Allegedly he had a very curious encounter (part of which is confirmed in his diary) with an eccentric but renowned mining expert who was serving in the ranks, but whose special ability was known to a member of Currie's staff. This individual, known as 'Foghorn' Macdonald because of his penetrating voice, was called in by the staff to give advice on a difficult tunnelling operation. After reading Macdonald's report, and without realizing the author was the soldier lounging in the corner of his headquarters, Currie vigorously rejected the recommendations saying that they made no sense to him. Immediately Corporal Macdonald interjected with the comment: 'Look here, old man Currie, you don't know the first thing about mines. I have forgotten more about them than you will ever know. You may say what you like about the rest, but don't you try coming it over me about the mine, just because you are the stud duck in this puddle.'[17] Unlike Haig, who gave up after his encounter, Currie found the episode amusing and accepted Macdonald's report. Once the ice had been broken, Currie usually overcame his shyness and could be very impressive. Among most of the officers of the 1st Division he inspired intense loyalty.

It is easy to underestimate the consequences of personal rivalries or personality clashes in any hierarchical organization. One tends to forget, for example, that a politician's greatest enemies and his real struggles are usually within his own party and not with the opposition. Even in armies, where authority is directly proportional to rank and rank is carefully graded, it is misleading to assume that personality plays no part in determining policy. Much of Currie's success can be attributed to his refusal to engage in personal disputes even when greatly provoked, a quality that helps explain the tremendous loyalty of his subordinate officers.

However, operations conducted in early 1916 served to increase personal frictions in the Canadian Corps until an open rupture among senior commanders occurred which Currie could not avoid and resulted in General Alderson's transfer. During the gas attack at Ypres a year earlier, mutual confidence between General Alderson and Brigadier-General Turner had been severely strained. Alderson, we should recall, was a regular officer with a long and successful career in the British army who displayed the qualities of a British gentleman. He was well liked by Currie. For his refusal to accept second-rate equipment, the Canadians were grateful. For many his introduction of wet-canteens on Salisbury Plain had granted him even more heroic proportions. Like Currie, Turner had had a long association with the militia, and he had won the Victoria Cross and the Distinguished Service Order when a subaltern in the Boer War. He was a brave, quick, and impatient man, who, during the Battle of Ypres, began to suspect that Alderson was not in control of the situation. Alderson had similar thoughts about Turner.

Small by Western Front standards, an action begun in March 1916 near the French village of St Eloi involved only Turner's division but had significant consequences for the entire corps. Turner took over a position from British troops: a series of craters blown in the German line were to be occupied by the 6th Brigade under the command of Brigadier-General H.D.B. Ketchen. Ketchen was a veteran of the Boer War and had served in the British army, the North West Mounted Police, and since 1901 in the Canadian Permanent Force. He had come overseas with the 2nd Canadian Division and directly owed his selection as commander of the 6th Infantry Brigade to Sam Hughes. The action at St Eloi was his first combat experience of the war. The area into which Ketchen's men moved came under a severe artillery bombardment as they were marching in. The gunfire lasted for almost two days and was so intense that it became necessary to rotate the battalions taking part in the attack earlier than had been planned. While the rotation was in progress, the Germans again attacked.[18] Four of the seven craters were overrun by the enemy. The 6th Brigade counter-attacked and two craters were recaptured. Unfortunately Ketchen reported that the ones recaptured were two which were still held by the Germans. There were several indications of the error; Currie suspected it as early as 11 April.[19] But the mistake was not realized in the 2nd Canadian

Division until April 16th. Three days later the Germans recaptured the two craters held by the 6th Brigade, and after a period of intense bombardment the front at St Eloi gradually became quiescent.[20]

By any standards, the action at St Eloi was a fiasco. Several mistakes had been made by the British troops before the Canadians moved into the area, and the Canadians had almost 2,000 casualties in their short tenure. After such an action it was normal for investigations to take place and they were quickly begun. Criticism after the fact is always simpler than on-the-spot perception, but criticism seemed merited, and the ubiquitous Sir Max Aitken became involved in the investigation. General Alderson was ordered to take 'severe disciplinary action' by the army commander, General Plumer, who apparently wanted to relieve both Turner and Ketchen for their share in the action.[21] The commander of the 27th Canadian Battalion was replaced, and General Alderson initiated an adverse report on Brigadier Ketchen. Turner refused to endorse the report on his brigadier, and Alderson then suggested that Turner be relieved. From Alderson's point of view this was the second occasion on which Turner had been confused about the location of his front. Turner apparently anticipated that Alderson would take some such action, and he appealed to Aitken to invervene. The British commander-in-chief, Sir Douglas Haig, had been keeping an anxious eye on the situation. As early as 16 April Haig recorded in his diary that Turner, 'though a VC, is not quite fit for his work.'[22] By 21 April Haig had penetrated to the heart of the problem. He reflected on it at some length in his diary:

General Plumer ... wishes to remove General Turner ... and Brig. Gen. Ketchen ... Another letter mentions "some feeling against the English exists amongst some of the Canadians ... " No doubt these two officers are not very efficient, but ... I doubt if we can find a Canadian officer with the training and knowledge necessary to replace Turner. But the main point is whether the danger of a serious feud between the Canadians and British is greater than the retention of a couple of incompetent commanders. After careful thought I have decided not to concur with Plumer as regards Turner but to keep him on. My reasons are that the conditions were abnormally difficult, under such conditions mistakes are to be expected, but that all did their best and made a gallant fight.[23]

Two days after Haig wrote these words, Sir Max Aitken paid a most important call on the commander-in-chief in France. He informed Haig, the 'Prime Minister of Canada makes a personal request that General Turner should not be relieved,' but that if Haig decided otherwise, the Canadian government would support his decision.[24] Haig had already decided to keep Turner and Ketchen and, according to Aitken, now proposed that Alderson would have to be removed.[25] During the course of the discussion it was arranged that an appointment would be created elsewhere for Alderson. Within a month the details had been worked out and Alderson became inspector-general of Canadian troops in England. On 19 May Haig chose Lieutenant-General Sir Julian Byng to be the new commander of the Canadian Corps.

On the surface it would seem that the British commander-in-chief was quite willing to sacrifice an ageing but active and efficient senior officer rather than risk Canadian ill-will by replacing two 'not very efficient' officers. However, General Alderson's replacement was not interpreted in this way by Currie or by most Canadian troops. On the contrary, it appeared to many that Alderson was 'a brave commander who was sacrificed to the Ross rifle' and to the whims of Sir Sam Hughes.[26] This popular view of the matter is considerably overdrawn. Indeed Lord Beaverbrook subsequently wrote that 'any history that tries to suggest that Sir Sam Hughes had responsibility for the removal of General Alderson, or that the issue arose in the remotest degree in relation to the Ross rifle, is not a history at all. It is a romance.'[27] Strictly speaking, Beaverbrook is correct. But the Ross rifle was in fact an issue at the time of the St Eloi attack, even though as far as Beaverbrook was concerned it was not connected with Alderson's removal. Lord Beaverbrook appears to have forgotten when writing the above that on 10 May 1916 he had warned Sir Sam that a very formidable attack on the Ross was developing.[28] However, Colonel Nicholson cautiously accepts Aitken's testimony and concludes that the '*immediate* cause of Alderson's removal' was not the 'differences of opinion between himself and the Minister of Militia regarding the use of the Ross rifle.'[29]

Yet it seems highly likely that the fiasco at St Eloi was also a convenient excuse for Hughes to get rid of Alderson. The withdrawal of the Ross from the 1st Division has been noted. Regardless of the experience of the 1st Division, the 2nd and 3rd Divisions (the latter was formed on Christmas Day 1915, under command of Major-General M.S. Mercer) had been armed with the Ross. Early in 1916, after a series of tests of both the Ross and the Enfield rifles, Alderson had expressed his position on the former in a letter to the chief of the general staff in Canada. His letter was reasonable and balanced. It listed the deficiencies discovered in the Ross, reviewed the history of tests conducted, and stated his personal opinion: 'I hold no brief for the Lee-Enfield,' wrote Alderson, '(the Martini was still the rifle when I commanded a company) and I did, and still do, as regards the 2nd and 3rd Divisions, discourage any crying down of the Ross ... What I shall not stop, however, is a *bonafide* report against the Ross should it come in after any future serious action that any part of the Corps may take part in.'[30] This letter was shown to Sam Hughes (with Alderson's approval), who replied to Alderson with a scathing 1,200–word denunciation. 'It is not worthwhile,' Hughes began, 'with men who know little or nothing about rifles' to discuss the alleged deficiences of the Ross. Complaints against the rifle, he insisted, resulted from the use of bad ammunition: 'Will you kindly permit me to suggest to you that it would be advisable that the Canadian Force should not find any of the bad ammunition in their pouches or on their persons? ... Your emphatic energy concerning what your intentions are, if you will pardon me, might better be directed to having your officers of every grade responsible in the premises [sic] to make sure that none of the defective ammunition again finds its way into the Canadian ranks.'[31] Seen in the best of lights, Sir Sam's letter was a stern rebuke, but he transformed it into a stunning insult by sending copies to all Canadian commanders in England and France down to the level of battalion commander.

Alderson made no reply. After failures with the Ross were reported at St Eloi, he sent a confidential questionnaire on the performance of the Ross to all unit commanders in the corps. Both Ketchen and Turner sent copies of the questionnaire to Hughes's representative in London. Turner advised that the replies in regard to the performance of the Ross should be ignored and complained that 'action is being delayed too long as regards Alderson.' Ketchen offered to furnish a narrative which might be used against Alderson.[32]

Throughout this long, painful controversy, Currie had repeatedly favoured the Lee-Enfield, and he may even have thought that Turner had espoused the Ross merely to save his position. In any event, he bitterly resented Alderson's dismissal, and given the coincidence of this action and the Ross controversy it is not surprising that he and the others should connect the two. Some of the heat was taken out of the situation by the tact of General Alderson's replacement. Sir Julian Byng worked well with the Canadians and helped restore harmony in the corps.[33] Byng would become the best-known and most popular of all the British officers who served with the Canadians. But Alderson's dismissal continued to rankle with Currie as an injustice for which Sam Hughes seemed responsible.

Following St Eloi, Currie faced his first critical test as a divisional commander. His command was engaged in a small but savage encounter near the village of Hooge, the Battle of Mount Sorrel. During the first stage of this fighting, from 2 to 13 June, the Germans attacked on the frontage of the 3rd Division, and in the fighting Major-General Mercer was killed. Mercer, along with Turner and Currie, had been a brigade commander in the 1st Division and at fifty-seven had been the oldest of the senior officers in the first Canadian contingent. Although the 1st Division was not directly involved in this action, it was Currie who was responsible for sealing the German penetration. On his own initiative he ordered forward part of the corps troops (units directly under corps headquarters) over whom he had no real authority. Later the 1st Division was chosen by Byng to make a full-scale counter-attack on 13 June after several postponements. On 2 June the 1st and 2nd Brigades were temporarily placed under command of the 3rd Division for an immediate counter-attack which was unsuccessful. Currie grouped his stronger battalions into two composite brigades and outlined a detailed artillery program. The attack, covered by a smoke screen made more intense by heavy rain, was an 'unqualified success' in the eyes of British observers.[34]

During his first year as a divisional commander Currie learned how to handle his new command. He appears to have made few mistakes in the process, but he was fortunate to have had relatively few severe tests. The greatest trial for the British armies on the Western Front would take place in the summer and autumn of 1916, with the Battles of the Somme, which lasted from 1 July until 18 November. According to Sir Douglas Haig's retrospective official dispatch, the object of the offensive on the Somme was threefold:

(1) to relieve the pressure on Verdun [which Falkenhayn had attacked in January].
(2) to assist our Allies in the other theatres of war by stopping any further transfer of German troops from the Western Front.
(3) to wear down the strength of the forces opposed to us.[35]

Currie's division did not move out of Flanders until August and did not become engaged at the Somme until September. A discussion of all the Somme battles is thus irrelevant here, but some general comment is necessary, since the campaign has become a subject of great controversy among military writers. The Somme was the beginning of attrition, or to use a more euphemistic phrase which still must appal humanists, 'the opening of the wearing out battle.'[36] Critics have been quick to excoriate the British command on these terms, and they usually indulge in head-counting to prove that Haig killed more of his own men than the enemy.[37] Liddell Hart with considerable accuracy claims that the 'Battle of the Somme closed in an atmosphere of disappointment, and with such a drain on the British forces that the coincident strain on the enemy was obscured.'[38] The British official historian did not agree. He insisted that success was achieved because the enemy 'realizing that his troops could not stand a second battering in the "Hell of the Somme" ... renounced trying to hold his ground ... and retired ... to the semi-permanent fortified line which he had prepared.'[39]

It is easy to be critical of the British leadership in the summer of 1916, but one wonders what the judgment on the Somme would have been if it had been followed by a brilliant success instead of Passchendaele. Possibly the Somme then would have been seen as a costly but necessary experiment. Without entering the lists against the generals, let us agree with Cyril Falls that at the Somme 'British tactics were in the main clumsy.'[40] Commanding a large military force is a ponderous task which compels a general to simplify most issues into clear-choice situations. A commander, moreover, must be able to pursue this logic without feeling that such simplification detracts from the rightness of his course. In short, the essence of military leadership comes partly from clarity of views, perhaps, indeed, from a structured personality's capacity to oversimplify. To the intellectual this trait often appears as the mark of a simple or narrow personality. Historian Brian Gardiner, for example, is critical of Sir Henry Rawlinson, one of Haig's army commanders, for continuing to co-operate with Haig after having criticized his plan of operations for the Somme. Though Gardiner seems to recognize that Rawlinson, after offering his criticism, had little choice but to co-operate – 'but this attitude was the very spirit of European armies' – he condemns him for chiding subordinates who had reservations similar to his own about the forthcoming battle: 'And soon Rawlinson too, was to be sniffing out the disbelievers among his officers.' Gardiner's remark that 'commanding officers were always right. They had to be; it was the only way the army would work,'[41] is made as disparaging comment on British generalship during the war. What the remark obscures is another problem only recently investigated by historians.[42] The British army was unwieldy, not only because its senior commanders were limited in imagination, but also because it was, from the battalion down, hopelessly undertrained. If such was the case for the British Army as a whole, it was 'true in spades' for the Canadian Corps. This fact became increasingly obvious to Arthur Currie as he pondered the Somme fighting. He was determined to change the situation.

Currie, a mere division commander, did not have Rawlinson's opportunity to criticize the plan for the Somme. Moreover, his division played a relatively minor, though bloody, part in the overall battle. But at the Somme, or at least immediately after it, Currie demonstrated an ability to analyse and to learn from analysis, a quality that hitherto he had not fully revealed. It was a quality lamentably lacking in most of the senior Allied commanders, a more serious handicap than the nature of the military structure.

In the first attack that the Canadians made at the Somme, Currie's 1st Division was to hold the corps front while the 2nd and 3rd Divisions assaulted Pozières Ridge. In a second attack on 26 September the 1st Division advanced on Thiepval Ridge. Currie's frontage bridged the highest point on the ridge and his advance did not keep pace with that of the 2nd British Corps on his left.[43] Despite repeated assaults, 'Regina Trench,' the German fortified front opposite the 1st Division, eluded capture until 21 October. Each successive attack was more disheartening than its predecessor, and each followed essentially the same pattern: intense artillery bombardment and a subsequent infantry advance. Each time the barrage ended, the Germans emerged from their dugouts and mowed down another crop of advancing Canadians.

It can be said that in carrying out these attacks, Currie displayed all the dull, unimaginative, insensitive qualities that most critics maintain were the characteristics of high command in the First World War. Why, they ask, did someone not refuse to attack? The answer is simple: to refuse was unthinkable. It was unthinkable for all soldiers because it would be interpreted as cowardice, and doubly unthinkable for senior officers because it would do no good. The attack would take place in any event; to refuse simply imposed the burden on some other unfortunate. Later in the war Currie was to become very adept at holding back on attacks when conditions were unfavourable. But at the Somme he had no opportunity to do so. Therefore he did as he was told; but afterwards he did not forget. Currie was determined to find out why the early attacks were unsuccessful and why they were so costly. Possibly he was influenced by the action of his then army commander, the much criticized (by Currie as well as others) and occasionally maligned General Gough. After an attempt to take Regina Trench on 8 October had failed to achieve more than a heavy list of casualties, Gough called for an investigation.[44] Such investigations, though hardly routine, were not unusual. But this was the first time Currie had been involved in one; and he was not satisfied with its perfunctory nature. Consequently, he conducted a private survey and submitted his own report on the failure of the attack.[45] Before putting pencil to paper he interviewed all available unwounded officers and at least three men in each company who had participated in the attack. His analysis spared neither himself nor his subordinates; and he found no scapegoats. Some of his discoveries were exceedingly unpleasant. In one of his battalions, for example, he found that the 'thorough elucidation of the plan ... was too much neglected.' In spite of the 'oft repeated orders of the Division,' another battalion 'did not hold rehearsals' for the attack. Although all company officers had explained the particular task to their men, using maps as a reference, 'this was not and never can be entirely satisfactory. To tell a Machine Gunner to take up his position at M.14.b.2.6. or a Bomber to establish a block at M.8.d.3.0. is an absurd order unless some other means of fixing this point has been explained.' Men were not sufficiently well trained for such an order to have any meaning.   But none of these things, singly or taken together, really explained the failure. Currie went on to state that the men had pressed the attack with 'great determination' in spite of everything done or left undone, in spite of wire obstacles that were intact, and in spite of enemy fire of 'hurricane' force. The soldiers who reached the enemy's lines 'used their rifles as clubs and did not give up as long as bombs were available.' And yet the attack failed! Here, according to Currie, was the real rub. It was possible, even under the adverse conditions at the Somme, to get into the enemy trenches. But once there the attackers could not hope to hold out unless reinforced and well supplied with bombs and ammunition. In existing circumstances this support was impossible. Given the fire-power of the enemy, reinforcements could be sent forward only if they could move safely through communcation trenches, and communication trenches could be dug only at night. New tactics were necessary to overcome these conditions. British attacks invariably took place at dawn; in future, Currie suggested, assaults should begin after mid-day so that night would cover reinforcement and supply activities.

This was only the beginning. Currie groped further for solutions. There was, he believed, 'no excuse ... for the lack of clearness ... in operation orders, for the fact that [one battalion] ... never rehearsed its task, nor gave sufficient explanation to the men. I found that one man had thrown away his Lewis Gun because he says it was too heavy to carry, yet had none of these things occurred, the wire would still have been uncut and the supply of bombs would have run out just as soon. All the lessons to be learned from these operations, All the points, and they are many, which can be improved, all the things left undone, done badly or which might have been done better, I shall take up ... with the battalions of the division.'[46]

At Ypres Currie had demonstrated an ability to deal with a fluid situation on the battlefield. In this report we find him struggling to get to the root of the British failures at the Somme. He was not satisfied by the accepted 'try again another time with more artillery' formula. As he was convinced that the men were doing their best, obviously some new method or system had to be devised. Fortunately he was given time to work out a solution for the tactical dilemma. On 17 October the Canadian Corps less the 4th Division, which had just arrived in France, went to a quiet section of the front just north of the city of Arras. While the holocaust at the Somme was moving inexorably to its bloody conclusion, and while statisticians were collecting preliminary figures to claim victory or prove defeat, Currie was reflecting on his experiences in the battle.

While Currie pondered his division's record, the eyes of all connected with the CEF were focused on the reorganization of the Canadian forces in England. Military efficiency in any force is a direct function of intelligent thinking, smooth channels of communication, and effective administration. Even under the best conditions, the Canadian establishment in England was a bottle-neck in the smooth flow of reinforcements from Canada to France. Poor administration and tangled communications transformed a potential trouble spot into a malignant bureaucratic abscess. For months it had been apparent to even the most superficial observer that the performance of the Canadian Corps in France was hampered by the cumbersome organization of the troops in England.[47] By May 1915 there was a seven-way split of authority in England. Militia headquarters in Ottawa communicated directly with the War Office; with the general officer commanding Canadians at Shorncliffe, Major-General S.B. Steele; with GOC Canadian Training Division at Shorncliffe, Brigadier-General J.C. MacDougall; and with Hughes's personal representative in England, Major-General J.W. Carson. At the same time, Brigadier-General Lord Brooke had a more or less independent position as GOC Canadian Training Division Bramshott, while Sir George Perley as acting high commissioner for Canada was continually consulted by the British government. Sir Max Aitken's position as 'Canadian representative' was nowhere clearly defined, and his seemingly wide authority confused everyone.[48] The creator of the system was Sam Hughes. But Hughes was only an agent, since the responsibility inevitably rested jointly with the Canadian cabinet and more specifically with the prime minister, Sir Robert Borden. Borden was a patient and not particularly perceptive man, but by October 1916 he had become aware that some kind of change must be made in the administration of the Canadian armed forces. After years of incredible provocation, he finally asked for Hughes's resignation on 9 November.[49] Meanwhile, a new organization, the Overseas Military Forces of Canada, had been designed to replace the haphazard system existing in England.[50] The formation of the OMFC has been described in detail in the finest piece of administrative history so far produced in Canada, Desmond Morton's *A Peculiar Kind of Politics*. It is clear in Morton's work that the architect of the new system was Sir George Perley, Canada's acting high commissioner in London. A chaotic system with no clear head or systematic channels of communication was transformed by Perley into an orderly structure which administered the flow of reinforcements from Canada to France, provided training for new arrivals, and provided medical care for evacuees. It was, moreover, a national system that ensured that Canadian troops were subject to Canadian control. Such an organization was an enormous step forward, but inevitably it would reduce the independence of the Canadian commander in France. The Canadian Corps commander became subordinate to the minister of overseas military forces as well as to the British commander-in-chief. Some of the irritation that Currie would later show towards Perley and the ministry unquestionably stemmed from the diminution of his independence.

Weary of Hughes's unbalanced behaviour, most Canadians in France welcomed the change.[51] A 1st Division diarist observed that 'there is now contentment among us all ... now that the inevitable has really happened ... Sir Sam has lost his job ... I do not like to kick a man when he is down but I am willing to break nine toes in kicking Sam.'[52] Unfortunately, it took time to mobilize the new organization. Borden and his colleagues, familiar with the structure of a government department, chose this rather than a military branch as their model. Sir George Perley, already a member of the Borden cabinet, became minister of the OMFC, and the new ministry was almost a duplicate of the Department of Militia and Defence in Ottawa. Perley's first act was to select a chief military adviser, confusingly (since there was already such a post in Canada) called the chief of the general staff. Byng had recommended that Currie be given the new post. Perley was prepared to take either Currie or Turner. But he accepted Turner on the grounds of his seniority and the fact that Currie seemed more likely to be useful in France. Turner took the post 'reluctantly' on the condition that if a Canadian should ever be offered command of the Canadian Corps in France he should have claim to the position as senior major-general in the Canadian forces.[53] As we shall see, Turner did a reasonable job as chief of the general staff in England under very trying conditions. However, at the time of his appointment, the move was greeted by Currie with some scepticism, not only because Turner's record in France seemed mediocre, but his appointment coming when it did gave rise to the suspicion that Hughes's dismissal would not make much difference. So far, the Canadian Corps had suffered at the hands of a politican who fancied himself a great general; now many, perhaps unfairly, feared that it would suffer from a general who wanted to dabble in politics. Luckily such was not to be the case, but suspicion died slowly.

While the new administration was clearing up Hughes's administrative legacy, the Canadian Corps in France welcomed a respite from the attacks of the Somme. In this lull Currie travelled to Verdun to inspect the battlefield on which so many French and German lives were lost in 1916. The trip was arranged for many senior British officers, and it gave Currie an opportunity to pursue the study of Allied tactics begun after the Somme.

Defending Verdun had been the major French endeavour in 1916. German bombardment had begun on 21 February; the final German attack was made on 18 July. By October 1916 the French had recovered sufficiently to be able to take up the offensive. Their attacks continued in December. One of the best accounts of Verdun described it as the 'First War in microcosm; an intensification of all its horrors and glories, courage, and futility.'[54] Currie visited the ancient fortress in January 1917, after the last French attack had been launched from it. He toured the battlefield, attended lectures by French officers, and was introduced to Nivelle, the man soon to replace Joffre as supreme commander. Following this visit, Currie wrote a detailed report which is not so much a critique of the battle of Verdun as an outline for future tactics.

Two things must be remembered about Currie's report. First, he used his visit to push ideas that were already developed in the Canadian Corps and in other British formations. A superficial reading of his report would suggest that most of the recommendations in the report came from French experience. In fact, the opposite was the case. Currie throughout the report pushes ideas already in practice or being developed within the British forces,[55] though he writes often as if he first encountered the concept at Verdun. Second, in the report Currie never questioned the rightness of making the main Allied effort on the Western Front. His commitment to an offensive strategy in Europe is best illustrated by the fact that he could find more important 'lessons' in the French attacks than in their defence of the city. Indeed he even found strategic justification for Haig's Somme offensive by correlating the dates of the maximum German penetration, 15 July, and the beginning of the British attack, 1 July. He concluded that 'success on the Somme was making itself felt.'[56] Basically, however, he gave scant attention to strategy. He was mainly concerned with discovering what an analysis of Verdun could demonstrate in order to reduce casualties and increase the chance of success in future battles.

Of particular note, indeed the greatest lesson to be learned from Verdun, was the French method of training infantry before making an attack. Assaulting divisions, according to Currie, were sent into the front lines to 'become as familiar as possible with the ground over which they were to attack.'[57] After a time they were withdrawn and then began a period of special training in rear areas on ground 'as similar to the area over which they had to attack as it was possible to find.' The emphasis in this training was on the platoon and company, each group studying the most effective way to accomplish its own particular task. Meanwhile, other troops in the front line undertook laborious and fatiguing preparations essential for the attack, digging communication and assembly trenches, establishing supply dumps, and repairing roads. While the assault forces were out of the line they were 're-equipped, re-clothed, fed particularly well, had entertainments provided for them, and consequently returned to the line absolutely fresh and highly trained.'[58] Training at the lowest level so that every man would know what to expect and what was expected was, in Currie's eyes, an essential ingredient for success; and his report described an ideal situation rather than what the French actually had done at Verdun.

Naturally, this preparatory infantry training had to be accompanied by careful planning and by sufficient artillery support and preparation. The key to success, however, was to ensure that the attack be 'made by absolutely fresh troops who had been specially trained for the work in hand.' Other factors were of course important. The British practice of leaving the trench line 'wave by wave' was unnecessary and also very costly in casualties among highly trained troops. The French had abandoned attacks in waves at Verdun. At the Somme attacks had invariably been made wave upon wave. Currie argued that 'it was pernicious to lay down such a doctrine ... [for] the factors governing [the method of attack] ... will readily suggest themselves to the minds of all who properly study the situation when making their plans.'[59] He also favoured the French practice of making an abundant distribution of maps and air photographs. Once the assault was under way, these guides were much more valuable to the officers participating in the attack than they were to those left behind to await results; but in the British forces it was the latter who were generously supplied.[60] Tactical features on the ground – hills, a row of hedges, and so on – should, according to Currie, become the objective of an attack rather than a line described on the map. Although the ground at Verdun consisted of features that were more sharply defined than those at the Somme, Currie insisted that current British tactics failed to make adequate use of ground cover. 'Our troops,' he reasoned, 'must be taught the power of manoeuvre.' They should move around strong points and take them from flank and rear rather than wait for artillery preparation which 'cannot be quickly and easily arranged for and is often not necessary.'[61]

Currie made numerous other suggestions for increasing morale and improving the effectiveness of the infantry soldier. But the bulk of his remaining comments dealt with artillery. He was lavish in his praise of the French use of the creeping barrage. The French had claimed that in their final attacks creeping barrages and preparatory bombardments were so effective that no hostile barrage was encountered by the advancing infantry. Questioning field commanders, Currie found that 'no Divisional Commander would agree with such a contention.'[62] But he was, nevertheless, impressed by the French artillery in general. Recommending adoption of a list of technical artillery procedures, he saw three general lessons that could be used with effect. He favoured placing all heavy artillery normally held at corps level under command of a divisional commander, who in the last analysis was 'responsible for the destruction of hostile trenches, obstacles, works and guns on his own front.' Secondly, he was impressed with French counter-battery fire (the section of artillery specifically designated to destroy enemy artillery): 'all counter-battery guns,' he argued, should henceforth 'be in one large group under one officer.'[63] During the last days before an attack, moreover, 'the location and destruction of the enemy's batteries' should be the 'chief occupation of the Artillery.'[64] In short, surprise could and should be achieved, even when artillery preparation lasted for several weeks. Later, as corps commander, Currie would argue for heavy artillery being held at corps level. Here, however, he is consistent with the arguments of divisional commanders from Fourth Army who believed that 'after the initial fire-plan had been fired,' divisional commanders should take over control of artillery from corps.[65]

Though many of its features may now seem commonplace axioms of elementary tactics, Currie's report on Verdun is highly significant. It seems, for example, only a matter of common sense to insist that the soldiers be told clearly what is to be expected of them if one is to hope for success in battle. It is necessary only to question survivors of the ranks or to read their memoirs to discover that men were not told in advance what they were supposed to do. R.C. Sherriff reflects the experience of thousands of young men in the British armies when he insists that 'one of the difficulties of a junior officer [in the First World War] was that nobody ever told him what ... attacks were intended to achieve.'

In the Second World War the generals would brief 'their officers before an attack. They would get them together and give them a clear preview. The officers would go back and explain things to their men, and every soldier would go into the attack as well informed as the generals in command. Nothing like that happened in the First World War. The Army Commander briefed his division and brigade commanders, who in turn passed on the information to the colonels of battalions. But it never got to the junior officers, who were to lead the men. Secrecy appeared to be the watchword, and you just waited and did what you were told when the time arrived.'[66]

As Currie did not challenge the Western Front strategy, one might argue that he is open to the same charges that postwar critics have levied against Foch and Haig. There are two answers to this criticism. First, Currie was not in a position, as were Haig and Foch, to change Allied strategy. Second, he can hardly be blamed for attempting to improve conditions within the framework in which he had to work. Naturally, it would be wrong to make too much of Currie's report. A close reading of it removes the danger of making extravagant claims and demonstrates that he discounted much that he was told. Currie did not accept French estimates of casualties on both sides at Verdun and made his own guesses; yet in his report he concluded that 'on grounds of casualties alone ... [Verdun] was a great victory.'[67] This statement seems to indicate that he was not able to free himself from the grotesque definition of success that the doctrine of attrition had introduced, namely that a calculation of casualties alone would determine the victor. In fairness to Currie, we should note that he was never satisfied to have that test of victory applied to his own command. His report shows that he was searching for a way to overcome the tactical deadlock on the Western Front and at the same time reduce casualties. Lord Mottistone, commander of the Canadian Cavalry Brigade, later recorded that Currie 'had an almost fanatical hatred of unnecessary casualties. Of all the men that I knew in nearly four years on the Western Front, I think Currie was the man who took the most care of the lives of his troops.'[68]

Currie wrote his report on Verdun in January and February 1917. During this time the only activity along his front was an occasional trench raid, which Currie, to Byng's annoyance, discouraged as being fruitless.[69] Early in 1917, however, commanders and staffs in the Canadian Corps began active planning and preparation for an attack on the ridge of ground near the village of Vimy. Here was Currie's first opportunity to put into practice the ideas that he had set out in his Verdun report. Byng adopted many of his suggestions. The Battle of Vimy Ridge is the best known of all Canadian actions in the First World War. At Vimy, for the first time in the war, all four Canadian divisions fought together under corps headquarters; and it was the only time during the war when all four attacked simultaneously. With understandable pride and only slight hyperbole, Colonel Duguid, himself a participant in the battle and later its official historian, wrote that the 'significance of Vimy in Canadian history ... lies in the fact that there the Corps was consolidated into one homogenous entity; the most powerful self-contained striking force on any battlefront.'[70] Later he claimed that Vimy was 'the greatest British victory since Waterloo' and also that 'it was the pattern ... for later ... Canadian attacks on the Western Front.'[71]

General Byng was responsible for most of the planning for the battle of Vimy Ridge and the credit for its success quite properly belongs to him. Nevertheless many of its features were foreshadowed in Currie's Verdun report. The battle was heralded by unheard of training, 'a full-scale replica of the battle area was laid out ... to the rear [in which units] ... rehearsed repeatedly ... from platoon to divisional level.'[72] To aid the infantry 40,000 specially drawn maps were circulated.[73] The preliminary artillery fire had three important features: first, its weight and length (it began on 20 March, two weeks before the attack); second, a concentration of heavy guns on counter-battery tasks; and, finally, it was carefully planned to achieve tactical surprise.[74]

Currie's division performed superbly. The attack took place on Easter Monday, 9 April, and forty-five minutes after starting time nearly all the first objectives were captured. Successive objectives were taken according to a preplanned timetable.[75] Vimy was a classic example of the 'set piece' attack. Careful planning, co-operation between artillery and infantry, good leadership, and sublime courage combined to produce an outstanding tactical victory; and it was the last major fight in which Currie commanded the 1st Canadian Division.

5

Corps commander

The success at Vimy Ridge was encouraging, but Currie remained convinced that there was still hard fighting ahead. In January 1917 he had predicted that the enemy would 'fight desperately until beaten absolutely. I do not think that he can be beaten this year; and I believe that next year he will fight more desperately than ever. The most foolish thing any of our people could do would be to imagine victory is so close that their efforts can be relaxed.'[1] After Vimy Ridge there was little reason, so far as Currie was concerned, to revise his earlier appreciation, and he maintained a healthy scepticism of predictions of an early peace. The summer of 1917, however, was to prove even more difficult than expected in Currie's cautious estimate. The Canadian attack at Vimy, in fact, had been only the most successful part of a much larger British operation, planned as a preface to an enormous French thrust, the Battle of the Aisne. This attack, the French high command had predicted, would knock Germany out of the war. Conceived by General Nivelle, who had replaced Joffre as French commander-in-chief in December 1916, the plan for the battle was one of the most flatulent plans of the entire war. When the French struck, the success achieved was a 'ludicrous fraction of what had been promised ... Instead of being miles behind the German lines, the French were barely clinging to toeholds in the enemy defences ... Unsaid, but fully understood by the whole Army, was the fact that Nivelle had failed to make good on even one of his grandiose promises.'[2] As a result, General Pétain became the third French commander-in-chief within a period of six months, and his first task was to quell the mutinies that began to break out in the French army. It was now the turn of the British to make great plans.

General Haig had agreed to co-operate with Nivelle's offensive, but he had long wanted to launch an attack further north, if only, as the editor of his diaries put it, 'because a success in Flanders would have had the effect of rolling back the whole of the German right wing; whereas success further south all too often merely meant the creation of a dangerous salient in the enemy line.'[3] To mask his intentions and also to meet Pétain's urgent plea that pressure be taken off the French until the mutinies could be subdued, Haig ordered that the Canadian Corps and adjacent British formations keep pushing the Germans in the Vimy area. As a consequence the 1st Canadian Division continued to move east of Vimy and captured the towns of Arleux and Fresnoy, small but intricate and frustrating operations.

Currie and his soldiers were soon to be involved more intimately in the British plan for 1917, but in the meantime other, seemingly unrelated events occurred that were to make this involvement more difficult for Arthur Currie. In April 1917 the British government decided to replace the commander-in-chief in Palestine. This decision on a remote theatre of the war was to have a direct and profound effect on Currie's career. General Allenby, commander of the Third British Army in France, was the choice for Palestine. Haig decided to replace Allenby with Byng which, of course, meant that yet another man had to be placed in charge of the Canadian Corps. Sheer chance, or perhaps fate, kept Currie in the running for this selection; for it was luck that saved his life on 2 June. Normally the divisional commander handed his messages to a runner, who would take them to the signals centre for transmission, but on 2 June no runner was available, and Currie himself took a message across to signals. As he did so, his headquarters received a direct hit. Currie was thrown to the ground, covered with earth, and received a nasty graze on his head from flying shrapnel. Those still in the headquarters were not so lucky: two were killed and sixteen wounded. The day after his 'lucky' accident Currie learned that he had been awarded a KCMG in the Birthday Honours list; three days later Byng told him that he was to command the Canadian Corps.

Such a promotion, after Byng's recommendation and Haig's approval, in any other case would have been a routine matter. In Currie's case the situation was not so simple. His promotion, in the first place, was embarrassing for the minister of overseas military forces, Sir George Perley. It will be recalled that when Richard Turner had been appointed CGS in England, he had insisted that if a Canadian were ever to be appointed commander of the corps, he, as senior major-general in the Canadian forces, would be considered. Perley was quite aware of his promise to Turner but probably was even more concerned that his efforts to untangle the Canadian administrative jungle in England should not go awry. To have Currie's appointment announced before it was confirmed by Canadian authorities was a direct threat to Perley's reorganization. This problem was easily resolved by a letter from Haig's military secretary which indicated that all arrangements and promotions in France were 'temporary' until confirmed by Canadian authority.[4]

On the question of who should be selected to command the Canadian Corps, Sir George Perley had few doubts. Turner, he knew was doing satisfactory work in England and was 'rather out of touch with the front after a six month absence.'

Currie, on the other hand, was 'considered most suitable for the Corps by higher command and also by the larger half of [the] troops.'[5] These views he immediately wired to the prime minister. Before Borden's answer arrived, Perley had come to his own solution. Turner would remain as CGS, but with powers extended to include a 'certain measure [of] authority over administrative matters at [the] front particularly on lines [of] communication.' Meanwhile both Currie and Turner would be promoted simultaneously, which would 'preserve Turner's seniority.'[6] Perley's solution was not unreasonable, since it would keep both Turner and Currie at the jobs they did best. He was relieved when the prime minister concurred, recommending that Perley should take the 'advice of higher command unless you see strong reason to the contrary.'[7]

While these negotiations proceeded, Currie's position was extraordinarily complicated. In the first place, he had been given very little warning to prepare himself for taking over his new command. Henceforth, he would be accountable for the entire corps, and so long as any part of it was in combat he always felt responsible for his men. The communiqué indicating that he was to step up reached him on 6 June, and two days later he was at corps headquarters struggling with the problems of the larger formation. Still to be settled was the issue of who would take his place as commander of the 1st Division.[8] Currie had recommended and Byng had accepted the commander of the 7th Canadian Infantry Brigade, Brigadier-General A.C. Macdonnell, as his replacement at 1st Division headquarters. Macdonnell, popularly known as 'Batty Mac,' was one of the few prewar Canadian permanent force officers who gained general's rank during the First World War. His promotion to brigadier had been fiercely opposed by Sir Sam Hughes.[9] Though Sir Sam was no longer minister of militia, further promotion for Macdonnell was to prove not easy.

Currie was convinced that Macdonnell was the best qualified for divisional commander of the senior officers at the front and thus was enthusiastic about his appointment. Sir Robert Borden, who had little knowledge of performance in France, believed that the appointment to the 1st Division of Major-General Garnet Hughes might well dampen the fire of criticism from Sir Sam. Perley had only recently settled an extremely awkward situation that had resulted when Sir Sam's brother, St Pierre Hughes, was dismissed from the command of the 10th Brigade. Perley, therefore, could hardly be against something that would reduce the attacks of the former minister. Thus he concurred with the prime minister's recommendation that Garnet Hughes be given the 1st Division. When Currie discovered that Hughes was being considered for command of the 1st Division, he immediately objected.[10] Perley called him to London on 14 June. The resulting interview, according to Perley, produced a 'most pleasant undertaking' among Currie, Turner, and himself.[11] The issues discussed, apparently, were command of the corps, new administrative arrangements between OMFC and the corps, and command of the 1st Division.[12] Unquestionably, Currie was easily satisfied on the relationship between himself and Turner. The real issue was Macdonnell's appointment. Currie interpreted the offer to Garnet Hughes of the 1st Division as a quid pro quo for his own appointment to command of the corps and refused to accept it. In his diary he noted that in the interview with Perley 'it was decided that I take the Corps and my attitude toward the appointment of Garnet Hughes was fully explained.'[13] It was not only explained, it was accepted by Perley. (Indeed, even before his meetings with Currie on 14 and 15 June Perley had supported the nomination of Macdonnell.) In the words of Desmond Morton, Perley 'had seen enough of the aftermath of Hughes's patronage and cronyism to recognize its price.'[14] Borden had stronger feelings about appointing Garnet Hughes, though he was not adamant about the matter. On 13 June he had wired Perley: 'If Garnet Hughes is acceptable for Division Commander, I would like to see him appointed but leave the question to your judgement.'[15] Later Borden would attempt to deny any involvement.[16]

In a letter written after the war, Currie too placed a rather different interpretation on the events in question. Then he argued not only that his own appointment was conditional on his acceptance of Garnet Hughes, but that this point of view was put forward, in Morton's words, with 'ruthless and irresponsible pressure.'[17] 'I refused,' Currie wrote, 'to accept command ... on any conditions which I thought would embarrass me.' He added that the 'main condition was that I should accept as my successor in the 1st Division Major-General Garnett [sic] Hughes.' Finally, he claims to have been 'importuned, coaxed, threatened and bullied. I was told that Garnett Hughes would have to get the 1st Division, that there was a combination in England and Canada for him that neither I, nor any man could beat; that his father wanted him to get the position and that God help the man who fell out with his father.'[18]

There are two puzzles here. One is the reason for which Currie rejected Garnet Hughes, which he never committed to paper. The other mystery that is undocumented is why Currie rationalized an interpretation of the negotiations over his appointment which was different than close inspection of the event suggests. Garnet Hughes, it should be remembered, was well known to Currie. Only five years younger, Garnet had been a friend in Victoria; Currie liked the younger man, and the affection seemed reciprocal.[19] However, Currie's biographer argues that the corps commander did 'not admire Hughes as a leader in the field.'[20] John Swettenham in his history of the Canadian Corps indicated that Currie considered Garnet 'an indifferent front-line soldier.'[21] In fact, there was a single occasion on which this opinion could have been based – Hughes's performance as brigade major during the gas attack of 1915. There can be no doubt that Hughes was confused in that situation. Equally there is little doubt that there were mitigating circumstances – an extremely difficult action, Hughes's first experience under fire, and other senior officers equally confused. This episode bothered Currie at the time, but it is impossible to be certain that it was the sole or even the main reason for his rejection of Garnet Hughes. Currie did not ever in writing accuse Hughes of being a poor leader in battle. He did, on the other hand, make it absolutely clear that he did not want him. When Hughes was given command of the 1st Brigade, Currie had argued that he was not sufficiently experienced as a combat commander. By 1917 it was still possible to make this argument, but it was much less cogent than it had been in 1915. Hughes had served for less than four months as a brigade major, he had been a divisional staff officer for nearly three months, and for almost sixteen months he had served creditably as GOC of the 1st Canadian Infantry Brigade.

With such a record, one could scarcely claim that Garnet was inexperienced, though it could still be claimed that his record was less impressive than those of other divisional commanders in the Canadian Corps. Major-General Henry Burstall of the 2nd Division had been a prewar permanent force officer and a graduate of staff college. He had come overseas in charge of the 1st Divisional Artillery. When the Canadian Corps had been formed, he became GOC of the Corps Artillery, served in that position for fifteen months, and then had taken over the 2nd Division. General Lipsett, commander of the 3rd Division, came overseas as commanding officer of the 8th Battalion, followed Currie as GOC of the 2nd Brigade, and after ten months had taken over the 3rd Canadian Division. When the 4th Division had been formed in April 1916, Brigadier-General David Watson of the 5th Brigade was selected as commander. Watson too came overseas with the first contingent as commanding officer of an infantry battalion. He served for almost as year in the position before taking over the 5th Brigade, where he remained for eight months before becoming GOC of the 4th Division. Brigadier-General Macdonnell, the man Currie picked as his replacement in the 1st Division, was a prewar permanent officer who had served in South Africa. Macdonnell came overseas as commanding officer of the Lord Strathcona's Horse and had served as GOC of the 7th Brigade since its formation in December 1915, except for three months spent recuperating from wounds. Each of these men had splendid records, but simply counting months in various positions of command would not be sufficient in itself to disqualify Garnet Hughes.

Perhaps Currie was negative towards Hughes partly because the suggestion for his appointment did not come from corps headquarters. Currie's subsequent correspondence with Sir George Perley confirms that he believed strongly that there ought to be 'no interference with my prerogatives in the matter of recommendations' for appointments.[22] On this matter the corps commander was unfair to Perley.[23] In any event, Currie believed that it was his right to make initial recommendations on appointments within the Canadian Corps, and he was particularly touchy about suggestions for appointments that came from England or Canada.

Probably, and the evidence is inferential, a key factor in Hughes's disqualification was his name. Sir Sam Hughes's influence had been so pervasive, his interference in appointments so well known, and his nepotism so obvious, that if Currie had accepted Garnet as GOC of the 1st Canadian Division, few could have believed that the old business of influence determining promotion was dead. When, after the question of the promotion was settled, the deputy minister of the Overseas Military Forces visited France, he found general satisfaction with both the new organization and Currie's selection of Macdonnell. He then reported to Perley that 'there could be no further question of raising Garnet Hughes' prospects.'[24] In short, if part of Currie's reason for not accepting Garnet Hughes was that he wanted to make a clean break with the Hughes system, it seems clear that he had done so. But if this was the case, it is quite likely that Currie had pangs of conscience about the matter. He owed his own appointment in 1914 to the influence of his friend Garnet Hughes. With the shoe on the other foot, Currie was not prepared to back Hughes for an appointment in the 1st Division. Thus Desmond Morton's claim that 'Currie's sense of martyrdom may have concealed a justifiably bad conscience'[25] seems valid. Given the evidence, this is probably as far as one can go with the puzzle about Currie's reasons for rejecting Garnet Hughes. It also offers a plausible explanation for the second question of why Currie changed his view on the negotiations concerning his own appointment.

On the second issue, however, there is something that should be added. The summer of 1917, as we shall see, was more difficult, frustrating, and disappointing for Arthur Currie than any other period during the war. During this time he took over the corps, dealt with complex military problems, settled his long-standing personal problems, participated in the great conscription issue, and discovered that it would not produce the men it promised. With the passage of time, it is surely not surprising that in his recollection of events one problem should become entangled with others occurring simultaneously. Currie probably did have a guilty conscience about Garnet Hughes. There was pressure to appoint Hughes, but it was not 'ruthless and irresponsible.' Currie was not 'importuned, coaxed threatened and bullied,' but it is quite easy to see how in retrospect he came to believe that he had been.

Before leaving England for France, Currie had an interview with Garnet Hughes which was long and heated. Hughes argued that he was the most senior major-general available for the 1st Division, and Currie plainly indicated that he would not back Hughes's appointment. If there were heat and pressure anywhere, it must have been during this meeting wherein former friends disagreed.[26] Hughes left the meeting feeling betrayed, and disappointed and promising revenge. Currie must have left frustrated and guilty, even if convinced of the correctness of his position.

Currie's biographer, Colonel Urquhart, has suggested that as soon as the command arrangements in France became public knowledge, a personal attack was launched on Currie, led by Sam Hughes. This attack, apparently, was based on the financial difficulties that Currie had left behind in Victoria in 1914. Urquhart alleges that Currie's enemies in Canada insisted that the debts be paid at once or legal action would follow.[27] Whatever the state of his debts, Currie, it should be recalled (See Chapter 1), had left Victoria having used the government uniform allowance to the 50th Regiment for personal purposes. He claimed on 25 June 1917, in a letter to the then commanding officer of the 50th Regiment, 'it is impossible for me to tell ... the efforts I have constantly made to meet the claim but I can tell you that for nearly three years the last thing I thought of at night and the first thing in the morning was this.'[28] His statement is probably the literal truth, since it appears that until June 1917 he had made very little effort indeed to redeem this debt. The only record that survives of an earlier attempt to take action is his letter of late September 1914 to Sam Matson asking Matson to get him time to pay. Yet on 25 June 1917, shortly after his interview with Perley that settled the question of command, Currie took the first step to pay off the debt. As commander of the Canadian Corps his pay jumped approximately 71 percent (from $24 to $41.24 per day), which one might assume would make it possible to pay the obligation quickly. In fact, the 50th Regiment was not reimbursed until September 1917, when Currie borrowed money from two of his wealthy subordinate officers, Major-General David Watson of the 4th Division and Brigadier-General Victor Odlum of the 11th Brigade. Subsequently Currie settled with these men by paying instalments which ended in 1919. For an individual caught in the vice of unpleasant circumstances, conspiracy is always a tempting explanation for these circumstances. However, conspiracy does not explain Currie's failure to take action to pay off the obligation, nor does it explain his decision to settle the matter in June. The only conspiracy was the subsequent action of Sir George Perley and Sir Robert Borden to cover up the corps commander's culpability.

After Currie wrote to him in September 1914, the loyal Matson made a substantial effort to help Currie. He sent Currie's letter to Borden, urging that Currie's case was one that merited 'generous treatment' and asking that Bordon should do his best 'to prevent an investigation until this poor unfortunate fellow has been given the chance he asks for.'[29] Matson's efforts to gain time and his subsequent and unsuccessful attempt to raise money for Currie have been carefully examined by R. Craig Brown and Desmond Morton.[30] They demonstrate that in spite of Matson's letter and a later anonymous letter from Victoria, it is not at all certain that the prime minister knew about Currie's action until after he had been appointed corps commander in 1917. They further demonstrate that only the polite and patient efforts of Moore, Taggart, the Glasgow manufacturers of the 50th Regiment uniforms, to secure their money kept the matter alive at all. Indeed, it moved with glacial slowness through the militia bureaucracy, coming to the attention of the militia council only on 15 June 1917. The council, practised bureaucrats all, simply referred the whole matter to the minister of overseas military forces of Canada, and the file that documented Currie's action reached the overseas minister on 21 July. There was no conspiracy of enemies here – only the lethargy of bureaucrats and the accident of the mails. Perley was shocked and appalled. He 'understood at once that the only possible outcome of further investigation would be a court martial and certain disgrace [for Currie].'[31] Perley instantly informed the prime minister that the matter would result in a scandal if it became public and offered to pay half of the amount personally if the minister of militia, Sir Edward Kemp, would put up the other half.[32] Borden replied that such action was unnecessary, since Sir Edward Kemp had arranged for the debt to be paid by the Department of Militia and Defence and the money subsequently recovered from Currie.[33] A draft order-in-council was prepared to pay off the Glasgow company but remained unsigned. Professors Morton and Brown have questioned this delay and found no definitive answer. They suggest, however, that the most plausible explanation of the delay is that 'someone had quietly intimated that Currie was finally making restitution and the potential scandal could be safely allowed to sink back into the shadows.'[34] It seems likely that this is the case, since Currie, as we have seen, had indeed begun to arrange to repay his debt.[35] He had informed the commanding officer of the 50th in June that the affair would soon be settled, and by 10 September he had borrowed the money from his two subordinates, and had begun to have the money transferred to Victoria.

While Currie was at last free of the direct financial obligation, he could never be free of the knowledge of what he had done. There is no evidence that he was aware that his action had been exposed to the militia council, the cabinet, and especially the overseas minister, Sir George Perley. All these people, in Morton's words, 'had exercised a beneficial discretion,' and had become 'accomplices in the cover-up.'[36] But they were not Currie's accomplices; he continued to carry his guilty 'secret' and to remember that Borden and Perley had had no initial objections to Garnet Hughes.

At the very least Currie's take-over of the Canadian Corps was something less than one might expect from a promotion. It seemed to him that he had earned the command of Canada's largest military formation on the strength of his ability, only to be questioned when he insisted on the right to appoint competent subordinates.

Throughout the experience he constantly faced the enormous responsiblity of commanding the entire corps. In these circumstances it is perhaps understandable that he occasionally was less generous in his dealings with Sir George Perley than he might to have been,[37] and perhaps even more surprising that he carried out his military responsibities so superbly.

The first major operaton that Currie directed from start to finish was an assault on the city of Lens. In this attack Currie was being asked to do two things, and the successful completion of one complicated the achievement of the other. First, he was to create a threat at Lens that would draw German attention away from the operations being conducted further north in Flanders; and second, he was to disrupt German reinforcement plans by destroying as many enemy formations as possible. Possibly because Currie was new at his job, the orders received by Canadian Corps from First Army for the Lens attack were considerably more detailed than usual. These orders dictated that the Canadians should break the German line south of the city and then advance by stages until the city was taken.[38] Such a plan, in Currie's view, took no account of the tactical features of the battleground and made the dual objective very difficult to achieve. Currie met General Horne on 10 July and persuaded him that the First Army plan must be replaced.[39]

Currie pointed out to Horne that Lens was dominated from the north and south by two hills – Hill 70 and Sallaumines Hill, respectively – which were precluded from the attack in the First Army plan. Each of these hills, in Currie's view, was a more important tactical feature than the city of Lens itself, and Hill 70 was the key to capturing the southern hill. Currie's basic idea was a modification of a theory advocated by the general staff officer in charge of planning at general headquarters, Brigadier John Davidson. The goal was to seize a tactical position of vital importance to the enemy which he would then be forced to retake. Once taken, the position would be held largely by preregistered artillery and machine-gun fire. As a modern student of tactics put it, this was 'typical of Currie, who used other people's ideas but did them better.'[40] Currie, in any event, persuaded the army commander to make Hill 70 the main objective, but Canadian plans were again complicated when the First Army ordered that 'all the ground [taken in any raid] must be held by rifle and bayonet alone if no assistance is obtainable from other arms.'[41] The order was almost preposterous. If followed, it would heavily handicap the success of the corps, since Currie planned to make a number of preliminary raids to destroy key defensive emplacements. Currie solved the issue merely by ignoring the army order and issuing instructions for immediate withdrawal after the destructive missions were completed.[42]

In order to achieve the objective of pinning down as many German forces as possible, it was essential to mislead the enemy into expecting a much larger attack than that of a single corps. If the Germans did expect a larger attack, then Canadian casualties would inevitably be heavy. Preliminary raids were designed to alarm the Germans and also to destroy key defensive works that would cause Canadian casualties when the real attack was made. Extensive gas shelling and dragging dummy tanks behind the lines served to increase further the enemy's apprehension, but the artillery barrages were carefully designed so that tactical surprise for the main attack could still be achieved. Currie planned for a lightning success and very quickly to consolidate the new position; then he could let the enemy wear himself out making counter-attacks.

Currie repeatedly postponed the final assault until weather conditions were perfect. Then, on 15 August, behind the protective fire of nine field artillery brigades, the Canadians attacked. Hill 70 itself was quickly seized and consolidated.[43] German counter-attacks continued almost unabated for three days, but the new line remained firm. Currie was delighted as the German attacks continued to be broken by artillery fire and collapse against the Canadian trenches. Between 15 and 18 August, he noted, 'there were no fewer than twenty-one counter-attacks delivered, many with very large forces ... Four German divisions were accounted for ... (and) our gunners, machine gunners and infantry never had such targets.'[44] The Germans continued sporadically until 25 August, each attack adding to the success of the operation. The German official history noted lugubriously that 'Even though we soon succeeded in sealing off the local penetration at Lens, the Canadian had attained their ends. The fighting at Lens had cost us a considerable number of troops which had to be replaced. The entire preconceived plan for relieving the troops in Flanders had been upset.'[45]

Thanks to Currie's careful planning, Canadian losses were less than expected; during July and August the Canadians suffered approximately 10,000 casualties while inflicting between two and three times that number on the enemy.[46] Still, the well-spring of Canadian reinforcements seemed to be rapidly drying up, and the events of autumn of 1917 were to prove costly in numbers of men. The Canadian attack at Lens was a part of the campaign in Flanders, since it was fought to keep German reserves from being sent to the Ypres area. But the Canadians were not to escape a more direct exposure to what Winston Churchill termed a 'forlorn expenditure of valour and life without equal in futility.'[47] To follow Currie's corps, however, we must have some understanding of the fighting that preceded its action.

The possibility of following up Plumer's success at Messines had been hinted at in the original order for Messines, but for a variety of reasons the possibility was forgone in June. The next phase was to be carried out by General Gough's Fifth Army and would not begin before a long delay. As Haig's biographer remarked, 'immeasurable ill flowed from this option.' The 'Third Battle of Ypres' – the formal name for the Flanders operations – began officially on 31 July, when Gough's army assaulted Pilckem ridge after a fifteen-day preliminary bombardment had pounded the earth to dust. During the week before the assault, sporadic rains mixed with the dust to make the ground very muddy for the attacking troops. On the evening of 31 July the rain became heavy and for four days it fell incessantly, bringing the Fifth Army to a standstill. The results: a maximum advance of 3,000 yards and 31,850 British casualties.[48]

'Third Ypres' consisted of eight separate battles and can be divided conveniently into three stages. Stage one, fought entirely under Gough's command, began with the attack on Pilckem ridge and ended with 'The Battle of Langemarck,' which was coincident with Currie's attack on Lens in the rainiest August for four years.[49] With Langemarck, the casualty total climbed to 68,000.[50] In the second stage Haig decided to switch the main effort from Gough back to Plumer. Hope for a major breakthrough was then abandoned, since Plumer planned a succession of three limited attacks designed to win the southern half of Passchendaele ridge.[51]

Perhaps the supreme irony of the campaign – if not the entire war – occurred in the three weeks between the end of the Battle of Langemarck and Plumer's battle of the Menin Road Ridge. During this interval the prime minister, Lloyd George, who had opposed the approval of the campaign, had ample opportunity to stop it and failed to do so. By the beginning of September it was obvious that Haig's action in Flanders was hardly about to achieve its grandiose objectives. Lloyd George after the war claimed that in June the war cabinet had agreed to Haig's offensive on the 'understanding that if the progresss ... made with the operation did not realize the expectations ... [of the planners], it would be called off and effective help rendered to the Italians to press their offensive.'[52] In fact Haig did not get such approval in June; it did not come until July, and unqualified approval of the war cabinet was not given until 25 July. None the less, Lloyd George, who could have stopped the fighting in September, made no move to do so. Perhaps the prime minister really did subscribe to the bloody plan that Sir Henry Wilson, then in charge of the Eastern Command, attributed to him: 'I believe,' wrote Wilson, 'that Lloyd George, knowing that Haig will not do any good has allowed him to keep all his guns, etc., so that he can, later on, say, 'Well, I gave you everything. I even allowed you to spoil the Italian offensive. And now, owing to gross miscalculation and incapacity you have entirely failed to do anything serious except lose a lot of men.' And in this indictment he will include Robertson, and then get rid of them both.'[53] In any event, Lloyd George did not stop the offensive. Instead he 'submitted with sullen fatalism' and allowed it to continue.[54]

Equally ironically, in Flanders all rain ceased. Cloudless skies and brilliantly sunlit days refined the mud once more to dust. For two idyllic weeks the soldiers in Flanders were warm, dry, and unhampered by malodorous sludge. To the German infantry it 'seemed almost inconceivable ... that even the peculiar British would fight in the rain and rest in the sun.'[55] In fact, there was no 'rest' for the British soldiers, who, under Plumer's direction, prepared for the next phase scheduled for 20 September. As darkness set in on 19 April, it began to drizzle, and by midnight rain was falling heavily. Luckily the rain stopped next morning, and Plumer's attack, meticulously planned, was successful. On 26 September Plumer launched his second thrust (the Battle of Polygon Wood) which was equally sucessful, but for the third stroke, Broodseinde, it was again necessary to attack in the rain. The consensus of opinion of the Battle of Broodseinde is that it too, despite the rain, was successful.[56] But the village of Passchendaele was still a mile away from Plumer's exhausted troops, and Haig now seemed more determined than ever to occupy the higher ground on which the ruined village sat.[57]

For the third stage of the Flanders campaign Haig planned a further series of three attacks, but the heavens had opened and turned the ground into a 'porridge of mud.'[58] Both Gough and Plumer recommended that the campaign should be stopped. Yet the line as then held was not good, and Haig insisted on pushing forward. Thus, on 9 October 1917 three assaulting divisions lost 7,000 casualties at the Battle of Poelcappelle, and on 12 October the 2nd Anzac Corps suffered through the mud in the 'First Battle of Passchendaele.' That day the German commander, Crown Prince Rupprecht, gave thanks in his diary: 'A break in the weather. Welcome rain, our strongest ally.'[59]

In the last battle of the last stage, Currie's command performed in the centre ring. On 3 October Currie was warned that his corps was to move north towards Passchendaele. He was less than pleased.[60] Canadian losses in the Hill 70 fighting had been heavy, and Currie realized that those in Flanders would probably be even greater. It seemed to him, moreover, that no appreciable good would come from continuation of the campaign. Thus, he protested vigorously against Canadian participation in the northern fighting. 'Every Canadian,' he later wrote, 'hated to go to Passchendaele ... I carried my protest to the extreme limit ... which I believe would have resulted in my being sent home had I been other than the Canadian Corps Commander. I pointed out what the casualties were bound to be, and was ordered to go and make the attack.'[61]

Aside from the heavy casualties that were bound to result, Currie realized that if his corps fought at Passchendaele, it would be impossible to participate in a forthcoming Third Army attack. General Byng now commanded the Third Army, and over the summer of 1917 he and Currie had discussed the possibilities of making a surprise attack by massed tanks and had drawn up tentative plans for such an experiment.[62] (When Byng, without the Canadian Corps, later made such an attack at Cambrai it proved to be the most successful tank action of the war.) More serious in Currie's mind than missing such an experiment was the possibility that the Canadians at Passchendaele would have to fight in the Fifth Army. Long after the war Currie claimed that he had threatened to resign if he were put under General Gough and the Fifth Army at Passchendaele.[63] There is no doubt that Currie complained about Gough, but the chances of his being placed in the Fifth Army seem quite remote, since the Canadians were to replace the 2nd Anzac Corps which had been under Plumer since the end of August.[64] Currie, in other words, was probably less exposed to serving under Gough in 1917 than he still assumed after the war. At the time Currie noted with displeasure the experience of the Canadians at the Somme while under Gough. Later he would also recall the misfortune of the Fifth Army during the German spring offensive of 1918. For the latter Gough's reputation has suffered, though he bore little responsibility for what happened. Regardless of the army in which the Canadians were placed, Currie was strongly opposed to participating in the Passchendaele fighting. The casualties that the campaign had produced so far and the tactical possibilities for continued fighting were more than enough to explain the corps commander's reluctance to move north.

Two facts connected with Currie's distaste for participation at Passchendaele are worth noting; for both are important points of dispute in the literature on this most contentious battle. First, Currie was not the only commander in favour of stopping the battle (we have already noted the objections of Generals Plumer and Gough), yet he ceased his protest and prepared to take part when the commander-in-chief requested him to. This submission was not simply because Haig insisted; rather it is a measure of Haig's influence on senior commanders. Currie later explained that Haig gave no reason for continuing the campaign but merely promised that 'some day I will tell you why, but Passchendaele must be taken.'[65] Haig was wrong about many things, but one should remember that he at least seemed to have enormous influence on those senior officers who knew him personally – so much so that he could sometimes persuade them to acquiesce in plans that they bitterly opposed. Secondly, even though Currie was opposed to continuing the attack, he was still a firm advocate of fighting the war on the Western Front. His basic objection to continuting at Passchendaele was that the tactical and strategic results of continuing the campaign were simply not worth the cost: more could be gained, still on the Western Front, by using other methods. In any event, when it appeared that his protest would not avert the attack Currie threw himself into the task of making the fight with the minimum cost in casualties.

It should be noted that Currie's attitude on Passchendaele was not formed in a vacuum. As soon as he learned of the possibility that the Canadians would go to Passchendaele, he asked General Lipsett and Brigadier Victor Odlum to go to that sector of the front, make a reconnaissance, and report back to him. Odlum had come overseas as second-in-command of the 7th Battalion and had taken over when his commanding officer, Lieutenant-Colonel Hart-McHarg, had been killed. Like Lipsett, he was a thoroughly experienced, intelligent officer. 'All you could see,' Odlum reported to Currie, 'was shell holes with a group of men in them, and you could look perhaps two hundred yards over and see the Germans in the same position. Both sides were just finished. They were down in the mud and there they were staying and they weren't even fighting.'[66] General McNaughton, then a lieutenant-colonel on the corps artillery staff, confirmed the distaste all Canadians shared for going to Passchendaele. 'Nobody wanted to go there,' he said. 'It isn't that we didn't want to fight, but when you fight you like to fight under reasonable conditions, particularly when you've got a good mechanism in which you have confidence. You don't want to be paralyzed by mud and terrain difficulties.'[67]

During April 1915, before the gas attack, the Canadians had held virtually the same front that they reoccupied in October 1917. But even the veterans of the gas attack found the landscape, which had been reduced to 'an unrecognizable waste of ridge and hollow,' totally alien.[68] Understandably depressed by the nature of the battlefield, Currie realized that the success of the coming encounter would depend to a large extent on the ability of his engineers and artillery. Consequently, he sent a strong contingent of sappers and gunners ahead of his infantry to the Ypres area.[69] Perhaps even more important, Currie secured the commander-in-chief's consent that the battle should not begin until the Canadian Corps was satisfied that pre-battle preparations had been completed.[70]

Dwarfing all other problems at Passchendaele was the question of the ground. The official historian records that over half of the battlefield in front of the Canadians was covered by water or very deep mud.[71] Not only was it almost impossible for men to advance across this ground, but it was equally impossible to bring up supplies, to concentrate men for the attack, to find stable gun platforms for the artillery or to evacuate casualties. During the last attacks launched by the 2nd Anzoc Corps at Passchendaele, sixteen men were required to carry one stetcher from the front lines, a job normally done by two bearers.[72] Currie put his entire engineer resources immediately to work, as well as those engineers received under command from Second Army. The corps chief engineer, Major-General W.B. Lindsay, from 17 October until the beginning of the Canadian attacks had 'a daily average of ten field companies, seven tunnelling companies and four army troops companies [of engineers] assisted by two infantry and seven pioneer battalions' at work in the Canadian sector.[73] Drainage canals were made wherever possible; road beds were improved; gun positions were stabilized; and supplies were stockpiled, so that a recent critic claimed the Canadian victory to be a triumph of 'aquatic engineering' and 'sheer courage.'[74]

One of the keys to success in Currie's view was to provide adequate support at all times for the assaulting infantry, and he was desperately worried that the artillery would not be able to do its share. He never rejected entirely the notion of a preliminary bombardment before an attack, but he put the greatest emphasis on the barrage that would cover the infantry advance, and on counter-battery fire to silence enemy guns. When, as at Passchendaele, the infantry had to struggle through mud to advance, the artillery task became all the more difficult. The infantry rate of advance could not be predicted accurately, and keeping the barrage just in front of the foot soldiers required not only careful planning but great flexibility in artillery arrangements and close liaison with the infantry. When the advance proceeded beyond the range of the artillery, the guns had to be hauled forward through the mud and placed in new firing positions. For the fire to be continous, some portion of the artillery would always be moving once the infantry attack had begun. Hence the need for adequate roads and gun platforms well forward of the starting positions prepared before the attack. Indeed, two of the most essential prerequisites for an attack in such complex conditions were very careful planning and close co-operation – qualities in which Currie excelled.[75] Daily conferences with his chief engineer and senior artillery officer became routine.

Immediately after his headquarters arrived in the salient, Currie spent an entire day checking his position. He discovered a number of disquieting facts. General Morrison, his reliable artillery chief, reported that only 220 of the 360 field guns that were to be taken over from the Australians were in working condition. Currie at once went to Second Army headquarters to demand that his deficiences be made good. Plumer's chief artillery officer contended that if Currie did not have the actual guns, he should have received indents for them during the take-over, and without the indents nothing could be done. The corps commander replied that he 'could not fight the Boche with indents' and the dispute was referred to Plumer himself.[76] The army commander came straight to the point, demanding to know how Currie knew the guns were not in position. Currie replied, 'I walked over this region, and many of the guns have disappeared altogether in the mud.'[77] The incident was typical. Currie learned of the trouble from his staff, then checked it out personally. Currie got his guns because he knew the situation and would not move until it was remedied. Throughout the preparatory phase of the battle Currie was almost continuously in the salient. Stubbornly he demanded reconnaissance and co-operation at all levels. In his post-battle report he wrote, 'I am convinced that this reconnaissance and close liaison between the artillery, the infantry units, and the staff, is vital to the success of any operation.'[78] Currie planned to secure Passchendaele ridge by three limited attacks which he originally hoped to begin on 24 October. When it became apparent that the engineer preparations were taking longer than expected, he recommended postponement until 29 October but agreed to begin on 26 October when the commander-in-chief insisted that time was crucial.[79] Because of the swampy ground directly to the front, the first attack was planned as a two-pronged advance on the corps' left and right where the ground rose slightly. The object of the attack was to carry the front approximately 1,200 yards forward, and one of the points that concerned Currie was that no easily discernible landmark could be selected as an objective for the first attack.

From 15 October the weather had been unexpectedly fine, and the engineers' work was facilitated by the fact that no rain had fallen. During the night of 25–26 October, however, there was a 'wet mist' which turned into heavy rain with the beginning of the attack. So far as most of the infantry were concerned, the attack followed the pattern of previous Passchendaele assault – the 'sea of choking fetid mud in which men, animals and tanks floundered and perished hopelessly' still had to be crossed.[80] Casualties were high: 2,481 from 26 to 28 October, though less in comparison with other actions than one might expect.[81] There were, however, certain novel features of the battle which are worth noting.

In the first place, the troops making the assault were fresh. Frequently in the past, when new troops had been available for an attack, commanders had kept these soldiers out of the front line until just before zero hour. This meant that the trip to the front lines – almost as enervating and dangerous as the journey across no-man's land – was made just before the actual attack, with the result that at zero hour the assaulting troops were more fatigued than the veterans who had been holding the front line. Currie ordered his men into the front lines slightly early, preferring to risk the possibility of casualties against the certainty that attacking with exhausted troops would produce even greater losses.[82] Secondly, the planning of the artillery barrage paid handsome dividends, because artillery fire did not run away from the infantry during the advance.[83] Although the attack met all the resistance Currie expected, it accomplished its basic purpose of securing the jumping-off position for the next thrust scheduled for 30 October. In the interim the work of the engineers continued unabated.

At 5:50 a.m. on 30 October the Canadian Corps again advanced, this time behind the protective curtain provided by 420 guns and howitzers. More important perhaps than the artillery support was the fact that the morning was clear and cold and no rain fell until late afternoon. Once again the front lurched forward approximately 1,000 yards at the cost of 1,321 killed, wounded, and missing.[84] Currie now rotated his divisions, replacing the depleted and exhausted 3rd and 4th Canadian Divisions by the 1st and 2nd. Unfortunately, while the Canadians were arranging reliefs, the Germans were doing exactly the same thing along most of the front. On 3 November the German 11th Division arrived from the Champagne area to take up positions along the front from Ypres-Roulers railway to the Mosselmarkt road. Along the rest of the front the 1st and 2nd Divisions faced the same opponents as had the 3rd and 4th Canadian Divisions.[85]

Battlefield communication has always been and still remains one of the key ingredients of tactical success. Throughout the First World War it was a problem with which most commanders struggled. Continuous wave wireless sets had been used with considerable success by the Canadians before Passchendaele. According to one expert the 'cw set' would be 'put to the supreme test' on the Passchendaele battlefield.[86] The freshness of the Canadian troops, the careful planning of the artillery barrage, and, most critical of all, clear skies, were obvious once the attack began.[87] According to the official account the attack began so quickly that 'the enemy's retaliatory fire, opening a few minutes later, fell mainly behind the advancing troops. Afterwards prisoners reported that the infantry followed their barrage so closely that in most cases the Germans could not man their machine guns before the attackers were on top of them. Almost everywhere the attack went well ... less than three hours after zero the village that had so long been an allied objective was securely in Canadian hands.'[88]

The rubble of Passchendaele village was at last captured, but the Canadian Corps was again weaker by 2,238 casualties. Haig recorded jubilantly in his diary that the losses were 'under 700 men' and the Canadian official history rather generously concludes that Sir Douglas's figures 'must have referred only to fatal casualties reported to him up to that time.'[89] Haig's most recent biographer, John Terraine, credits the capture to the 'brilliant organization and method' of the Canadians.[90]

A final attack was still deemed necessary before the campaign could end. It was designed to gain the remaining high ground north of Passchendaele village. The fact that additional reliefs were undertaken by the Germans does not seem to have operated to the attackers' disadvantage. Indeed, precisely the opposite was the case: the German units were now so disorganized that many were unsure of their own boundaries.[91] Other equalizing factors were the heavy rain that fell when the attack was launched on 10 November and the fact that the Canadians were no longer as fresh as they had been during the previous assaults. In spite of the advance, the results of the attack were hardly salutary, for the entire line about Passchendaele now formed a dangerous salient. 'The new tongue of ground' gained on 10 November 'jutted out even more awkwardly and now could be fired into not only from three sides but slightly from the rear as well.'[92] A final loss of 1,094 men by Currie's command ended the Passchendaele campaign. On 14 November the relief began, and six days later Currie once again resumed command of the old Lens front.

Third Ypres has become the most contentious subject in the English literature of the First World War. Yet Arthur Currie has received relatively little attention, in spite of the fact that it was his command that captured Passchendaele and ended the campaign. In the dispute the points of issue are many, and they arise partly from the curious attitude of the British official historian, General Edmonds, who over the years in conversation 'might demolish the reputations of the higher commanders – even Haig – but [who] in print ... was far more circumspect.'[93] The tremendous loss of life in the campaign focused popular attention on Passchendaele, as did the abominable conditions under which it was fought. Though the British casualties were actually less than those suffered during the Battles of the Somme in 1916, Third Ypres epitomized to many the extraordinary stupidity and inhuman aloofness of the generals who ordered such slaughter. To those who were appalled by the role of the professional soldier in the First World War, it was a hideous example of unrestrained generalship. Haig has been portrayed by the civilian protagonists in the debate as 'a stubborn, fame-hungry, cold-blooded, deceiving oaf, and his [Passchendaele] campaign as a military abortion unparallelled in the history of the western world.'[94]

Beyond doubt, the high command made egregious errors in the campaign. In the most ardent defence of Haig, his 'gravest and most fatal error' is conceded to be the decision to give the main role to the Fifth Army under General Gough.[95] Many other charges have been levelled against the commander-in-chief, but 'since the debate is endless and by its nature cannot lead to a conclusion,' one turns to the 'repellent but more tangible process of 'counting heads.'[96] Even here there is much controversy. In the British official history German casualty figues are adjusted from 217,000 to 400,000, and the British loss is placed at 244,897.[97] A Canadian compilation reckons British casualties at approximately 260,000, compared with 202,000 for the Germans, but sidesteps the conclusion that this calculation seems to suggest, claiming instead that the 'Somme, costly as it was to the Allies, began the destruction of the German Army. Passchendaele carried the process a long step forward.'[98]

The campaign has fascinated historians. It was 'a long grim ordeal, its horror forever etched on the minds and hearts of those who fought there.'[99] But this assessment has led critics automatically to assume that 'tactics were always bad.' Actually, the individual battles – those of the Canadian Corps at any rate – were very cleverly conducted and by a commander fully aware of the horror his men faced. Currie's experience goes far in support of the claim that 'tactics were never more skilful' than at Passchendaele.[100] One might argue, of course, that Currie's divisional generals or brigadiers should have equal recognition or that the entire credit for the smooth functioning of the Canadian attacks properly belongs to General Plumer. Both Plumer and the Canadian divisional commanders deserve great praise; teamwork was an essential element of Canadian success. Brigadier Odlum of the 11th Brigade later observed that 'Currie was a man with remarkable intelligence. And when we gathered together ... for discussions he would listen to us as we argued amongst ourselves, and we did argue, but ... in the end, [he] would sum up what was said and draw deductions from it ... He had that mentality that made it possible for him to pick things up, to listen to others and gather from them.'[101] Brigadier-General J.A. Clark of the 72nd Battalion recorded that 'Everbody with any common sense was going to conserve his force and protect his men from casualties to the absolute limit and that was Currie's theory. That was instilled by him into every Commander, and the Battalion Commanders, of course, they were the key to it because some Battalion Commanders could conserve lives better than others. The man who wasted lives, well, he would lose his job.'[102]

Currie's role in the battle of Passchendaele is also important with respect to the controversy regarding civilians and professional soldiers. Lloyd George saw the campaign as the natural outcome of a war directed by incompetent professional soldiers. He charged that in the British army no prewar civilian rose above the rank of brigadier-general: 'the ablest brains did not climb to the top of the stairs and they did not reach a height where politicians could even see them.'[103] Yet the majority of men and regimental officers in the army had been civilians when the war broke out. Thus, claims the British official historian, the British army from 1916 to the end of the war was 'an amateur army, with a very small leaven of professionals.'[104] This does not substantially answer Lloyd George; as long as the 'leaven' was spread evenly over the top, the army was essentially professional. The essence of the charge, moreover, is that the professional soldiers, such as Haig, deliberately suppressed the military careers of promising amateurs or prewar civilians – presumably because the professionals feared they would lose control of the war. C.E.W. Bean, the Australian official historian, comes closer than General Edmonds to a genuine rebuttal when he argues that Haig's constant support of Monash [the Australian Corps Commander] ... throws a vivid light on the inaccuracy of the constant implication ... made by Lloyd George that Haig was prejudiced against civilian soldiers and tended to suppress them.'[105] But Bean's argument itself is not entirely adequate.

In the first place Lloyd George was willing to admit that 'the only exceptions' to the suppression of civilian soldiers were 'to be found in the Dominion forces ... General Currie ... and General Monash ... were both in civil life when war broke out. Both proved themselves to be brilliant military leaders and went right through to the top. It means that their being officers in unprofessional armies gave full play to their gifts.[106] Secondly, he suggested that if an amateur soldier such as Currie or Monash had been allowed to rise higher, to the command of an army or to the position of commander-in-chief, the course of the war would have been radically different, and the tragic slaughters on the Western Front would have been avoided. In short, an amateur would have followed quite a different strategy for the war – presumably akin to that Lloyd George had advocated.[107] In this view Currie and

Monash struggled upwards, in spite of the fact that they were civilians and in spite of their radical notions.

Without examining a multitude of case studies, it is impossible to refute positively the first charge – that within the armies raised in Britain professional soldiers repressed amateurs. Currie's case, however, suggests that Lloyd George's argument is a shaky one. Currie, it should be recalled, started the war as a brigadier-general, mostly because of the paucity of trained regulars in Canada.[108] As a brigade commander, the chances of his surviving while learning of war in France were, relatively speaking, guite good. The same is true of other colonials, such as Monash, who rose to high rank during the war. But in the British armies there were many more senior professional officers to begin with, and so a civilian soldier at the start of the war began his career with a lower rank. The chances of a British amateur who began the war as a captain of surviving the learning period were obviously much lower than those of the colonial who began as a brigadier.[109] In other words, the composition of the British army partly explains the slow promotion of amateur soldiers, without resorting to fanciful arguments concerning 'repression.' We should recall also that while Currie did not hesitate to oppose higher professional officers if he thought the reasons for such action sufficient, one of his most difficult tasks during the summer of 1917 was to advance a prewar professional soldier to the command of a division. On the question of friction between amateurs and professionals Currie was emphatic. 'My fight,' he afterwards recorded, 'was not with the regular officers at all. It was with the Canadian authorities in London.'[110]

It is worth noting that after the war Lloyd George's thesis was given considerable support by the stories of returned men, who contributed to the common view of the 'military mind' – 'by necessity an inferior and unimaginative mind; no man of high intellectual power would willingly imprison his gifts in such a calling.'[111] This notion was as common and as overdrawn in Canada and Australia as it was in England and the United States. Frequently citizen soldiers judged professionals on the most picayune personal experiences.[112] Just as frequently they were so revolted by war that a professional soldier became noxious simply by association. For one who had 'seen so much death – and brains and blood – and marvellous human machines smashed like Humpty-Dumpties ... [who] had bound up a man without a face ... [and] had stood by the body of a man bent backward over a shattered tree while the blood dripped from his gaping head,' it seemed natural to hate armies and those whose profession it was to lead armies.[113]

The second part of Lloyd George's claim – that successful amateurs opposed Haig's strategy – is disproved by the 1917 campaign in Flanders. To be sure, Currie was opposed to participating in the campaign and favoured making an end to the battle. But, and this must be stressed, Currie did not oppose Haig's strategy of fighting the war on the Western Front; rather his objections to continuing the campaign were based on tactical grounds. Currie was not the only general who advocated different tactics on the Western Front. Bidwell and Graham in the book *Firepower* show that many British divisional commanders had worked out tactical ideas very similar to Currie's. Currie, however, as commander of the Canadian Corps, was in a better position than his British peers to push such ideas forward. Even after the war Currie maintained that Passchendaele had been an 'expensive' operation, but he never opposed Haig's fundamental strategy. In discussing Haig and the Ypres campaign after the war, Currie wrote in a vein that surely would have enraged Lloyd George: 'There were always those in authority in England who wanted to fight the war in many places other than on the Western Front, and so he, (Haig) who held strongly that the issue must be decided there, was often very much concerned when Divisions which he badly needed were sent to other places. Much has been written and much has been implied concerning his troubles with those whom we may call the politicians. He had to withstand from them much criticism and much interference, but he never complained bitterly about these things, but always held out with the greatest patience for what he knew to be right.'[114]

To recapitulate, Currie commanded an army corps for only the second time in the Passchendaele battle. He was thrust into this position when both his old and his new commands were actively engaged with the enemy and when his personal affairs were in a highly embarrassing condition. When he became corps commander he insisted on the right to appoint his own subordinates, but he did not challenge the ill-defined nature of Turner's 'administrative authority' in France, which was to prove the cause of considerable friction during the coming year. In spite of these handicaps, Currie handled his corps with extraordinary tactical skill.

Perhaps a special word on the success of the Canadians is in order; for in the summer of 1917 Currie's command had a record of which, not unnaturally, he was extremely proud. It had been the Canadians who took on elements of five German divisions at Hill 70 and who seized Passchendaele ridge, finishing the campaign. There is little doubt that such success was in large part due to effective leadership and sound planning by Currie and other senior officers. It was, equally, the result of the truly astonishing courage of the men who had to wrestle their way through the mud. But the outcome of Passchendaele rested on other factors as well. The Canadians, after all, were relatively fresh, while the Germans were exhausted. The artillery barrage that covered the Canadian advances was meticulously planned to stay just in front of the attacking troops. And, not to be ignored, the Canadians frequently had the good luck to make their attacks when there was no rain, an advantage the British and Australian troops less often enjoyed. In short, success was not the simple result of Canadian fighting superiority over other forces in the Allied armies. Many people, mostly Canadians, nevertheless came to believe that the Canadian Corps was the only force capable of taking Passchendaele. Unwittingly perhaps, Haig contributed to this notion. Currie later observed that Haig 'always left you feeling he had supreme confidence in your ability to carry through successfully the task which he had assigned to you.'[115] Currie realized that Haig 'seldom showed any emotion,' and as a consequence the commander-in-chief's appeal for success at Passchendaele seemed to take on a special significance. In any case Currie came to believe that it was not 'too much to say ... that the victory of the Canadians at Passchendaele kept the Allies in the war.'[116]

6

A new doctrine

After the capture of Passchendaele ridge, Currie received his share of the victors' honours. In July he had been knighted by King George v. He was now fêted by the French and Belgians. On 22 November he received the Croix de Guerre with Palm from the hand of the French minister of the interior, who effusively hoped that Currie would become the 'Duke of Passchendaele.' In December he simultaneously received the Belgian Croix de Guerre and became an 'Officier grand de l'Ordre de la Couronne.'[1]

The heady praise and the handsome decorations did little to alleviate Currie's most stubborn problems. Of these difficulties the most exasperating (it seemed to involve and inflame all other issues) was keeping his command at full strength. Since the first contingent of Canadians had arrived in France, the problem of reinforcements had been vexing. It had now become critical. The total size of the Canadian army always had been determined by Canadian political leaders, and they had steadily increased the size of the expeditionary force. In November 1914, while Currie and the 2nd Brigade marched on Salisbury Plain, a second contingent had been authorized. In July of the following year, just before Currie was given command of the 1st Division, the total number under arms was increased to 150,000. In October 1915 this number was expanded further to 250,000. On New Year's Day 1916, a little better than two months before the fighting of St Eloi craters, Sir Robert Borden announced that Canada was to place half a million men in uniform.

Borden and his colleagues were accountable, not only for the total size of the Canadian force but also for the method by which the army was kept up to strength. From the beginning Borden and Hughes had insisted that membership in the army would be voluntary. Theoretically, so long as volunteers were available (in 1914 and 1915 there seemed to be a super-abundance), maintaining the force would be simple. Unfortunately, flaws in the theory developed rapidly. The difficulty was an inefficient organization of the flow of replacements mainly caused by the interference and the ill-considered methods of Sir Sam Hughes. Hughes's resignation, the formation of a sound organization in England, and the army's growing experience, led eventually to the introduction of sensible procedures. Just before his resignation, however, Hughes had authorized the formation in England of the 5th Canadian Division under the command of his son. The 5th Division did not proceed to France (hence, as we have seen (Chapter 5), the desire to give Garnet Hughes a 'fighting' division). New arrivals from Canada were earmarked for this 'home-defence' division rather than replacing casualties suffered by the Canadian Corps in France.

During the winter and spring of 1917 it increasingly became apparent that there were simply not enough volunteers to fill both of these needs. At Vimy Ridge the Canadian Corps had suffered 10,602 casualties in six days; but only 4,761 men had volunteered during the entire month of April 1917.[2] Finally, on 18 May, the last day of Nivelle's abortive Battle of the Aisne, Sir Robert Borden announced in the House of Commons that the Canadian government intended to end the system of voluntary enlistment and 'to provide, by compulsory military enlistment on a selective basis, such reinforcements as may be necessary to maintain the Canadian Army today in the field as one of the finest fighting units of the Empire.'[3]

Borden's decision sparked one of the most acrimonious political debates in Canadian history, which soon divided the country on racial rather than party lines. It produced the most bitter anti-English feeling in Quebec since the Riel Rebellion. It split the Liberal party, elements of which entered a coalition government, and it destroyed the seventy-five-year-old leader of the party, Sir Wilfrid Laurier. The next quarter-century of Canadian politics would fail to erase the effects of Borden's stand.

One would expect that the leader of a military force desperately in need of reinforcement would heartily advocate any measure that would assure him men. At first Currie took this attitude; but as the summer of 1917 progressed (and as the need for reinforcements became more critical) Currie no longer seemed such a warm advocate of conscription. Indeed, during the last months of 1917 he tried to disassociate himself from the measure.

The explanation of this evolution of attitude is found in the events of the latter half of 1917. Often generals are criticized for the seemingly dehumanized manner in which they reduce living men to numbers. There is something fundamentally abhorrent about calculating the possible losses for an impending attack, and the man who launches an attack when fully aware of the probabilities is frequently deemed insensitive at best, inhuman at worst. However, critics usually fail to point out that the general who does not study numbers carefully is usually responsible for the greatest number of casualties. Currie paid the closest attention to the losses

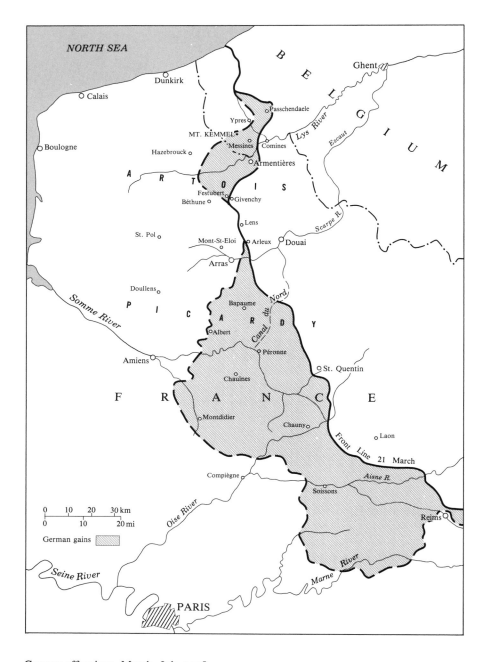

German offensives, March–July 1918

suffered by the corps and to the numbers of reinforcements reaching it. He was firmly convinced that sending an under-strength unit into battle almost always resulted in greater losses than if that unit fought under the same conditions but at full strength. These forbidding statistics were always in the forefront of his mind.

In June 1917, when Currie expressed his support of conscription, he stated simultaneously in a letter to the leader of the Ontario Liberal party his willingness to do anything to support compulsory service. Everyone in France, he wrote, is 'anxiously looking to see what the result of [Borden's] conscription proposals ... will be.' Then he added: 'I attribute a great deal of our success to our fighting organization. If our units are not kept up to strength that organization breaks down, and success cannot be expected in the same measure. Furthermore, if our units are kept at full strength, the morale of our troops remains very high: whereas if units are allowed to become weak in numbers, the morale suffers accordingly. I pray that you will not relax your efforts in seeing that everything possible is done by Canada to furnish the necessary drafts of officers and men. The troops expect it – let them not be disappointed.'[4] About the same time Borden decided to make use of Currie's promotion to gain further support for the introduction of compulsory military service. On 18 June he wired Perley: 'As soon as Currie is appointed I shall send a message of congratulations to him. It would be well if in his reply he should make clear the need for reinforcements to maintain Canadian Army Corps at full strength.'[5] Currie showed no reluctance whatever in complying with this prearranged political strategy. Upon receiving Borden's message of congratulations, he replied: 'It is an imperative and urgent necessity that steps be immediately taken to ensure that sufficient drafts of officers and men are sent from Canada to keep the Corps at full strength.'[6] In short, it is clear that at the end of June 1917 Currie was solidly behind the introduction of compulsory military service and was prepared to back the measure fully.[7]

Less than five months later his correspondence shows a marked change in attitude. He was still in favour of compulsory service, of course, but he showed no enthusiasm for the proposition and had many doubts about its efficacy. By November 1917 it seemed to Currie that 'months had already been wasted, and even if the men who are being called up now are got into training at once [a course that was virtually impossible] we shall need them very badly before they will be fit to send. If they don't come at all within three months I feel that this Corps may still consist of four Divisions, but of probably only nine [instead of twelve] Battalions each; in six months it would probably consist of only two Divisions, and in a year from now not more than one.' Canadians, Currie complained, had been 'deceived' about the nature of the reinforcement situation. They had not been told clearly by those in authority how critical the situation was becoming, and this was unfair to the men already in France. Canadian soldiers in France, in Currie's view, were 'committed until peace is declared. If no others are sent to help them they can look forward to nothing else but to be killed or permanently maimed. Many of our men have already been wounded three or four times, yet the exigencies of the period demand that they be again sent to the firing line.'[8] In December his attitude became even more hostile. Although he believed that Canadian soldiers in France would vote 'overwhelmingly in favour of seeing that nothing is done to delay the operation of the Military Service Act,' he told Sir George Perley flatly that 'it is too bad that we are bothered by an election,'[9] implying that an election would probably do little to improve the situation regardless of how the soldiers voted. As the election approached, Perley went to France hoping to persuade Currie to buttress the government's chances by sending to Canada a further message on the necessity of conscription. He received an uncompromising refusal from the corps commander.[10]

On 10 December, just a week before election day, Currie demanded a public statement from Perley. He had discovered that opponents of conscription were circulating rumours of incompetence within the Canadian Corps, and his disgust with the situation was clear and explicit. He wanted Perley to make an official statement denying such scurrilous reports. 'You know how I have striven to keep clear of politics,' he told the high commissioner, 'but both sides seem determined to mix me up in it. I do not consider that it is fair that in the propaganda issued by the Government that my name should appear so prominently. When it does, the Opposition of course consider it good political tactics to throw mud, and some mud always sticks when thrown. To have gone through what anyone who has been here for three years has had to go through, ... would almost justify one in hoping that your own countrymen would not refer to you as a murderer.'[11]

The most obvious explanation for the corps commander's changed attitude would appear to be his growing resentment at being involved in the debate developing in Canada over the introduction of conscription. He acknowledged that his request for a statement by Perley on 10 December was stimulated by a letter signed by a number of Canadian editors and addressed to 'General Sir Arthur Currie, or the Acting Commander of the Canadian Corps,' indicating to him that 'in the minds of these gentlemen there was a doubt as to whether I was in command of the Corps, this doubt having arisen from statements which I understand Sir Wilfrid Laurier and others of his party made in Canada to the effect that I had been removed from command of the corps owing to inefficiency and the excessive number of casualties at Passchendaele.'[12] Without doubt Currie resented inferences made about him by politicians and journalists in Canada, but his anger and his changed view of conscription had a broader basis than resentment over attacks on his personal reputation. To ascribe Currie's reaction to selfish pique completely misrepresents his position. The reasons for his changed frame of mind about conscription can be found in the events of the summer of 1917.

As we have already seen, the months of that fateful summer were difficult for Currie. He had faced the possibility of public exposure for his expropriation of the uniform allowance in 1914, though he was taking steps to make retribution. He had undergone the difficult process of taking over command of the corps and arranging for his successor in the 1st Division. He had faced the sobering responsibility for the operations in which the Canadian Corps was almost continuously involved. From time to time, there intruded on his routine reports of the election campaign in Canada.

Conscription had been formally announced by Sir Robert Borden on 19 May 1917; but the Military Service Bill did not pass its third reading in the House of Commons until 24 July. Further delay ensued while the prime minister, who had promised not to introduce conscription until after a general election, negotiated with pro-conscription Liberals on the formation of a union government. More delay was essential until the ground was prepared for an election by the passage of the Military Voters Act and the War-Times Election Act. Meanwhile the provisions of the Military Service Bill were amended, compromised, and redrafted, making them increasingly acceptable as the basis for a broad union government. Exemptions, appeal procedures, and various deferrals all had to be worked out, and their impact was to make the act more politically acceptable and, in Currie's eyes, less effective. Parliament was not dissolved until 6 October 1917. While Currie's divisions were en route to Passchendaele, Borden announced the formation of a union government of Conservatives and pro-conscription Liberals. As the election approached and the debate in Canada became more intense, Currie and other senior officers were faced with the toll of casualties. Between April and October the corps had sustained approximately 40,000 casualties. Replacements were arranged by the new Overseas Military Forces of Canada, yet despite this vastly improved organization for Canadian administration there were frustrations.

The circumstances surrounding the simultaneous promotion of Currie and Turner have already been discussed (see Chapter 5). Turner's authority, as we have seen, was not adequately defined at the time of his promotion. Turner occasionally was also difficult to work with, and the deputy minister of overseas forces eventually resigned after a series of disputes with him. Even the prime minister noted Turner's awkwardness and considered replacing him.[13]

However, trouble arose more quickly between Turner and Currie. In July 1917, without reference to Currie, a number of minor appointments in the Canadian Corps were made by the Canadian headquarters in London. After his difficulty in appointing Macdonnell to the 1st Division, Currie was furious, and he reacted vigorously. 'Instead of asking me for my recommendations,' he wrote to Sir George Perley, 'or permitting me to make recommendations, you make suggestions as to who should get the appointments and force me to agree to your suggestions or oppose them. This puts me in a false position and I maintain it is most unfair.' He concluded that 'If I am to command this corps, surely it is for me to say who should be recommended to fill the appointments rendered vacant ... Am I not the most cognizant of all the factors which bear on the case [?] ... I am quite sure you personally are not in accord with this attempted interference, but some of your assistants are, to my mind, to put it most mildly, just a little too enthusiastic for their friends ... I am only too anxious at all times to do everything possible to promote and preserve harmony, but I most respectfully submit that, as I am the one who must assume final responsiblity for the efficiency of the Corps, there must be no interference with my prerogatives in the matter of recommendations.'[14]

The corps commander believed that General Turner was behind this attempt to interfere with the Canadian Corps. Indeed, Currie was always suspicious of Turner, and he held him responsible for the inadequate training of reinforcements in England.[15] Existing evidence indicates that Turner could be factious but he was not malicious. When Currie's conduct of operations was severely criticized after the war, Turner, on two occasions, took a vigorous stand in support of Currie.[16] Some of the misunderstanding between Currie and Turner resulted from ambiguities in the system of communication between Overseas Military Head-quarters in London, the Canadian Corps, and British General Headquarters in France.[17]

Currie's relationship with Perley was already made difficult by the fact that Perley had urged Currie to accept Garnet Hughes. Currie probably did not know that Perley had offered to pay half of his debt, and he clearly showed him no gratitude. Indeed, during the latter part of 1917 Currie suspected that Perley was issuing propaganda in his name for the election campaign in Canada, a suspicion that was supported by statements made by anti-conscription Liberals in Canada. For example, the charge by Frank Oliver, a prominent Alberta Liberal and one of the architects of the developing split in the Liberal party, that 'when we have a political general in command of our forces I want to be assured that our battles are not being fought for political effect,'[18] cut Currie to the quick and increased his resentment towards Perley. Had Borden's cabinet reorganization in October, in which Sir Edward Kemp became minister of the overseas military forces, removed Perley from the scene, perhaps Currie's attitude would have changed. But Perley remained in England as Canadian high commissioner, and he continued to act as overseas minister until Kemp arrived in England in January 1918.

For Currie the frustrations of the summer of 1917 seemed endless. Many were perhaps magnified or distorted, but the pressures were real and the casualties were real. Most officers in the Canadian Corps focused on the need for replacements. Currie was less interested in how the supply of reinforcements for the Canadian Corps was secured than he was in its happening. It began to appear that as the need for reinforcements steadily grew, the government inexorably postponed or whittled away the guaranteed provision of men. Borden had promised conscription at the beginning of May. The Military Service Bill did not pass the House of Commons until 24 July and would not be effected until after a general election. Since the election would not take place until December not a single conscript would be called until January at the earliest. It would be weeks, even months, after that before trained soldiers would appear in France. Meanwhile, the British commander-in-chief predicted that within a few months Allied forces would 'meet a strong and sustained hostile offensive.'[19]

Sir Arthur Currie's attitude towards conscription took little or no account of the complicated situation in Canada or of the thorny question of race relations which underlay the issue. It could be argued that his outlook was simplistic or naïve. However, it was founded only on the realities that faced his command in France. In the spring he had been prepared to overlook the previous incompetence of his political masters. He had been willing to forget the past, the scandals of Hughes's administration, if only the politicians would, for once, do what was within their power alone and solve the reinforcement crisis. As the need for reinforcements increased, it appeared that a solution was postponed. Politicians seemed more concerned with foisting unwelcome subordinates on him and with using his name in electioneering than in fulfilling their responsibility to the Canadian Corps. In his blackest moments this was Currie's perception of situation. During the summer and autumn he had faced perhaps the most difficult military tasks of his entire career. He had confronted them squarely and successfully, only to be humiliated and insulted by politicians in Canada who had never seen the trenches of Flanders. As is often the case with shy and awkward personalities, Currie at heart was a very sensitive man. The thought of additional and unnecessary casualties resulting from sending under-strength units into battle was genuine torture to him. His view may have been one-sided, but given the pressure under which he operated, his increasingly sceptical attitude to conscription – even his refusal to co-operate with Perley by sending another message of support for the government – becomes understandable. Likely the most galling fact, however, was that in England there were already enough men to bring the corps up to strength and beyond. Under the command of Garnet Hughes the 5th Division trained and, at full strength, simply sat in England. For almost a year it had been performing the role of 'home defence' and could not be tapped to provide the men so desperately needed by the corps in France. Indeed, during the election campaign the men of the 5th Division had been promised that the 5th would never be disbanded.[20]

The reinforcement problem not only affected the Canadians; it was equally acute in the other British forces. Between January 1917 and January 1918 the total British and dominion strength on the Western Front had declined by almost

100,000, although the number of divisions in service had increased. This situation and other factors produced a gloomy prognosis for the winter from the commander-in-chief, who told his army commanders on 3 December that the 'general situation on the Russian and Italian fronts combined with the paucity of reinforcements which we are likely to receive, will in all probability necessitate our adopting a defensive attitude for the next few months. We must be prepared to meet a strong and sustained hostile offensive.'[21] Faced with such an inauspicious prediction for the future and with his own ranks depleted, Currie could draw small comfort from the fact that his sector of the front around Lens was relatively quiet.

Currie was also troubled by existing organizational and training arrangements in the corps which he felt could be more expeditiously handled, and he was anxious to make changes to improve the corps' tactical efficiency. Reflecting on the situation that existed in late 1917, he recalled almost a year later that it had been necessary for signallers and machine gunners 'to do as much training in France as they do in England.'[22] It had always been Currie's 'clearly-held purpose,' according to one of his subordinates, that Canadian combat troops should lack nothing in the way of support and assistance during battle. To achieve this aim throughout the summer of 1917 he had encouraged changes in artillery organization and procedure. The reason was explained by the commander of the corps heavy artillery: 'The complement of guns in the Canadian Corps proportional to Divisions engaged, was never unusual but invariably in and after Vimy and through the intelligence and command organization which came to be built up, the guns available were kept firing on useful targets long after the prearranged barrages had been completed. In the result the infantry had the benefit, on due occasion, of more than *double* the rates of ammunition expenditure achieved in other formations in like circumstances.'[23] As a result of the Passchendaele experience, Currie was also contemplating organizational changes in the engineers and machine gun corps when, quite suddenly, the entire question of reorganization, reinforcements, and the 5th Division erupted to produce one of the most serious policy debates of the entire war for the Canadian forces.

British authorities precipitated the issue. To bring all units up to strength they decided to change the establishment of an infantry brigade from four to three battalions, and to use the men from the disbanded battalions as reinforcements. Henceforth an infantry division would contain nine instead of twelve infantry battalions.[24] At the same time the chief of the imperial general staff proposed that the Canadian forces should be similarly reorganized. This request made good sense so far as the principle of military standardization for all British forces was concerned, and the War Office was anxious that the reorganization should include the 5th Canadian Division. The War Office proposed further that the Canadians made surplus to establishment should not be used as reinforcements for existing divisions but should form an additional division, the 6th Division. Then, both the 5th and 6th Divisions could be sent to France.[25]

Implicit in such a reorganization was the break-up of the six Canadian infantry divisions into two corps and the formation of a Canadian army. Currie perceived that the suggested reorganization would be well received by many officers. 'Such a move,' he observed, 'would be popular in many quarters. It would mean an additional Corps Commander, several new Divisional Commanders, at least six new Brigade Commanders and quite a number of additional Staffs, at least 50% more of the latter than we have now.'[26] It would also mean a new army commander, and Currie naturally would have a strong claim for this position. In fact the proposed change was more radical than at first glance it might appear. Unlike a division, an army corps and its superior formation, an army, were more or less amorphous formations. That is, the size and composition of a corps or an army varied from time to time as did the task it faced. There were, it is true, fixed corps and army headquarters establishments and a body of soldiers known as corps or army troops, permanently under control of the corresponding headquarters. But the size of a British corps or army varied according to the number of divisions that it possessed at any given time. However, the Canadian Corps, to which Canadian divisions had become more or less permanently attached, was in effect a permanent organization. Each of the divisions, it is true, served for short periods under other corps headquarters, and many times the Canadian Corps was temporarily augmented by the attachment of British divisions. The difference between the Canadian Corps and a British corps was that the Canadian divisions always returned to the mother corps and spent most of the time under its command. More significantly, the corps headquarters played a more important role in the Canadian than in a British corps.

Currie's proposals for organizational changes would increase rather than diminish this difference; for he was primarily interested in changing the composition of corps troops. Tactical efficiency, Currie insisted, was directly related to unit organization and could be improved or retarded by organizational changes. Basically, he was satisfied with the existing infantry structure, if it could be maintained. The experience of Passchendaele had suggested to him a number of organizational changes in the supporting arms. He was not pleased, for example, with the British arrangement of three engineer companies in a division. Similarly, changes in the signals service and machine gun corps seemed to be desirable. When he reorganized, he planned to put these services directly under corps headquarters.[27] If the War Office scheme were adopted, such changes would be hard to implement and the infantry structure, which he thought worked well, would be subject to change for the worse.

The importance of Currie's argument against the proposed changes in structure and of his substitution of a different arrangement cannot be over stressed. Their implementation meant that, in the short run, the reinforcement problem would be solved for the Canadian Corps and also that Currie would not receive a promotion and the command of an army. However, the long-term effects were more significant. The reorganization that Currie undertook, when associated with the special training program he would institute in the spring of 1918, puts him among the most imaginative tactical thinkers on the Western Front. Currie's emphasis on supporting arms was similar to the approach that led to the devastating success of the German attacks in the spring of 1918. Indeed many of the enemy's successful tactical innovations were matched in Currie's subsequent training program.[28] Monash, usually reckoned as the most brilliant of Allied generals, came to conclusions about supporting arms that were very similar to Currie's.[29] After the war Currie's views on the twelve-battalion division were confirmed by the French tactician, Colonel Lucas.[30] Currie's tactical thinking was neither as penetrating nor as brilliantly comprehensive as that of postwar thinkers such as Liddell Hart and J.F.C. Fuller; but his reorganization and his training scheme demonstrated that he was struggling with some of the problems – increased mobility and better communications, for example – for which they later found solutions.

In January 1918, however, Currie's main problem was to prevent a step backward, to hold off a retrograde reorganization of his infantry divisions. He was particularly disturbed by the alacrity with which the British proposal was accepted in London by Canadian authorities. When he was first informed of the proposed reorganization, there was already considerable agreement at OMFC headquarters in favour of creating two Canadian corps; and the commanders of the proposed new units were tentatively selected. The more he thought of it, the more it seemed to Currie that the real pressure for such a reorganization came from within the Canadian headquarters in London rather than from the War Office.[31] Consequently, he asked Sir Edward Kemp, the new overseas minister, to come to France to discuss the situation. Currie managed to persuade Kemp that the matter was too serious for quick action and that any changes should be thoroughly studied.[32]

The British, it seemed, were making the change of structure because their reserves of manpower were low. For political effect they decided to reduce the strength of a division rather than reduce the number of divisions. Until now the 5th Canadian Division had been kept in England because it was believed to be impossible to reinforce five divisions in France. Basically conditions had not changed: it would be weeks, probably several months, before the Military Service Act could produce trained reinforcements. Yet now it 'was proposed ... to put more men in the field than ever before, thereby disclosing a condition of reserves directly opposite to that with which the British were confronted.'[33]

While briefly in London in December, Currie found headquarters to be the bed of rumour that is usually the case in military organizations. Inevitably rumours at a rear headquarters involved the commander at the front. Given the difficult summer and fall that Currie had endured, he perhaps reacted to such rumours with more heat than was prudent.[34] On the other hand, he did not lose sight of the main issue. He became more than ever determined to focus on the essential problem of whether or not a reorganization would add to the fighting strength and efficiency of the Canadian forces. Writing to one of his brigadiers temporarily in Canada, Currie pledged that nothing would influence him in 'sanctioning any change, or any new organization which I do not believe to be the best interests of Canada's fighting forces.'[35]

Currie sought the advice of his own staff and, on 5 February he had a hurried interview with Haig before returning to England to put his case to Sir Edward Kemp.[36] By 7 February he had come to a decision that he outlined in a lengthy memorandum. Carefully pointing out that the situation that prompted the change in the British forces did not apply to the Canadians, Currie stressed the fact that Sir Douglas Haig did not insist on the Canadians following the British precedent.[37] Haig, it seems, was under the impression that even in the British forces the reorganization would be a temporary expedient. In time, Haig hoped to replace the disbanded battalion in each British brigade with 'an American Battalion, thus serving the double object of restoring the four Battalion organization which has stood the test of experience and ... of training American Troops.'[38] Currie believed that Haig's plan involved a very sensitive national issue. Placing American troops in Canadian higher formations would merely 'invite' diaster. He was disturbed even more by the possiblity of destroying 'strong feelings of Esprit de Corps and comradeship' if existing brigades were broken up. His main thesis was based on more tangible issues. 'The main object in view, both of the War Office and of Canada, is to put the greatest possible number of men in the fighting line at the least expenditure of manpower and money. This object may be gained more economically than by accepting the present suggestion.'[39]

Currie noted that the proposed reorganization would create six new battalions. A battalion in attack was about 600 strong. Thus the added striking power would be about 3,600 men. To provide this increase it was proposed to create at least three new brigade staffs, a new divisional staff, a new corps staff, perhaps even an army staff, which in his estimation was 'increasing out of all proporation the overhead charges.'[40] Currie had an alternative proposal. First, the 5th Division should be disbanded and its men posted to understrength units in the corps. Then, 100 additional men should be attached to existing battalions in the first four divisions without altering the infantry structure of the corps in any way.

This gives a total increase in striking power of 4800 without increase of staffs ...

Experience has shown that the machinery of each of the fighting battalions is capable of dealing with this increase and I know of no difficulties of supply or administration which cannot be easily overcome ... The time may come when Canada may find it difficult to produce the reinforcements, necessary to maintain the Corps at the establishment, increased either by the addition of six Battalions or by the addition of 100 men per Battalion as I suggest. I submit that in this case it would be far easier to reduce Battalions to normal establishments [i.e., less the 100 additional men] than to reduce the number of Battalions or the normal establishment of a Battalion. The bad effect on efficiency of the latter alternative has been sufficiently proved.[41]

Currie made two additional points. First, he demonstrated that if the War Office scheme were accepted, it would be necessary to bring in a large number of British staff officers, since there were not enough trained Canadians to fill the additional appointments. That Currie was not averse to the use of British staff officers when necessary was already quite well known. Thus his point was bound to be taken seriously by those who were anxious for the corps to be a purely Canadian formation. Finally, he noted that there were not enough 'personnel for specialist army services' for the War Office scheme to be implemented at short notice.

Sir Arthur Currie made his case carefully; and he secured Kemp's support for his own idea of adding 100 men to each existing infantry battalion. On 9 February orders were issued in London for disbanding the 5th Canadian Division and posting its men to the corps in France.[42] For the time being, at least until the Military Service Act could become operative, Currie's proposal resolved his greatest difficulty. No longer would he be plagued by a lack of reinforcements.

Currie's next problem was to tackle the reorganization of supporting arms. To allow more efficient communication within the corps and, in particular, to create new lines of communication more speedily during a battle Currie had already authorized a considerable increase in the personnel of the corps signal service.[43] In early 1918 the most pressing remaining need seemed to be changes in the engineer organization and an increase in the number of machine guns in the corps. To accomplish the latter, in March Currie authorized the reorganization of the Canadian Machine Gun Corps. Eventually it was to become a kind of mobile reserve of medium and heavy machine guns mounted in armoured cars and directly under the control of the corps commander.[44]

Before any thorough solution for engineering difficulties could be attempted, however, the Western Front was once again thrown into crisis condition. In 1918 the British armies were stretched across 126 miles of northern France, from just below the northern coast to below the Oise River. During the early months of the new year Sir Douglas Haig was under tremendous pressure. His frontage had been extended by twenty-five miles, giving the British army a total of 126 miles of front. He was convinced that the Germans were preparing a massive attack; his divisions against his wishes had been reduced from twelve to nine battalions; and he was limited further by inadequate reserves.[45] In March Haig's pessimism was justified by Ludendorff's attempt at a gigantic breakthrough. The Germans planned to punch through the British line on the Somme at Peronne and then to swing north, rolling up the British flank as they went. A second breakthrough would then be effected in the north near Armentières, and the British would be caught between the two German forces. Ludendorff's hammer blows began on 21 March, just a week before rioting broke out in Quebec City in opposition to the Military Service Act.

The German plan, in the short run, was spectacularly successful – in four days enemy forces advanced fourteen miles, the greatest advance on the Western Front since 1914.[46] Indeed, as John Terraine has written, 'the stunning violence of the German bombardment ... ; the huge weight of the infantry attack ...; the fog which ... nullified much of the British defensive system; the total annihilation of forward units; the breakdown of communications; the new German tactics of infiltration ...; all these elements added to the thousand-and-one harrowing details of defeat in the field and sudden retreat, have lent tones of awe and wonderment to the narrative of the "March Offensive." '[47] In all, the Germans unleashed four great attacks between 21 March and 18 June. All the Allied gains of the past two years were obliterated. The seriousness of the threat is hard to overemphasize. It resulted in the appointment of General Ferdinand Foch as commander-in-chief of the Allied armies.

The ultimate effect of the attack, unlike that of the Quebec conscription riots which long remained a symbol of corrosive dispute, was not great. Indeed the German effort spelled the end of the potential of German armies to take up the offensive. 'Ludendorff had cast the dice; once again the gray clad hosts had moved almost within sight of the spires of Paris. The Germans had captured about 225,000 prisoners in their 1918 offensives, inflicted a total of almost one million casualties; yet their triumphs were a "victory without a morrow." '[48]

Throughout the fighting of the German offensive the greatest Allied need was for additional soldiers; to contain successive German drives, Haig again and again had to thin out formations not actually under attack. Throughout this fighting the Canadian Corps maintained its position near Lens, almost exactly between the two areas of German penetration. Not unnaturally, therefore, Haig made heavy demands on Canadian manpower. On 23 March the 2nd Canadian Division was taken under command of GHQ Reserve, and the 1st Division was moved to First Army Reserve. This left Currie to hold some 17,000 yards of front with only two divisions. On 26 March the 3rd and 4th Divisions were detached from his command, and Currie's headquarters was sent into reserve. 'Under the pressure of circumstances,' Currie recorded, 'the four Canadian Divisions were to be removed from my command, placed in two different Armies ... and under the command of three different Corps.'[49]

Currie recognized that in such a crisis desperate redispositions had to be made; but he was also of the opinion that the results achieved from a piecemeal disposition of the corps would be less than if it could be engaged as a collective unit. All Currie's efforts thus far had been towards strengthening the corps rather than individual divisions. To his own officers he frequently stressed that 'a corps with four divisions was the logical tactical organization' for success. This assertion was based on his conviction that the division was 'too small an organization to get the full benefit of artillery' and other support.[50] He now made these views known to his army commander, General Horne, and to Haig's chief of staff, and suggested that the corps should be reunited as quickly as 'the tactical and administrative requirements of the moment' allowed.[51] Currie stressed the fact that he did not wish to 'embarrass the Chief [Haig] in the slightest degree' by his request. However, he added that, when separately employed, Canadian divisions did not achieve the success they should: 'From the very nature and constitution of the organization it is impossible for the same liaison to exist in a British Corps as exists in the Canadian Corps. My staff and myself cannot do as well with a British Division in this battle as we can do with the Canadian Divisions, nor can any other Corps Staff do as well with the Canadian Divisions as my own. I know that necessity knows no law and that the Chief will do what he thinks best, yet for the sake of the victory we must win, get us together as soon as you can.'[52]

Within twenty-four hours of sending his message, the 3rd and 4th Divisions were back under Currie's headquarters. By 8 April the 1st Division had also returned, although the 2nd did not rejoin the Canadian Corps until 1 July. This quick reunion, however, was not the result of Haig's acceptance of Currie's logic. When Currie requested that the Canadian divisions be returned to his control, he sent a copy of his letter to Sir Edward Kemp, who in turn relayed a copy of its content to Lord Derby, the British secretary of state for war.[53] Derby then informed Haig that it was 'the Canadian Government's desire' that the Canadians fight together. Haig later admitted that it was this communication that caused the corps reunion.[54] As a consequence, for a short time there was hard feeling between Haig and Currie.

Engaged in a life or death struggle with Ludendorff, Haig had little time to digest Currie's request. He strongly resented the pressure to reunite the Canadian Corps that came through political channels. Currie's army commander, General Horne, took a similar view and was inclined to think that Currie's letter implied criticism of the quality of British forces. On 14 April Horne called on Currie and made it plain that he objected to 'any reflections on [the] fighting ability of British

Divisions.'[55] Currie was, in fact, being critical of the British forces. He had already noted in his diary that 'many British troops are not fighting well. This is what I expected ... would be the case.'[56] He was not critical of British forces because they were British; his opinion was based on military considerations, namely, his well-known dislike for the nine-battalion division which he had opposed so strenuously in January. In Currie's view one simply could not expect troops to fight as well under the organizational arrangement the British had adopted. This distinction was lost on Horne. Sir Arthur was annoyed when Horne proved so obtuse, doubly so because Currie shared with Haig and other British commanders resentment towards Lloyd George's diversion of troops to other theatres.[57]

Piqued by the interview and by Horne's failure to comprehend his position, Currie reflected, 'they do not want the truth, they want camouflage and they're getting it. Oh God, how they are getting it and how the British people are getting it in all the balderdash being published in the Press.'[58] Meanwhile, Horne reported to Haig that he thought Currie was 'suffering from a swollen head,' which in turn provoked Haig. 'Currie,' Haig wrote, 'wishes to fight only as a 'Canadian Corps' and gets his Canadian representatives in London to write and urge me to arrange it. As a result the Canadians are together holding a wide front near Arras, *but they have not yet been in the battle*! The Australians on the other hand have been used by divisions and are now spread out from Albert to Amiens and one is in front of Hazebrouck.'[59]

It is hard to know exactly what Haig meant by his italicized phrase. If he kept the corps out of battle as a punishment for Currie's stand, he was being less vindictive than Lord Beaverbrook's pen sketch of the commander-in-chief suggests and less inventive than indicated by Liddell Hart. Beaverbrook described Haig as 'frank, truthful, egotistical, self-confident and malicious,'[60] Hart wrote that the commander-in-chief possessed a 'calm unimaginative acceptance of whatever fate may have in store.'[61] The comparison between the Australians and Canadians is also interesting in the light of a letter Haig wrote to his wife a little more than a month earlier. 'I spent some time today with the Canadians. They are really fine disciplined soldiers now and so smart and clean. I am sorry to say that the Australians are not nearly so efficient.'[62]

General E.L.M. Burns, after experience in the Second World War and in United Nations forces, saw the episode as a 'continuing difficulty.' The Canadians, he observed, 'their sentiments of nationality greatly intensified in the war, [wanted] ... to fight all together in a homogeneous Canadian higher formation; and the British commander, faced with a very difficult tactical problem ... [wanted] to solve it by moving the most conveniently placed divisions to meet the threat.'[63] Currie argued strongly that the corps should be reunited as quickly as the crisis would allow; but he did so for the simple reason that he believed such a move would be militarily wise. Haig, on the other hand, thought Currie's arguments were based on a selfish, chauvinistic desire to have Canadian soldiers commanded by a Canadian general. Currie, of course, on other occasions and particularly after the war did write and think in nationalistic terms; but in this case it is apparent that he was thinking in purely tactical terms. The nationalistic element was later introduced by the politicians. The Canadian prime minister did not learn of the episode until 3 May. He then wrote, 'any proposal to break up the Canadian Army Corps would be strongly resented in Canada and would have the most unfortunate effect upon public opinion.'[64] Derby had apparently foreseen what Borden's reaction would be. The supreme irony of the situation came when Lord Milner, from his record in South Africa an unlikely candidate to encourage 'colonial' nationalism, assured the Canadians that 'even on purely military grounds – and apart entirely from consideration of National sentiment' the Canadian Corps would in future be kept together.[65]

On 7 May, 1918 the Canadian Corps, less the 2nd Division which remained under the Third Army until 1 July, moved out of the line into general headquarters reserve in the First Army area. The threat caused by the German attack was still critical. Apparently, Haig was planning to use the Canadian Corps to counter-attack.[66] While the corps awaited the commander-in-chief's pleasure, Currie had a private interview with Sir Robert Borden in which he was highly critical of the British high command for losses sustained during the German offensive and the Passchendaele campaign. Borden came away convinced that the Allied defeats were due to 'lack of foresight and incompetent leadership.' Currie was obviously angry during this interview, but he made it clear to Borden that the problem lay in the officers who surrounded Haig and insulated him from the front – not in Sir Douglas himself. Currie thought that Haig's intelligence service was particularly at fault. He told the prime minister that 'the reports of the Chief Intelligence Officer at British Headquarters were so useless and misleading that when he [Currie] recognized the signature he always tore them up and threw them into the waste-paper basket without reading them.' Haig's director of military intelligence had been, evidently, no favourite with the Canadian Corps commander. Currie maintained that there were 'many British divisions well organized, highly trained and competently led,' but the inefficiency at GHQ and the inadequacy of some officers meant that everyone suffered.[67]

The fact that Currie said nothing directly against Sir Douglas Haig and that during the summer and autumn of 1918 he was to become more devoted than ever to the British commander-in-chief, is chiefly a sign of the latter's remarkable ability to secure the loyalty of his subordinates. Later in the year, perhaps to mitigate any implied criticism of Haig, Currie made a point of informing Borden that 'Sir Douglas Haig himself told me that in the dark days of last spring, the one comforting thought that he had was that he still had the Canadian Corps intact, and that he could never regard himself as beaten until the Corps was put into battle.'[68] Haig, it would seem, though he was quite unable to impress those whose authority was superior to his own, could communicate with his officers. Unlike his chief, Currie could and did impress his political superiors. After interviewing Currie, Borden cabled his cabinet colleagues in Canada that the corps 'has come on wonderfully since last year and this is due not only to the courage, resourcefulness and intelligence of the men, but to the splendid and unremitting work of the officers, and to Currie's great ability. I believe he is the ablest Corps Commander in the British Forces; more than that I believe he is at least as capable as any Army Commander among them.'[69]

7

The last phase

Unfortunately there were far too many senior officers in the First World War who, to the enormous cost of those they commanded, never seemed to understand that hard patient study and detailed planning were more important ingredients for success than flamboyant mannerisms or slavish attention to dress. On the other hand, those who did hold such tenets and who, because they did not attract attention by their personal peculiarity or smartness, were often overlooked. This, in some measure, was the fate of Sir Arthur Currie.

Currie was never flamboyant, and he could hardly be called smart. He lost considerable weight as he became older, and his appearance grew more distinguished, but during the war he was still a massive man, ill-suited by nature for tight military clothing and unlikely from his appearance alone to cut a dashing figure. Someone from the press would probably find him cool, for he had a very sharp prejudice against most newspaper reporters which can hardly have enhanced his public image. An interviewer, none the less, would probably be impressed by Currie's formal courtesy and would soon find himself drawn by Currie's charm which always shone in a small group. His postwar secretary later noted that in an interview with Currie 'all pretentiousness seemed to melt away.' She added that 'When you were across the desk from him he knew in a few minutes just what you were ... he had the great gift of very simply knowing and understanding human nature.'[1]

The trouble was that relatively few people had the chance of seeing Currie in this way. On the podium or in writing he gave a very different impression. His letters were often acerbic, and his statements frequently seemed pompous. His correspondence with Sir George Perley showed little attempt to understand Perley's problems and often seemed ungenerous. Yet when the two men met, difficulties were usually quickly overcome and solutions seemed to work smoothly. For most soldiers, contact with the commander of the Canadian Corps came at the formal review or through an order he had written. Currie's proclamations to the corps were sometimes extremely unpopular. At the time of the German attacks in 1918, he issued a special order to the Canadian Corps which ended with the words, 'to those who will fall I say 'You will not die, but step into immortality. Your mothers will not lament your fate, but will be proud to have borne such sons!"' One veteran recorded that this message 'evoked a jeer from every trench and dugout.'[2] It could scarcely have pleased many mothers. Often Currie seemed to have a talent for picking just the wrong phrase in addressing troops. On one occasion he told survivors of a battalion returning from the line 'that is the way I like to see you, mud and blood.'[3] Such statements, however typical of military idiom, belied everything that Currie had worked to achieve. Currie in many ways was his own worst enemy, and these statements illustrate his inability to be a popular leader. In front of a large audience he became abrupt, formal, and often spoke inappropriately. In the words of a veteran of the 11th Battery, Canadian Field Artillery, General Currie 'did not seem to have the gift for stroking fur the right way.'[4]

In front of a parade other senior officers almost always made a better impression than Currie. The crusty old regular, 'Batty Mac' Macdonnell of the 1st Division, the well-connected and wealthy Watson of the 4th Division with his forage cap always at a jaunty angle, the dashing Seely of the Canadian Cavalry Brigade, or the young McNaughton of the Heavy Artillery were all more likely than Currie to fit the image of a leader. But among friends or in small groups he lost his awkwardness; with his defences down he could laugh at himself, curse with fluent saltiness and be very human. In other words, he then demonstrated precisely those characteristics that might have been admired by the troops but were so conspicuously absent when he was with them on formal occasions.

Often it took very little to penetrate Currie's shell, as a corporal in the 10th Regiment discovered: 'I was standing in the courtyard ... and General Currie was taking a stroll through ... there were several of the boys around the courtyard and Currie walked along with his head down looking at the stones in front of him as he was walking, and didn't say anything. I should have brought everybody to attention when Currie was going by because I was a corporal at the time, and he stopped me and asked my why I didn't. That was the military man in him. But do you know what I said to General Currie? "Sir I thought your mind was otherwise occupied. That is why I did not wish to disturb you." He said, "Thank you, Corporal," and he walked on. Now the man was human.'[5] He was a highly sentimental man, which, along with his sensitivity, perhaps explains why he insulated himself from groups. From intimates he roused not only admiration but also fierce loyalty. Brigadier Ross, who became general officer commanding of the 6th Brigade while Currie was corps commander, thought of him as a 'first class man. I'm quite sure that he always had the welfare of the troops at heart, and, from remarks he's made to me from time to time, I know he had.'[6] Ross says that 'Currie would come into your dugout in the front line, would take out your maps, you would discuss things, and his ideas were reasonable and he was interested and would make suggestions.'[7]

Even someone critical of Currie's awkward public appearances and ill-chosen words acknowledges that 'at no time, even among the men who could not mention his name without some coarse allusion to his personal appearance, [was there] any question of his military skill. I always believed that Sir Arthur Currie was the best technical commander the corps had had.'[8] In the First World War there were obviously too few 'inspirational' leaders; but there were also few who possessed other military qualities that Arthur Currie had in abundance. Currie instinctively grasped the problems of modern war. Yet he never relied on instinct alone to provide solutions. The successful fight to maintain a twelve-battalion infantry division was only the beginning of Currie's structural changes in the Canadian Corps. During March, while Ludendorff's offensive continued, he carried out a number of experimental changes in the ratio of heavy to light machine guns within the corps which strengthened his resolve to reorganize this branch of the service. At the end of the month he was able to begin permanent changes which were to bring handsome dividends in the last months of the war when machine gun patrols frequently 'operated as far as 2,000 yards behind the German front line, while motor lorries and armoured cars, carrying machine guns and their teams, on several occasions went clean through the enemy front, dropping guns and teams where required as they went.'[9]

Passchendaele had confirmed a suspicion that had long been growing in Currie's mind, namely, 'that the old British organization of three Engineer companies to a division was insufficient.'[10] Until the spring of 1918 the bulk of the labour on engineering projects such as roads, bridges, and entrenchments was provided by infantry soldiers who worked under engineer supervision. Not only did this activity take the edge off the fighting troops, but it put the engineers under the indirect control of various infantry commanders, frequently more concerned with the fatigue of their men than with the completion of a particular project.[11] It was perfectly natural for an infantry commander to want to rest his men, but often the work was vital to a coming attack. The solution for the problem was to disband the various special engineering units and all the engineer units of the 5th Division and to streamline completely the engineer organization with the corps.[12] The details of the new engineer reorganization came from the chief engineer, Major-General W.B. Lindsay, and his staff. But Lindsay's work was possible only because of Currie's approval and encouragement. Henceforth each Canadian division was to have attached to it an engineer brigade consisting of three battalions of 1,000 men each, so that in future the engineers would have a large enough labour force within their own ranks to complete any task. 'In the old days,' Currie later remarked, 'we were often forced to ask the infantry to fight a battle one day and perform engineering work the next.' But in the last months of the war 'much of the success of the Canadian Corps ... was due to the fact that [there were] ... sufficient engineers to do the engineering ... we did not employ the infantry in that kind of work.'[13]

From May to July 1918 the corps enjoyed one of its longest respites from front line duty in the entire war. During this time Currie was extremely active. With the reorganization of his engineers and the machine guns well under way, he turned his attention to 'the machinery both to receive, train and dispatch reinforcements from England and to deal with returned casualties,' and he made several revisions and improvements in these areas.[14] He knew that it was impossible to forecast the length of time his command would remain in reserve. He sensed that operations in future would be more open than the close trench fighting of 1917; and he was determined to lay down a 'definite Corps tactical doctrine' that would fit 'the different organization, the greater strength, and the particular methods which characterized the Canadian Corps.'[15] Because he did not know how much time he would have before going back into action, Currie directed the new training to begin at brigade level. This would give maximum scope to staffs and, while keeping the men occupied, would give them as much rest as possible.[16] Much of the Canadian training, Currie admitted, was inspired by the translations of captured German documents circulated by GHQ. After studying these documents, the corps staff issued instructions outlining 'the methods of Employment of Artillery, Engineers and Machine Guns in combination with the tactics of the Infantry.' The aim of each tactical exercise and every staff paper was to instil the twin notions of 'cooperation and mutual support' among all arms and services.[17] As time passed and there was no call to take a place in the front line, he ordered more concentrated training for smaller units. The greatest emphasis at the lowest level, he later wrote, included 'how to overpower resistance in an area defended by machine guns in depth using covering fire and smoke grenades: how Batteries of Machine Guns should cooperate in assisting Infantry to get forward; and how sections of field artillery could best carry out and advance in close support of attacking Infantry.'[18] Currie's interest lay not only in the structure of his command and in the evolution of a tactical doctrine. He was vitally concerned with the weapon technology from which his tactical doctrine was derived. New techniques to improve weapon mobility or accuracy always received Currie's blessing. He was fascinated by the new tanks becoming available in increasing numbers on the Western Front. Currie believed in the potential of the aeroplane as a military weapon, and he strongly recommended the creation of a Canadian flying corps which he hoped would operate exclusively with his corps.[19] He was impressed by the success of the large number of Canadian pilots in the Royal Flying Corps; and his desire to have a Canadian air force was partly, at least, based on the view that an air force would be very useful in peace time. 'Our men have done well in the Flying Corps,' he wrote in November 1917, 'and I think it would be an additional incentive to them to know that in battle they were serving Canadian troops ... Secondly, I think it would be a good thing to begin such an institution now, because when we go back to Canada, I believe it will be then considered advisable to have a Canadian Flying Corps, and if we begin it now, we shall be in a better position to have an efficient organization when that time arrives.'[20] In May 1918, although he was still enthusiastic about the use of aeroplanes, he regretfully noted that since the Canadian authorities in England were not impressed with the idea, a Canadian flying corps would probably not be founded.[21]

Few would deny that the analysis of organization tables or weapon characteristics is dull fare compared with accounts of successful campaigns. Yet it was Currie's abilities in such routine but very important areas that set him apart from most commanders of his time as a man who understood the requirements of modern warfare. Generals are frequently accused of preparing for the last war, but in Currie's plans and aspirations one can see elements of progressive thinking.

Speaking broadly, two tactical schools of thought evolved after the First World War. The so-called Blitzkrieg technique, developed mainly by B.H. Liddell Hart, was adopted by German forces in the 1930s and very nearly won Europe for Hitler when the Second World War broke out. The essence of Blitzkrieg was to attack quickly with highly mobile forces which bypassed heavily defended centres of resistance to strike the enemy's communication and command systems. The other school of tactical thought, developed in France and based on the concept of linear defence behind a line of fortification, received concrete expression in the Maginot Line. Just as military theorists at the beginning of the First World War had underestimated grossly the defensive power of machine guns and artillery, so the Maginot concept egregiously under-estimated the offensive capabilities of the aeroplane and mobile armoured forces. The concrete gun explacements and machine-gun 'pill-boxes' of the Maginot Line were bypassed by Hitler's drive to the sea.

One can detect elements of both of these doctrines in Currie's reorganization. His preoccupation with machine guns and his emphasis on co-operation between artillery and infantry can be regarded as evidence of linear thinking. Even the use of combat engineers might suggest this if Currie had used the engineers solely to repair field works and to restore broken lines of communication. Naturally the corps commander was anxious to improve the engineers' ability to restore defensive installations, but obviously he was also concerned about the engineers' ability to assist the infantry to advance rapidly. The change in the Canadian engineer organization, moreover, was partly arranged to facilitate the introduction of new equipment such as the 'Inglis' portable bridge and prefabricated gun platforms.[22] Currie worked hard to develop training exercises that would familiarize 'all Arms and Services with the difficulties, both administrative and tactical, inherent to a surprise attack intended to penetrate suddenly to a great depth.' He was determined that 'all Commanders and Staffs' in the corps would be as knowledgeable as possible 'with the handling of troops in open warfare.'[23] The entire thrust of Currie's reorganization, the essence of his tactical doctrine, his willingness to experiment with new weapons, and above all his desire to increase mobility while reducing casualties – all these qualities make him appear very modern in comparison with many of his colleagues.

While Currie was refashioning the Canadian Corps, the German offensive was rapidly losing momentum. Just as rapidly American troops and material were arriving in France, their mere presence providing a tremendous fillip to the morale of British and French veterans. Gradually the Allies prepared to strike back at the enemy. A modest action near Hamel by the Australian infantry and British tanks on 4 July prepared the way for larger offensives and brought considerable attention to the Australians under Sir John Monash, almost the only commander in British forces universally regarded as 'brilliant.'[24] The essence of many of Monash's ideas on war had already been incorporated in Currie's reorganization and spring training. 'The true role of infantry,' Monash later wrote,

was not to expend itself upon heroic physical effort, not to wither away under merciless machine-gun fire, not to impale itself on hostile bayonets, not to tear itself to pieces in hostile entanglements ... but on the contrary, to advance under the maximum possible protection of the maximum possible array of mechanical resources, in the form of guns, machine-guns, tanks, mortars, and aeroplanes; to advance with as little impediment as possible; to be relieved as far as possible of the obligation to fight their way forward; to march to the appointed goal, and there to hold and defend the territory gained; and to gather, in the form of prisoners, guns and stores, the fruits of victory ... A perfected modern battle plan is like nothing so much as the score for an orchestral composition, where the various arms and units are the instruments, and the tasks they perform are their respective musical phrases. Every individual unit must take its entry precisely at the proper moment, and play its phrase in the general harmony.[25]

Monash's success at Hamel made his superiors anxious to expand this victory into a bigger operation. Thus a plan was conceived to launch a British attack, developing the Hamel success, in the vicinity of Amiens. General Foch was eager to free the important rail junctions at Amiens, and Haig, too, became steadily more sanguine regarding the prospects of such an attack. To help the British, Foch agreed to place the entire French First Army, on the British right flank, under Haig's tactical control for the attack, and to have the French Third Army also co-operate on the southern flank of the First Army. The main blow was to be delivered by the British Fourth Army under Rawlinson. The Canadian and Australian Corps were selected to attack side by side in the Fourth Army area.[26]

The resulting Battle of Amiens, launched on 8 August 1918, was one of the most successful attacks made by the British on the Western Front during the entire war. Ludendorff described that attack as a 'black day' for the German Army and later wrote that 'the 8th of August put the decline of ... [German] fighting power beyond all doubt.'[27] It should be stated at once that Currie's role in planning the battle was minor. He first learned of the possibility of Canadian participation in an attack at Amiens on the afternoon of 20 July when he was given only the barest outline of the attack and warned that absolute secrecy was essential.[28]

Two features of the pre-battle arrangements are particularly relevant: first, why the Canadians were selected to participate; second, the arrangements that Currie would make to facilitate Canadian participation. The use of the Canadian Corps at Amiens carried with it a certain hazard, for the corps had to be moved over thirty miles, and if such a move were detected by the Germans it would warn them of the impending offensive. Why then, should such a risk be taken? The Australian historian C.E.W. Bean claims that both the Canadians and Australians were 'treated as picked shock troops' and adds that 'it seems possible that on Haig's mental list of his shock troops, the Canadian Corps was marked before the Australian ... He [Haig] appreciated their [the Canadians'] strength – four battalions in each brigade and 10,000 reinforcements in the depots behind them ... Not only had the Canadians been practically intact since Passchendaele, but the Australians gave him more anxiety in several respects.'[29] The Australian refusal to implement the death penalty for desertion was one of the 'respects,' since Haig considered this humane aberration 'a danger to his army's discipline.'[30] Haig's biographer substantiates Bean's claim that 'most British line divisions were by now neither morally or materially the equal of Dominion divisions.'[31]

Naturally, it has pleased the national pride of Canadians to regard their corps as a *corps d'élite*. History textbooks from Canada tell us that 'there was no form of fighting in which her [Canada's] sons were not outstanding,' or that 'to the Germans, the Canadian Corps was a bright spear of battle [which] ... had come to stand for sudden, and calculated, and murderous attack.'[32] Implied in such statements is the notion that the Canadians were such good fighters because they were Canadian. In fact the condition of the corps was due less to the innate fighting qualities of Canadians than to the fact that it had not been used to stem Ludendorff's offensive, and that it had been carefully reorganized, reinforced, and re-trained by Sir Arthur Currie. A second factor is also important. Monash made the use of the Canadian Corps at Amiens practically a condition of Australian participation. During the planning stages of the assault General Monash was urged to aim for the greatest possible depth of advance. He agreed to do so, "if you give me safe support on my right flank" ... Rawlinson suggested several corps for this purpose but Monash shook his head until the army commander mentioned "The Canadians." Monash leapt at this suggestion.'[33]

Once the Canadian Corps had been selected to participate in the Amiens attack, Currie's role in making preparations became more important. The first problem was to move the corps to the Amiens area, and Currie made suggestions that substantially accounted for the surprise with which this manoeuvre was achieved. He sent two infantry battalions and a number of medical and signal units north of Vimy to set up an advanced headquarters in the vicinity of Kemmel, where the signallers erected their sets and began sending dummy wireless messages to deceive the enemy into thinking the corps was moving north to Flanders.[34]

It is always difficult to determine the success of such ruses. The Canadian official history concludes: 'German intelligence noted the presence of Canadian units with the Second Army, but evidently did not draw the desired conclusion. Prisoners ... stated that the enemy expected an attack astride the Scarpe rather than in Flanders.'[35] In Currie's log-book a captured German staff officer is recorded as indicating that an attack at Amiens had been expected because of British air activity, but that it had not been considered imminent.[36] Ludendorff indicates that the attack on 8 August came as a surprise.[37] For security reasons Currie was not allowed to mention the impending operation to more than a handful of his staff – even division commanders were ignorant until 29 July. Although he could not disclose the nature of the coming operations, he immediately ordered preparation for a bogus attack on a defended locality in front of the Canadians which approximated the area over which his corps would operate at Amiens. Currie stated that tanks would be available for this operation (though the corps had none at that point); he urged commanders on all levels to impress the essentials of tank-infantry demonstrations and ordered that 'the greatest possible number of officers should witness them.'[38] To a considerable extent Currie's plan was successful; for when the corps arrived at Amiens, many men were suprised to find how closely their operational task resembled the exercises they had recently been practising.[39]

The task of the corps at Amiens was difficult. The Luce river, flowing diagonally across most of the Canadian front, presented a daunting obstacle, since all the bridges over it had been destroyed. The corps was to attack on a three-division front with the Australians on the left (or north) and the French 31st

Corps to the right. Each assaulting division was allotted a battalion of forty-two tanks, while the 4th Canadian Division in reserve was allotted thirty-six tanks. Notwithstanding the exercises arranged to demonstrate tank-infantry co-operation, Currie feared that his command might not maintain proper liaison with the tanks. Thus, he ordered that an infantryman be detailed to ride in each vehicle to aid the tank commander in maintaining contact with the infantry outside.[40] In the hope of achieving total surprise, no preliminary artillery bombardment was to take place; but tanks and infantry would go forward under cover of a creeping barrage, sustained by 'leap-frogging' field artillery once the attack began. The Canadians were also to be assisted by No. 5 Squadron Royal Air Force, which was attached to the corps.

To describe briefly the course of any battle from a corps or army level and, at the same time, to convey the intense physical strain, the horror, and the heroism that surround the individual soldier is virtually impossible. General Monash believed that in a well-planned battle 'nothing happens, nothing can happen, except the regular progress of the advance according to the plan arranged ... It is for this reason that no stirring accounts exist of the more intimate details of such great set pieces as Messines, Vimy, Hamel, and many others. They will never be written, for there is no material on which to base them. The story of what did take place on the date of the battle would be a mere paraphrase of the battle orders prescribing all that was to take place.'[41] Currie later summarized the results of the attack in a few words: 'By afternoon the Canadian Corps had gained all its objectives with the exception of a few hundred yards on the right ... but this was made good the following morning. The day's operations ... represented a maximum penetration of the enemy's defences of over eight miles ... The surprise had been complete and overwhelming.'[42]

The effect of the attack was indeed overwhelming. According to Cyril Falls 'the tanks unsettled the Germans' spirit and the Canadian soldiers killed them, rounded them up, or chased them back in flight.'[43] The second day of battle, 9 August, was less successful; but the advances were still impressive. 'Substantial progress was made', Currie observed, 'and by evening the average depth of our advance was about four miles, with a maximum of $6\frac{1}{2}$ miles at some points.'[44] On this day Currie also noted that the 'enemy's resistance stiffened considerably' as fresh troops were rushed in to stem the Allied advance. Meanwhile, breakdowns and casualties had left the Canadians 'with only a few tanks available for support.'[45] However, Fourth Army ordered that the attacks be continued and on 10 August Currie pushed forward again, having replaced the 1st and 2nd Divisions by the 4th. The attacks continued throughout 10 and 11 August but without the spectacular success of earlier efforts.

The Canadians and Australians had by now reached the old Somme battleground of 1916 and Currie was convinced that this ground could not be taken easily. Careful reconnaissance and air photos revealed that trenches were numerous and that the old battleground had been restrung with fresh barbed wire and obstacles in anticipation of further attacks. Currie therefore forcefully indicated to army headquarters that future success in this sector was likely to be extremely costly. Since the enemy was perfectly familiar with the ground, his artillery, in all likelihood, was preregistered on all possible avenues of attack. Surprise would be almost impossible to achieve. 'If it is absolutely necessary to carry out this attack,' Currie continued, before a new assault was mounted, an interval of time would be essential 'to give the impression that we are not going to proceed further at present.' But an even better plan would be 'that the Canadian Corps be taken out of this line; that the supply of tanks be replenished; then let us go and make an attack somewhere else, where I believe we can do equally well, if not better than we did here. I believe if we made an attack on the Third Army Front in the direction of Bapaume, and in conjunction with an attack by the French from their present line, we could force the Boche to evacuate the position he holds on this side of the Somme without attacking them.'[46]

Currie's letter convinced the army commander. When Haig learned that Rawlinson had doubts about continuing the operation, a conference was arranged. At the meeting Rawlinson put forward essentially the same view as Currie had, that the attack should be stopped, and in support he brought with him Currie's letter and air photos of the German defences.[47] General Monash later formed the impression that it was Currie's argument more than Rawlinson's that influenced Haig to postpone and finally to cancel further attacks in front of Amiens.[48] Whether this was so or not, the fighting at Amiens was ended. Currie regarded the battle as a 'magnificent victory' and attributed the success to good training, good discipline, good leadership, and 'splendid support and cooperation' from all arms, all services, and all ranks.[49]

As already noted, although he was partly responsible for breaking off the action, Currie had little to do with planning the Battle of Amiens. His role is rarely given much prominence in a discussion of the battle. Yet practically every consideration of the battle includes a comparison of the Australian and Canadian forces as as whole. Currie himself was impressed with the Australians at Amiens and he wrote to Monash that 'no troops ... [ever] had given us as loyal and effective support.' Both contingents, according to Cyril Falls, were very good though the Australians were 'of a rather different pattern, perhaps even more clever tactically but at lower levels apt to be less careful of detail.'[50] There were instances, of course, when closer attention to detail by both contingents would have paid dividends. There were other obvious differences of dress and accent; but on the whole most observers seem to agree with Falls. The commander of the Canadian Heavy

Artillery later remarked that the 'Canadians stood for planning and coordination while the Australians stood for individual initiative.'[51] Arthur Lower, who served with the Royal Navy and subsequently became a distinguished historian, claimed that people in Canada believed that 'their boys combined the steadfastness of the English with the ingenuity of the Americans'; while to those in France, 'it was a matter of observation that they had not quite that embarrassing degree of individualism which possessed the Americans or Australians and they were not afflicted by the Englishman's unwillingness to be thorough.'[52]

However intriguing, such generalizations, like articles of religion, are matters of individual belief. Perhaps part of being Canadian is to have greater respect for fellow citizens than for Canadian leaders. The success of the Canadian Corps at Amiens was of course the result of fine qualities found in Canadian soldiers. Surely it is no slight on these soldiers to claim that their success was, at least in equal measure, the result of the efficient military organization and system that Sir Arthur Currie had built. Similarly it does not lessen Monash's reputation to insist that Currie understood modern war and created in the Canadian Corps an admirably efficient military instrument. General Monash testified indirectly to this when he remarked, after learning that the Canadians were to return to Arras, that Currie's men would do well there because 'it was a country lending itself admirably to operations requiring careful organization.'[53]

If the battle brought little in the way of recognition from his countrymen, for Currie it marked the beginning of the most sustained series of offensives in the entire war. Though it actually lasted ninety-six days, this period is generally called the 'Hundred Days.' In this period the Canadian Corps participated in a series of spectacular operations which produced some of the greatest victories and the highest casualty counts for Canadians in the entire war. Between 8 August and the end of hostilities elements of the Canadian Corps were in action almost continuously. More than 42,000 Canadians became casualties in the last four months of the war.[54] The gains, like the losses, were considerable. Currie himself calculated that the Canadians liberated 228 cities, towns, and villages and that they confronted and overcame elements of forty-seven German divisions, or nearly a quarter of the German forces on the Western Front between 8 August and 11 October.[55] This sustained drive really began with the Amiens battle. Sir Douglas Haig, more convinced than ever after Amiens that the Germans could not endure much longer, was upset to discover that the government in London thought that the summer of 1919 would be the decisive period of the war. However, Haig was prepared to disregard 'the cautious counsels' of his government and 'to risk his reputation by assaulting the ill-famed Hindenburg Line – the strongest defences on the whole German front.'[56] In his design a special task was reserved for Currie and his men: to advance from the city of Arras towards Cambrai.

The breakthrough east of Arras, achieved by Currie's men between 26 August and 3 September, was not the last of the formidable tasks undertaken by the Canadians in the final days of the war. Breaking through the Canal du Nord defences between 27 September and 10 October was one of the most technically difficult tasks ever performed by the corps. After crossing the canal, the Canadians captured the city of Cambrai and then pushed on through Valenciennes and Mons. This historic town was occupied early on 11 November. Throughout the 'Hundred Days' the Canadians were practically never out of the line. Counting Amiens, five separate major offensives were mounted (Amiens, Arras, Canal du Nord, and Cambrai, and the drive through Valenciennes to Mons). Over eighty miles of enemy territory were occupied, twenty-three miles of it in just over six days. In this period 32,000 prisoners moved through the corps cages, and more than 600 field and heavy guns became Canadian prizes.[57]

In the Hundred Days, of course, all Allied forces made considerable gains, but the achievements of the Canadian Corps were outstanding. For the corps commander it was the most successful as well as the most demanding period of the entire war. Because the attacks took place so rapidly, tactical planning had to be accelerated. Because the advances were so substantial, enormous logistical demands had to be anticipated, and supplies and replacements had to be moved further and faster to be at the right place at the right time. Also, as it became clearer each day that the war would not last much longer, plans and administrative arrangements for demobilization and other transition requirements had to be made to prevent chaos when the fighting stopped. All these tasks, moreover, had to be undertaken while fighting was still in progress, fighting as difficult, as arduous, as any so far undertaken. Never were Currie's abilities so taxed or so manifest.

A detailed narrative of the action in this period is hardly necessary; for in the literature on the fighting one finds virtually no disagreement over the magnitude or importance of Canadian success. There are, however, some features in this achievement that have been little analysed. A reading of prebattle orders for any of the actions in the Hundred Days, for example, shows that Currie's insistence on formulating a corps doctrine was paying handsome dividends.

Describing the normal procedure of issuing battle instructions in British forces from the point of view of a junior officer, Major-General Howard Essame later claimed that before every battle, 'there descended on us an immense spate of paper – operation orders, appendices and sketches, to be followed by amendments and, later, amendments to amendments. By the time we moved back to the line, the file was nearly a foot thick and quite unintelligible.'[58] Earlier in the war this procedure had been common in the Canadian Corps. When a corps battle order was issued, it would be repeated by each subformation, division, brigade, and battalion, growing inexorably at every repetition. By the time it was repeated to an infantry platoon commander, it had become a huge, indigestible, and meaningless mass of information. In addition to the main battle order, supplementary orders were issued to artillery, machine gunners, engineers, supply services, and so on.[59]

By August 1918 the process of issuing orders and having them multiply as they passed down the line had been almost reversed. Currie's headquarters would issue a comprehensive battle order to all infantry divisions and supporting arms and services. Each subcommander would then extract from this general order the purpose of the whole operation and the instructions relevant to his own formation. The latter would be automatically elaborated in subformation orders and quickly forwarded to the next lower formation. In approximately three to eight hours the corps commander's order would reach the lowest private soldier and would do so in an intelligible manner. The infantry private knew the general objective of his own brigade and the specific task of his platoon; he knew who was working to his left and right and what support was available to him; he was given special instructions for specific obstacles that lay in this path; he knew when and where he would receive his next rations, the location of the field dressing station and when he could expect to be relieved. The artillery gunner, meanwhile, had learned the exact type of barrage or bombardment that would have to be fired; he knew when his guns would have to move forward and the location of their new positions. The service corps and engineer privates knew the general purpose of the attack and the precise roles they were to play. This entire procedure took place smoothly as the general order issued by Currie was expanded and contracted automatically at every level.

War by its very nature is an untidy business. The size of the Canadian Corps meant that even exemplary systems of communication would occasionally fail. None the less, Currie knew that without an improved means of transmitting plans to the lowest level the extended operations of the last stages of the war would be chaotic. Increasingly in the future the ranks would be filled with conscripts who would be led by inexperienced junior officers. On the whole, the testimony of those who participated suggests that the new system was a vast improvement. One who criticized Currie's rapport with the rank and file acknowledged that the Canadian soldier gave Currie full credit for his tactical ability, noting that the rank and file 'as far as they could judge, ... thought well of his technical skill as a commander.'[60] F.F. Worthington of the Canadian Machine Gun Corps, who also thought that Currie 'was not an inspiring man,' insisted that one knew that he 'never went into a battle that wasn't carefully prepared and thought out.'[61] H.S. Cooper of the 3rd Battalion claimed that Currie 'wouldn't let the Corps go in unless he was satisfied that everything was done that should be done.'[62] Gregory Clark of the 4th Canadian Mounted Rifles, who after the war became one of Canada's best-known journalists, said of Currie's system of preparation: 'The grand important thing was that he gave us maps, down to Lance-Corporals. Prior to that only officers and gentlemen were allowed to have maps. Currie said, "Maps down to section leaders," because he knew who fights the battles. It's the sections.'[63]

Currie's willingness to experiment with both old and new weapons is another aspect of the operations of the Hundred Days which is often ignored. Occasionally this willingness to experiment backfired, but on the whole it proved beneficial. As early as the autumn of 1917 Currie had been enthusiastic about working with tanks at Cambrai; and as we have seen, he was disappointed when his corps was selected to go to Passchendaele instead. He had been equally enthusiastic about tanks at Amiens and had done his best to initiate his command in the special use of these weapons before that battle. During the Amiens offensive, however, Currie had been concerned about the large number of tank losses. In an effort to conserve the tanks at Arras he stressed 'the necessity of exercising the greatest economy' in the use of tanks and ordered that as a 'general principle tanks should follow rather than precede the infantry.'[64] While this tactic may have helped preserve a few tanks, it was not the most effective method of employing the weapon, and Currie subsequently reversed this order of attack.

At the Drocourt-Quéant Line Currie also experimented with his motor machine gun brigade as an independent mobile force. The commander of the Corps Machine Gun Brigade was a French officer, Brigadier-General Brutinel, who served with the Canadians for most of the war and who occasionally had 'fantastic notions regarding the use of machine guns.'[65] Brutinel, for example, was convinced of the effectiveness of using machine guns to 'thicken up' artillery barrages. Currie did not record his thoughts on the use of machine guns in this manner, but he allowed the practice to continue and thus gave it at least tacit approval. It is surprising that Currie should have failed to recognize the misuse of this weapon. Although before the war machine guns had been used for indirect fire, the weapon's effects were largely wasted when the target could not be observed. On the other hand, Currie did not allow his machine guns to operate only as artillery; as soon as the preliminary bombardment was finished, the machine guns were rushed forward to provide 'that sustained, observed, flanking fire, which is the supreme safeguard to a captured position while it is being reorganized for defence.'[66] Indeed, Currie's use of mounted machine guns and cyclist troops worked extraordinarily well in many cases, particularly in the closing days of the war, when troops had to move greater distances.

It was still Sir Douglas Haig's hope to send cavalry through the German line once a gap could be punched in the enemy defences. Haig was so enthusiastic about the possibility of success in this regard that before crossing the Drocourt-Quéant Line he made a point of visiting Currie's headquarters on four consecutive days to 'outline future policy.' During the final visit Currie gave his own opinion quite firmly. 'I do not think they [the cavalry] will be of any great advantage to us,' and he was able to point to the considerable success of his mobile machine gun brigade as proof of the efficacy of such a force compared with cavalry.[67] Currie was far ahead of the commander-in-chief in recognizing the limitations of cavalry, just as, according to G.S. Hutchinson, the Canadians were ahead of the British in clever use of the machine gun. Hutchinson claims that the Canadian Machine Gun Corps quickly brought itself to a 'high state of efficiency ... Neither directed nor prejudiced by a command with preconceived notions got from South Africa and manoeuvres as to the purpose of weapons, the corps at once developed a highly scientific and closely coordinated scheme of mutual support among its companies.'[68]

After cracking the German defences at the Canal du Nord and capturing Cambrai, there had been no respite for the Canadian Corps; resistance remained stiff until the very day of the armistice. Throughout this last month of operations, Currie concentrated on the operations of his command with persistent and perceptive devotion. He seemed remarkably in tune with events as they developed and frequently anticipated the needs and reactions of his troops. He foresaw, for example, that the medical facilities of the corps would be taxed by the necessity of caring for civilian sick and wounded during the final advance; and he did all in his power to have the medical service of the corps extended to cope with this additional burden. Three special hospitals and several dressing stations for civilians were established.[69] Similarly, Currie recognized that lengthening supply lines would place increasing burdens upon supply services and he brought special detachments of railway troops forward to repair existing but damaged heavy gauge lines within his area and also to push light railways as close as possible to the infantry.[70] With his own supply lines reasonably secure, he continued to worry the army commander about the supply to the Canadian Corps; on 20 October he observed that 'our Higher Authorities do not seem well enough organized to push their rail heads forward fast enough.'[71]

Currie also worried about the attitude of his command with respect to the enemy. He had never been a 'soft' commander, but he did have certain principles with regard to the treatment of enemy prisoners. He became suspicious that at least a few Canadians were shooting prisoners rather than sending them to the corps cages. Cruelty is a part of every war, but Currie was concerned over this particular brand of sadism; and he was perplexed about a remedy. Since our men 'have lived amongst and talked to the French people here,' he wrote from Valenciennes, 'they have become more bitter than ever against the Boche.'[72] Documentary evidence to support his suspicion is slight. In the records that have been preserved in Ottawa there is little that would positively support Currie's suspicion. However, at least one company commander reported that 'It was impossible to avoid taking so many [prisoners] as they surrendered in batches of from 20 to 50, but some very useful killing was also achieved.'[73]

Two related matters during the last month of war served to take up any free time the corps commander had available. One of these was the continued opposition that seemed to emanate from Canadian headquarters in England. 'I do not wish to quarrel with the authorities there,' he wrote to a friend late in October, 'but the manner in which training has been carried out has never been satisfactory, though I do see by the speeches made at the big dinner they held on the anniversary of the arrival of the First Contingent in England, it was plain that the credit for the Corps' victories belonged chiefly to the work done in England. I am afraid the old gang is still doing business.'[74] Currie's suspicion of Canadian authorities in England was magnified when he learned that a plan for demobilizing the Canadian forces was nearly completed.

Demobilization would present enormous problems, not only in France but in England and Canada as well. These problems had been under consideration in a desultory fashion at the Ministry of Overseas Military Forces since April 1917. Sir Edward Kemp, shortly after taking over as minister, had ordered that the planning be accelerated. Gradually a scheme evolved which emphasized 'economic rationality rather than soldier psychology.'[75] The Canadian planners thought the process of moving more than a quarter-million men back to Canada could best be achieved by dissolving all existing CEF units and reassembling men according to twenty-two dispersal points in Canada. Accompanying this reassembly was an elaborate documentation process during which each soldier would fill out thirteen separate forms and answer 363 separate questions. Confronted with this plan in early October 1918, when he was preoccupied with the operations still under way, Currie reacted strongly. Understandably proud of the Canadian Corps, he rejected out of hand the idea that its units should be so quickly disbanded. He wrote to Kemp suggesting that 'the most wonderful fighting machine in the world's history' should be shown to the Canadian people – perhaps in a review on the Plains of Abraham.[76] The idea of a grand review of CEF units was a ridiculous notion which, on reflection, Currie dropped. However, he insisted that the major units of the Canadian Corps be returned intact to Canada. On 6 November he outlined his views on demobilization to the minister and recorded with some relief that Sir Edward had come to 'very satisfactory conclusions' on the subject.[77]

Demobilization was to prove a more difficult problem than either Kemp or Currie anticipated, but while active operations continued, few soldiers could afford to worry about it. Currie's attention was concentrated on the Canadian Corps' approach to Mons, the Belgian city from which the British Expeditionary Force had retreated so hastily in 1914. Meanwhile, armistice negotiations with the Germans had begun. On 29 September Hindenburg and Ludendorff had jointly advised the Kaiser that negotiations for an armistice should take place; and by early November the terms of an armistice were almost final.[78] At 6:30 a.m. on 11 November a message was received at Canadian Corps headquarters which stated that hostilities would cease at 11 o'clock that morning.[79] This information was relayed as rapidly as possible but in some cases did not reach the front line troops until approximately 9 a.m. In the meantime Mons had been taken and elements of the corps had pushed some five miles east of Mons.[80] The delay in transmission was of little consequence, because practically no fighting took place after Mons had been cleared.

The news was received everywhere with mixed emotions. Sir Robert Borden was in mid-Atlantic en route from Canada to England and he noted in his diary that 'revolt has spread all over Germany. The question is whether it will stop there. The world has drifted far from its old anchorage and no man can with certainty prophesy what the outcome will be. I have said that another such war would destroy our civilization. It is a grave question whether this war may not have destroyed much that we regard as necessarily incident thereto.'[81] Reflections on the course and outcome of the war for the time being seemed to be left to those, like Borden, more remote from the scene of conflict. Most soldiers who had fought so hard and long for the end of the war accepted the news of the armistice passively. Currie, in his diary, recorded simply that 'in the morning a wire came from the Army informing us that the Armistice was to come into effect at 11 a.m. when hostilities would cease. At 10 o'clock I inspected the 1st Brigade.'[82] Many contemporary accounts mention the oppressive silence that settled on the Western Front at 11 a.m. on 11 November. Some soldiers who, like Currie, could remember Ypres, Vimy, and Passchendaele found the transformation of that hour very difficult. Memories of home, previously banished from thought in all except unguarded moments, now rushed back and flooded the mind.

8

Inspector-general of militia

The armistice was welcomed by everyone; but for Currie it brought only temporary relief from the intense strain of the last four months. By his own reckoning he had worked an average of seventeen hours a day during this period, and he was exhausted. The end of the war, the end of killing and fighting, the end of daily casualty lists, was an extraordinary fillip, but Currie's responsiblities were still great. There were fresh burdens to be shouldered which contained few of the satisfactions of commanding a formation in action. His most bitter disappointment was a new round of the whispered criticism that had so concerned him in 1917.

In October 1918 Sam Hughes had written to Sir Robert Borden levelling accusations at Currie which were soon to be made public. Hughes claimed that the Canadian Corps had been subjected to 'massacres ... where the apparent object was to glorify the general in command, and make it impossible, through butchery, to have a Fifth and Sixth Division and two Army Corps.'[1] Currie did not immediately learn of Hughes's attacks, but he did discover other rumours of a disquieting nature. Apparently there were 'some senior officers in England [who] spend most of their time visiting and condoling with the wounded; intimating to the latter that the casualties in the Canadian Corps have been altogether too high.' In Currie's view this was the 'cheapest and meanest form of criticism that a small person could conceive.'[2] He was probably right, but the fact that he allowed rumour and gossip – always abundant in any army – to distress him so, is evidence that the corps commander was not immune to the widespread let-down that followed the armistice.

With the fighting ended, more than anything else in the world the average soldier wanted to go home. So long as an armistice existed, armies could not be disbanded for fear that the enemy would again take up arms. Probably few ordinary soldiers thought about this aspect. Those who grasped the notion that some unlucky devils would have to form part of an army of occupation, none the less had little sympathy for the problems of bureaucrats trying to find sufficient shipping to bring home not only Canadians but Australians and Americans. For Canadian railway officials, who claimed that no more than 20,000 soldiers could be moved from the Atlantic region to the rest of the country each month, the ordinary soldier had no time whatsoever. Yet in the dead of winter, Canadian soldiers could be repatriated only through Halifax and Saint John. Thus the single most limiting factor in bringing soldiers home was the capacity of railroads in Canada.[3] Explaining to a soldier who had endured years or months or even weeks of the Western Front was not likely to boost morale. A member of the 49th Battalion summed it up very succinctly: 'Myself, I had been in France for three years and the army for four, and I didn't want to go the Rhine, I wanted to get to hell home out of there.'[4]

This let-down, perfectly understandable and natural though it may have been, complicated the already difficult tasks facing the corps commander following the end of hostilities. The Canadians were required to provide two divisions for the army of occupation. Normally the corps staff would have handled the move of the 1st and 2nd Divisions routinely without the close supervision of the corps commander, but Currie became more and more concerned with the details of the march as a series of events threatened to transform the advance from a routine march into a horror show. The first difficulty was weather. Following 26 November several days of rain closed all secondary roads. Currie noted the additional strain imposed and began to worry about supply. By the end of November, the supply system to the Canadian Corps had almost collapsed. In his diary Currie wrote, 'trains are arriving several days late, and the result has been simply chaos. I have never experienced in France such evidence of mismanagement.'[5] To ease the situation, Currie commandeered trucks from every conceivable source, including his own Machine Guns Corps. With supplies coming into the corps on Canadian vehicles, the advance soon began to move again, only to be delayed temporarily by more serious developments.

Because the armistice could be replaced by hostilities at any time, Canadians, like other Allied soldiers, were warned to be ready to fight. To be so prepared and also to relieve the overburdened transport system hard pressed to keep the soldiers moving towards the Rhine supplied with food and essentials, Currie ordered that Canadians march in steel helmets and full equipment. This order was bitterly resented by men who believed the war was over. At Nivelles on the evening of 17 December men of the 7th Brigade began to protest. An artilleryman arriving in the town recalled that 'I saw quite a gathering in the square and a fellow up on a bandstand or something or other and he was haranguing the troops. "Will we carry our packs tomorrow?" And you'd hear a thousand voices say, "No! What are we going to do? Sit down." And the next day they sat on the side of the roads and wouldn't move until at last some of the the sergeants got around and talked them into it. I thought they had a fair grouch. Why should soldiers who have been through Hell have to carry a sixty pound pack on their back as well as their arms and ammunition, and I say "They've got a legitimate kick." '[6]

'Legitimate' or not, the episode at Nivelles represented a breakdown of discipline, and it was not the only case. When units of the 2nd Division crossed the Rhine, one artillery battery defied an order to remove greatcoats for the formal march past. It was raining and the men apparently refused to get soaked simply for a formal salute. As Professor Morton has noted: the 'explanation for both events was sagging discipline and negligent officers.'[7]

In part, his fear of a disciplinary breakdown following the armistice moved Currie to insist that units of the Canadian Corps should return to Canada without being disbanded. In a letter to Sir Edward Kemp written on 23 November the corps commander played his trump card for demobization by units. 'I feel I cannot dwell too strongly on this matter of discipline,' he wrote. 'I know its value. It has been the foundation of our strength and the source of our power. It has been the principal factor in the winning of our battles and is worth perserving for the national life of Canada. For God's sake do not play with it, for you are playing with fire.'[8] Currie's argument persuaded both Kemp and the prime minister, who in turn persuaded their cabinet colleagues to accept Currie's plan of disbanding corps units intact. Borden and Kemp were also impressed by the fact that the Australians appeared to be demobilizing by units. But neither man, nor Currie for that matter, noticed a fundamental difference between Australian and Canadian procedures. The Australians did demobilize by units, but each unit was split between early and late comers overseas. All the long-service soldiers were then demobilzed by units ahead of short-service soldiers, who could also be demobilzed by units at a later time.[9] The weakness of the Canadian system was that many of the corps units that were first to be demobilized contained high percentages of Military Service Act conscripts who had only recently arrived in France. Undoubtedly this helped produce the bitter riots that broke out in Canadian demobilization camps in England. The worst of the riots, where five men were killed and twenty-five wounded, occurred at Kinmel Park which was the 'kind of organization Sir Arthur Currie had warned against. It was a random mixture of combatants and non-combatants, conscripts and "Old Professionals," mixed with the professional misfits who drift to the rear of any army.'[10]

Although neither Currie nor any other Canadian official spotted the flaw in the Canadian system that would contribute to the difficulties in England, in France there were relatively few problems. Aware that there were a few malcontents and that everywhere men would be anxious to get home, Currie took steps to see that soldiers were not left with time on their hands. He encouraged the development of educational programs, rehabilitation training schools and sports. Above all, he insisted that 'the greatest possible freedom ... [be] allowed all ranks.'[11] He changed the situation at Cologne when he discovered that the military governor refused to allow off-duty Canadians into the city. Currie noted that 'that there are more restrictions placed on the conduct of our own troops than on the Germans,' a situation he was not prepared to tolerate.[12]

Happily both the period of occupation in Germany and the entire process of demobilizing the CEF were shorter than had been anticipated. During late January the Canadian divisions in Germany were withdrawn to Belgium and the repatriation process began immediately. Within five months two-thirds of the overseas force were back in Canada, and the process was completed in less than a year.[13] As demobilization proceeded, Currie's duties as commander diminished, but he was still busy with many ceremonial and official functions.

In the January honours list Currie received the GCMG, and later in the month he was awarded the American Distinguished Service Medal.[14] In February, at the invitation of Sir Robert Borden, he spent ten days in Paris as an observer at the opening of the peace conference. Shortly after his arrival in Paris, Currie had a quiet dinner with Sir Douglas Haig after which the British commander-in-chief confided 'why Passchendaele had to be taken.' The discussion was recorded by Currie in his diary, and it is particularly interesting, since it demonstrates that Haig put forward his argument that 'Passchendaele was fought to save the French' earlier than is generally believed. Currie reported that Haig

gave me as his first reason that owing to the mutiny in the French Army (which he said was of large proportions) the British had to fight in order to prevent the Germans from attacking the French, low spirited as they were. He also mentioned that in the hope of securing the submarine bases on the Belgian coast it was decided to fight, as fight the British Army must, in the Ypres sector. He also referred to the fact that there was a Peace Party in England and to the very severe fighting which the British Army had had. He said that in order to help restore the morale of the French Army and the British people he was determined to finish the fighting of 1917 with a victory.[15]

Haig's most recent biographer argues that the basis of Haig's fight for the French argument was a letter written in 1927 and that Haig's own 'day-to-day comments do not bear it out.'[16] His conversation with Currie indicates that Haig's confusion was not the result of the 'lapse of ten years' but that as early as 1919 Haig had begun to rationalize his 1917 campaign as a crusade to save the French.[17]

Further chats with Haig or anyone else were prevented when Lady Currie, who had joined Sir Arthur in Paris, fell victim to the influenza that was then reaching epidemic proportions in Europe. For the rest of his time in the French capital

Currie stayed at his wife's bedside in the Majestic Hotel. His discussion with Haig, however, coincided with knowledge of the criticism Sir Sam Hughes was circulating in Canada covering his conduct of operations in 1917 and 1918. In the winter of 1919, when Currie was writing his official report on the operations of 1918, these attacks persisted and Currie brooded on them. Throughout the war Currie's primary aim, apart from looking for the ultimate defeat of the enemy, had been to reduce casualties to a minimum. Now, with the fighting ended, he was being accused of reckless wasting of lives, and that charge hurt him a great deal.

He had been delighted in early December when the War Office published a statement which to his mind proved that casualties in the Canadian Corps in 1918 were less, in proportion to strength, than in the British Army. It was true, of course, that the Canadians had faced none of the devastating German attacks in the spring of 1918; but the corps had not been exactly idle during the Hundred Days. Reflecting on the last operations and on Hughes's attacks, he wrote to a friend that

I was able to put into these operations every ounce of strength that I possessed, and I can truthfully say that for three months I averaged at least 17 hours a day ... This brings me to what you have said is in the mind of a former Minister of Militia. However much one would dislike his slinging of mud, I cannot see how I can stop him. The man is a liar, is at times insane, and apparently is a cur of the worst type. I put in four years at the front and am one of very few who have never been away. In those four years I have never commanded a force which ever failed to carry out the mission assigned to it. I am proud of that record. To say that casualties have been excessive is an easy thing to say; but I can imagine nothing meaner, more ungrateful and untrue. Had that man had his way, the Corps would still be armed with the Ross rifle, which caused more unnecessary casualties by far than any other factor I know of. Had he had his way, or had his friends their way, the several appointments in the Corps could not have been held by the best man, but by his friends. Merit would not have counted, but what would have placed them there would have been their willingness to lick his boots. Apparently he chooses to utter his foul lies where he has the protection of the walls of parliament. Only a coward would behave such. I have never intended to go into politics, but if he does what he says he will do, I will not rest until I have (to use his own words) 'skinned the skunk.' I have faced too many dangers and pitfalls in the last four years to be afraid of him. I am now, as always, without pull. If my record in this war can be tarnished by such as he, then I don't much care.[18]

But Currie did care a great deal, and he did have some 'pull' and was prepared to use every ounce of it to counter Hughes's statements. He asked a friend to inquire whether General Mewburn, the minister of militia, or Sir Thomas White, the minister of finance, would support him in the House of Commons.[19] In March Hughes launched another attack on Currie. This time he read his October letter to the prime minister to the House of Commons and assailed the Canadian capture of Mons on 11 November. 'Were I in authority,' the ex-minister declared, 'the officer who, four hours before the Armistice was signed, although he had been notified beforehand that the Armistice was to begin at eleven o'clock, ordered the attack on Mons thus needlessly sacrificing the lives of Canadian soldiers, would be tried summarily by court martial and punished so far as the law would allow. There was no glory to be gained, and you cannot find one Canadian soldier returning from France who will not curse the name of the officer who ordered the attack on Mons.'[20]

Such a charge by the man who for a considerable time had been in control of the Militia Department was simply fantastic. The man who had given Currie his first appointment in the CEF, was accusing him of 'butchery,' 'needless slaughter,' and 'needlessly sacrificing the lives of Canadian soldiers.' Several members of the House who had served under Currie immediately rose to his support. Regardless of all the evidence to the contrary that might be produced, the damage had been done. 'It is very easy to cast aspersions or to put blame on any person, and it is very hard to overtake these aspersions once they have gone amongst the public.'[21] Unfortunately members of the government, who perhaps still were reluctant to oppose Hughes directly, initially left Currie's defence to private members. Not until 14 March did Sir Edward Kemp pay any tribute to the corps commander, who, he said, 'was ever considerate of the men under him,' tepid praise indeed compared with the warm thanks that Kemp had tendered General Turner.

Currie had never been particularly fond of Sir Richard Turner, and he remained unimpressed with Turner's abilities as a commander or as a chief of staff.[22] Considering the rivalry that had always existed between the two men, it is not surprising that he came to believe that Turner was also against him. In his correspondence Currie never made direct reference to Turner, though many of his allusions were only thinly veiled. He wrote to one of his aides of 'an officer in England of as high rank as myself' who had contributed to rumours of high casualties.[23] Turner was the only other Canadian lieutenant-general. Existing evidence tends to indicate that Currie was wrong about Turner is this matter. From his combat record alone it was obvious that Turner was not a particularly good commander; but he did not attack Currie behind the latter's back. Indeed on 3 April 1919 Turner sent a cryptic letter to Kemp protesting 'malicious lying statements' made against Currie which in Turner's opinion were 'bred and fostered by disgruntled and discredited officers.'[24]

By July Sir Robert Borden had returned to Canada from the Paris Peace Conference. One of his first acts in the House of Commons was to pay tribute to the men of the Canadian Corps. In regard to the commander of that corps, the prime minister stated:

There has been a whisper of criticism that he was not sufficiently mindful of his duty to safeguard the lives of those under his command. In my judgement no criticism would be more unjust. Indeed, I know that on more than one occasion and especially on one noteable occasion, he took a stand in defiance of military precedent, a stand which would have been impossible except for his independent position as a Canadian General, a stand which involved risk to his own status and reputation. That stand he took for one reason and one reason alone: his duty to avoid needless sacrifice of the troops under his command. No General at the front more fully realized that solemn duty and during the last eighteen months of the war there was no General whose judgement was more respected, none whose ability and thoroughness were more relied upon, than he who then commanded the Canadian Corps.[25]

Borden's words did much to put the criticism to rest. In any event, Currie had decided that the best plan would be to ignore Hughes's attacks so long as they were confined to parliament. After all, as he wrote to one of his officers almost a year later, if Hughes 'didn't call me a coward and a murderer he would call me a drunkard or a roué.'[26]

As the demobilization of the Canadian Corps proceeded, Currie was faced with another disconcerting decision. What was he to do when he returned to Canada? He was not anxious to take up the real estate business in Victoria; and other prospects were hardly more encouraging. On 10 July, shortly before he was due to leave England, Currie was offered the post of inspector-general of militia in Canada, although he was not told what his salary or duties would be.[27] He refused to give a final answer but agreed to discuss the possibility with General Mewburn when he reached Canada. Thus when Currie left England in August, his future seemed to be almost as uncertain and scarcely as exciting as when he had left his home in 1914.

When he arrived in Canada, the prospects were no brighter; he accepted the position he had been offered. This last phase of his military career, from his return to Canada on 17 August to his resignation from the army, lasted only eleven months. In fact it was even shorter; for Currie was on leave for some three to four months of that time. It was a frustrating and disappointing experience. The sudden release from the tension of battle and the frustrations of the last few months in Europe seemed to overtake him simultaneously. Currie arrived home mentally and physically exhausted. 'The first four months after my arrival in Canada,' he later told one of his old comrades, 'I felt wretched in health.'[28]

He had accepted the position of inspector-general, hoping that he would have the opportunity to perform an important and useful service; but his experience in the job did little to lift the depression into which he slipped on arriving home. His first disappointment was the coolness of his official welcome in Ottawa. Could it be that Hughes's charges were actually believed? Scarcely a week after Currie's arrival, as if in answer to the question, Sir Sam launched his most caustic tirade. This time Hughes was even more personal; he assured the House that that fellow Currie was 'a coward, unworthy of association with his fellow-men and women.'[29] After reviewing Canadian battles from Ypres (where, he said, Currie first proved to be a coward) to Mons, he focused on the last action of the corps. 'Mons was not a city of great importance,' he said, 'I would not give the snap of my fingers for it. It is a nice little place, but to sacrifice the lives of Canadians on the eve of the armistice was quite out of place and more a piece of bravado than an attempt to help the great cause of liberty at an acceptable time.'[30] Clearly Sir Sam was losing his grip. His imbalance showed more clearly than ever before, and many members of the House warmly defended the corps commander. The government's attitude was to ignore this attack as unworthy of response.

Currie was unable to take such a lofty position and would have preferred a more vigorous government defence. Sick and disappointed, he probably failed to recognize immediately that 'the Government forces were drifting aimlessly on a sea of troubles, in the doldrums of indecision and inertia.'[31] Borden himself was ill: in November his doctors insisted that he retire. Other members of the government with whom Currie was acquainted were either occupied with more pressing affairs, or were preparing to resign. Rowell, absorbed in delicate problems of foreign policy, left the government in July 1920. Perley remained in England. Kemp, inexplicably, said nothing. Mewburn, also ill, had already decided to retire from public life. Mewburn's decision was especially disappointing; for Currie had come to admire him, and he felt his chances of doing useful work as inspector-general would be much reduced by Mewburn's retirement.[32] Illness and resignations were only two of a multitude of problems that faced the union government in the autumn of 1919. There were many indications of an impending economic depression. In May 1919 the most serious labour dispute in many years had begun in Winnipeg. Evidence of agrarian unrest was provided in November, when the United Farmers of Ontario swept the Ontario provincial election. In January the formation of a new Progressive party gave further indication of discontent among farmers. Laurier's death in January 1919 had saddened many unionist Liberals, and, the war having been over for almost a year, many of them began to think of returning to the Liberal fold. In short, Borden's union government was falling apart: the reason behind the coalition no longer existed.

In the summer of 1919, not all these factors were apparent to Currie. He realized that much of his dissatisfaction resulted from the natural dislocation of all society in what he deemed the 'pregnant days of reconstruction.'[33] At the same time, he knew that it was necessary to have patience; more than once he insisted that in the long run he had 'every confidence that the good sense of our people will prevail.'[34] None the less, he was still much troubled by the spirit of materialism which seemed to frustrate and infuriate many of the soldiers who had fought in the war. 'It is not the Canada I expected it to be,' he wrote shortly after his return, 'I came back from the war feeling that all the suffering and sacrifice must have meant something. But I found, as others have done, that there was little change – that there was at any rate no change of heart. Men were fighting for the dollar in the same persistent way. There seemed to be little difference in the viewpoint towards life, little indication of any growth of national spirit and very little appreciation of the world situation and its attendant problems.'[35]

When he took the job of inspector-general, Currie had hoped to initiate a thorough reorganization of both the militia and the permanent force. But after only a few weeks on the job he wrote to a comrade still in England that 'the position was not quite what I had in mind when you and I discussed my probable future employment.'[36] So far as the militia was concerned, Currie was determined to rectify the difficulties created by the wholesale raising of new battalions during the war, and also to insure that each battalion of the expeditionary force was perpetuated by a militia battalion. He was astonished to find that the notion of perpetuating CEF battalions was vigorously opposed. Some people, he remarked, want to forget 'that there was such a thing as the Canadian Corps as soon as possible.'[37] In order to have a useful militia force it was necessary, in Currie's opinion, to have an efficient staff organization and a small but well-organized permanent force. He planned to build the permanent force around a nucleus of officers who had served in the Canadian Corps. Many of these men did come into his headquarters as staff members; but once again Currie met resistance to his wishes. The reorganization was much more prolonged than he thought necessary and as a result many of the officers he hoped to bring into the postwar army 'got tired of waiting to see what would happen' and entered other occupations.[38] Even more frustrating, however, was the difficulty encountered in pensioning off prewar permanent soldiers who had spent the war in Canada and who now blocked positions Currie was anxious to fill with his own nominees.[39]

Sir Arthur favoured some form of universal compulsory military training, if only in the militia or cadets. However, he knew that universal training would not be popular in the war-weary country, especially if it were officially proposed by the Militia Department. In his estimation, the matter of universal training might best be suggested by

such organizations as the GWVA [Great War Veterans Association]. They ought to realize that much of the dissatisfaction amongst the returned soldiers is primarily due to the unsatisfactory way in which the manhood of our country served during the war, and they must realize that the only fair and democratic defense organization is one where everyone will be required to place his service at the State's disposal. However, if we from this office advocate universal training, we shall be charged with endeavouring to foster militarism, an entirely erroneous conception, of course. Certainly no Political Party will put such a plank in their platform, unless pressure comes from some large body of citizens.[40]

Universal military service, even in cadets, was a most unlikely possiblity in postwar Canada. Sentiment throughout the country, Currie recognized, was 'overwhelmingly against any form of universal training.' Hence the best plan was 'not to attempt to force the issue and proceed meanwhile with other things.'[41]

By statute the permanent force was fixed at 10,000 all ranks, but Currie was forbidden by the government to recruit more than 5,000. By refusing to build proper accommodation, moreover, the government restricted the numbers even further.[42] 'We have tried our best,' Currie noted, 'to make what we have into a well-balanced force, but yet I cannot get the government to provide such necessary organization as a Signal Corps.' During the winter and spring of 1920 Currie pushed strongly for a reorganization of the defence department. The creation of a single Department of National Defence, including navy, army, and air force under the direction of a single minister, was the most forward-looking military reform in the interwar period. Although Currie advocated just such an organization in the winter and spring of 1920, it did not materialize until 1922, two years after his retirement.[43]

As usual, Currie found that his salary was inadequate; even his promotion to general did not rectify the situation. In January 1920 he remarked that those officers and men who went directly back into civil life after the war were 'very much better off financially. Any increase in rates of pay has been more than offset by the high cost of living.'[44] Currie must have known that there was a very marked difference between the financial treatment of officers in Britain and that of those in Canada after the war. The normal practice in Britain was for parliament to grant a substantial cash payment to high-ranking officers in appreciation of their services. Haig, for example, received £100,000, and Sir Julian Byng was awarded £30,000. In Haig's case the reward was made at the insistence of Winston Churchill, hardly one of his most ardent supporters.[45] Sir Robert Borden apparently thought that Currie should be similarly rewarded; and he suggested to his colleagues that 'Parliament should grant him [Currie] a reasonable sum.' When there were objections to this proposal, Borden dropped the idea and it was never again put forward.[46] In fact, the objections stemmed from the government's determination to refuse a bonus to veterans – an acknowledgment that Currie placed in a much higher category than his own financial well-being.

Sir Arthur's disappointment and frustration increased daily. Even a simple act such as sending an official letter of thanks to British officers who had served with the Canadian Corps during the war seemed impossible to accomplish. Currie suggested to Borden in the spring of 1919 that official letters would be a gracious act, and he provided the prime minister with a list of British officers to whom the letters should be sent. Despite repeated reminders from Currie, the letters were never written.[47] Currie found the disparity enormous between commanding a unit in war and serving in the Canadian forces in peace. Disheartened by his failure to get through the endless red tape and bureaucracy of Ottawa, he observed that 'when conducting affairs in the Field you simply went ahead and did what you thought was right and did it at once.' But as Inspector-general there seemed 'to be no freedom of action: financial considerations, political considerations, personal considerations and all sorts of other things retarding what one considers progress.'[48]

Sir Arthur realized that a certain amount of political influence on militia forces was probably inevitable, but he could not accept the notion that every decision on military matters should be made in the light of the political circumstances of the moment. 'In these days,' he wrote disgustedly to a friend, 'Governments ... do not lead the people, they simply try to guess what the people want and govern their policy and action accordingly.'[49] As his distaste with the position of inspector-general grew, Currie considered entering politics.[50] However, his disgust with political influence in the Department of Militia and Defence was great enough that he was easily dissuaded from this course by his friends. What he seemed to dislike above all was the implication, repeatedly advanced, that the position of inspector-general was a reward for services rendered, a none-too-subtle hint that he should keep his mouth shut and be thankful.

Currie's unhappiness was genuine, but much of the dissatisfaction, of course, rose from the enormous changes that took place as the country and the army moved from a war to a peace footing. For four years he had daily accepted risks of injury and death, not only for himself but for all those he commanded. Along with those risks came a quite remarkable freedom of action, unknown in any civilian occupation. Throughout history commanders in war have had to make quick decisions. So long as the commander is successful, his decisions are rarely questioned. At the end of war the risks are gone and so is the freedom. For four years the cost in dollars of equipment, supplies, training, and organization seemed of little consequence when compared with the saving of soldiers' lives. For four years no one had questioned the commander who was working for victory and for saving the lives of his soldiers. This situation ended virtually overnight. In peacetime the army's budget was severly limited. To the politician the armed forces had a very low priority. Who in a war-weary population could relish expenditures on defence, when for four years the army had absorbed so much money? The standard question for any issue touching the army was 'how much does it cost?'

During the war Currie had become a professional soldier, but he had no experience as a professional soldier in peacetime. In any event, no professional soldier alive had witnessed anything like the shift from war to peace that occurred after 1918. He was not so naïve that he believed the peacetime army would parallel his wartime experience, but the limitation on his power and ability to act as inspector-general was certainly much greater than he had anticipated.

Quite suddenly, in April 1920, an escape from these frustrations was presented to him by the board of governors of McGill University in the form of an offer of the position of principal and vice-chancellor of the university. Although Currie had doubts about his training and ability to handle such a job, his hesitation was only momentary. During the same month he accepted the appointment. His resignation as inspector-general was received by the Privy Council on 30 July. A military career of major importance then ended. Writing to a well-wisher he said that he left the Department of Militia with a few regrets; for he had still hoped to make certain changes in the defence organization. And he added, 'from the attitude of the people generally, and that of the Government in particular, I have come to the conclusion that it would be a long time before these ideas would result in anything practical. In a way it is a relief to get away from here. I always disliked intensely holding a Government position. There were many you know, both in the Government, and outside of it, who considered that I was given the position of Inspector-General, as a reward, and I never relished being placed in such a position. I like Montreal and its citizens and believe that I am likely to be happier there than in any other place in Canada, outside of Victoria.'[51]

Canada's most distinguished soldier left the army with a great sense of relief.

9

The old soldier

Unlike the old soldier in the song, Arthur Currie did not 'just fade away' after he resigned from the army. Without ever having attended a university, he became principal of a distinguished university. He held two orders of knighthood received from George v, and he had earned American, French, and Belgian decorations. After the war he received honorary degrees from American, British, and Canadian universities. In the early 1920s the man who had commanded the Canadian Corps would have been recognized by any well-informed Canadian. At McGill he was just another university president, albeit a good one, and he would never again achieve the prominence that had been his as commander of the Canadian Corps.

A military career is not always ended by a simple resignation. On retirement Currie received a sword of honour from his former officers which was a symbol of their shared, never-to-be-forgotten, experiences. Many of his close friends remained in the armed forces, and he carried on a voluminous correspondence with these ex-colleagues until his death. Many of the speeches which, as university president, he made constantly, alluded to experience during the war. He never ceased to plead on behalf of veterans of all ranks – for jobs, pensions, or other assistance from government and individuals.[1] Frequently, when trying to solve an administrative problem at the university, his mind must have reviewed precedents or analogous situations from his military experience. Nevertheless, his relief at leaving an active military career was genuine, and throughout the 1920s, except for one or two brief episodes, his attention and his energy were given to his work at McGill. After becoming principal, he was inclined to shun any connection with formal military activity. He rarely appeared in uniform, and he dropped his subscription to the *Army Quarterly*.[2] When he was asked to help organize an empire-wide drive to raise funds for the purchase of Douglas Haig's family estate as a gift to the ex-commander-in-chief, he was reluctant to participate and observed: 'I suppose one must take some action, but ... there are many other matters at home here which would appeal to our people as more worthy of consideration.'[3]

From time to time Currie still thought of entering politics. On one occasion he was urged by Arthur Meighen to stand as a Conservative candidate, and Lord Atholstan, owner of the *Montreal Star*, even suggested that he might become leader of the Conservative party.[4] Such overtures ignored Currie's adherence to the conservative tenets of the Canadian Liberal party. On another occasion Sir Robert Borden was convinced that Currie was laying the groundwork for a political career. The episode took place in September 1924 when Currie addressed delegates of the Citizen's Research Institute of Canada. Drawing on his wartime experience, he talked of the difficulties that ensued when the advice of experts had been ignored. Public reaction to the speech was slight, but Sir Robert, then retired and engaged in drafting notes for his memoirs, reacted vigorously. He was convinced that Currie was preparing a political career for himself by public statements critical of the wartime administration. Either unaware of or unconvinced by Woodrow Wilson's statement to the effect that being president of the United States was relatively simple after having been president of a great university, Borden recorded that Currie would find the organizing of a government 'a harder task than he did the leading of the Canadian Corps in France or than he does the heading of McGill University.'[5]

Earlier the same year Currie had been considerably annoyed when he had been pressed to enter political life by an old friend from British Columbia. 'You would have me believe,' he wrote, 'that all my friends on the coast consider that I am sinking into oblivion. What would you have me do? Get up on the housetops and crow every morning like a noisy rooster? ... I have had from here just as much encouragement to go into political life as anything you have ever suggested and all sorts of temptations have been offered, but I am not particularly interested. Anyone who comes into such active and close association with 3,000 young men each year – men who are going to be the leaders in professional life, in public life, in commerce, etc. – is not likely to sink into oblivion.'[6] Currie also refused an offer by the prime minister, Mackenzie King, to become Canada's first ambassador in Washington, a post subsequently accepted by Vincent Massey. Whether he regarded the diplomatic job as essentially political, and thus undesirable, it is impossible to say; but clearly he preferred McGill and Montreal.[7]

Even without the student revolts and campus unrest more recently associated with universities, the job of a good university president was demanding. The task required patience, tact, persuasiveness, foresight, a robust constitution, an instinct for acquiring funds and persuading people, and, not least important, a conviction of the importance of the institution one served. With such characteristics few men have been abundantly endowed, and Currie had his limitations. Yet he appears to have been remarkably successful as principal. He was able, in spite of his own inauspicious financial history, to raise funds and enhance the university despite general hard times and economic difficulties. Without any real knowledge of *academe*, even without a university education, he was able to win the respect and, more important, the affection of his academics. Stephen Leacock once remarked that he had 'known many college principals and presidents – a poor lot most of them, with a few brave exceptions here and there. But there never was one that matched up with General Currie.'[8] Perhaps his success with academics stemmed from the fact that with age he found it easier to unbend, and he thus appeared less pompous. Or, perhaps his tendency to pomposity was less apparent or less offensive to academics than to soldiers. Most probably, however, Currie's success with his academic colleagues was rooted in his willingness to work for them. As ever, he regarded himself as the spokesman for a team, and thus he did not engender the mistrust that so often is attached to more hierarchical-minded university presidents. In the words of one observer: 'there was little in his military career to suggest that he would make a great principal ... yet he succeeded; and the academic world, usually jealous of an "outsider" who has been granted power, regarded him with affection and respect. His decisions were prompt and fair; he could pass without effort from great dignity to jovial friendliness; he knew even very junior members of his staff and kept himself informed about their personal problems.'[9]

Currie's success was partly the result of his attitude towards students. His courtesy to younger students became almost legendary on campus, and many an alumnus testifies to the sense of astonishment on this or that occasion when he discovered that the affable gentleman to whom he had just been chatting was the university principal.[10]

Given the arduous social responsiblities, to say nothing of speaking engagements and official duties, which were the principal's lot, one of the difficulties Currie faced throughout his McGill days was his declining health. He suffered a series of more or less minor troubles rather than a serious illness; but each attack of sickness drained his strength and left him exhausted.[11] For one devoted to the idea of service, it is no easy task to ration one's strength for the long haul. This fact was increasingly apparent to Currie throughout the 1920s. In 1921 and 1922 he was forced to cancel his engagements and rest. Partly to break his routine, and also because he was keenly interested in foreign policy, Currie followed the program of the Institute of International Affairs. Indeed, he was one of the founders of the Canadian branch of the organization, and he made an effort to attend important meetings of the parent body overseas – thus interrupting his heavy schedule at McGill and also indulging his interest. From May to September 1927 Currie was out of Canada attending meetings of the Institute in Honolulu. Returning to

Canada refreshed and relaxed, he was greeted by a nasty surprise. On 13 June 1927 the *Evening Guide*, a newspaper with a limited circulation of approximately 1,000 published in the small town of Port Hope, Ontario, had printed an article that would change Currie's life.

A press release describing the unveiling of a commemorative plaque at Mons, Belgium, was the excuse which the *Evening Guide* used to print a vicious attack on the Canadian officer responsible for sending troops into Mons on 11 November 1918. The article was a direct accusation of incompetence and inhumanity on the part of the Canadian Corps commander. It resurrected publicly the charges made by Sam Hughes after the war. For the first time an open attack against Currie's wartime leadership was made in a public journal, albeit a rather insignificant one. The article charged that 'it is doubtful whether in any case there was a more deliberate and useless waste of human life than in the so-called capture of Mons.'[12] The question was: how would Currie respond?

Sir Arthur was not informed of the article until some time after he had returned to Canada in September 1927. For five months Currie debated whether to take legal action. He had longed for a chance openly to disprove the campaign of slanderous rumour that Sam Hughes's privileged statements in parliament had started. However, to rush headlong into a lawsuit would involve substantial risks. Many of his friends advised him to forget the incident.[13] Who read the Port Hope *Guide*? Could anything be gained in a situation where a popular local paper was attacked by someone from the big city? Could the jury really be expected to make a sensible decision on military questions beyond the understanding of a layman? Was it not more dignified simply to forget the incident? These and similar considerations were pressed on the ex-corps commander, who, no doubt, had reservations of his own. There was always the risk that his financial indiscretion of 1914 would become public. The article, after all, had been written by W.T.R. Preston, who in 1927 published a book of memoirs that contained an exaggerated account of the military voting in 1917.[14] Preston had been a 1917 Liberal scrutineer in England, had gained the nickname 'Hug the Machine' and possessed a taste for nasty invective. In the end, however, Currie decided to serve notice of suit for libel against the newspaper, specifically against Preston, author of the article, and against F.W. Wilson, owner, editor, and publisher of the *Guide*. Currie then attempted to settle out of court. He explained to Wilson, in detail, the operation in Mons, demonstrated that the *Guide's* account was false, and asked for an official retraction. Wilson refused: what had been written, he contended, was substantially true.[15] The trial was on.

Trial proceedings began on 16 April 1928, but the course of events was largely determined in the 'examination for discovery' at which Currie was asked more than 200 questions about his movements on 24 April 1915. Hughes's allegations of cowardice during the first gas attack were well known to the defence attorney. At the trial itself it was quickly established that the article in question did indeed refer to Currie. The piece claimed:

There was much waste of human life during the war, enormous loss of lives which should not have taken place. But it is doubtful whether in any case there was a more deliberate and useless waste of human life than in the so-called capture of Mons. It was the last day; and the last hour, and almost the last minute, when to glorify the Canadian Head Quarters staff the Commander-in-Chief conceived the mad idea that it would be a fine thing to say that the Canadians had fired the last shot in the Great war, and had captured the last German entrenchment before the bugles sounded eleven o'clock, when the armistice which had been signed by both sides would begin officially ... The men were sent on in front to charge the enemy. Headquarters, with conspicuous bravery, brought up the rear ... Of course the town was taken just at the last minute before the official moment of the armistice arrived. But the penalty that was paid in useless waste of human life was appalling ... Veterans who had passed throught the whole four years of war lie buried in Belgian cemeteries as the result of the 'glories of Mons.'

Headquarters Staff assembled in the centre of the town as the eleven o'clock signal sounded that the official armistice was effective from that hour. Along the route that they had carefully and with safety made their way to the centre of the town, passing the dead and dying and the wounded, victims of their madness. It was common talk among the soldiers that while the staff were congratulating themselves upon the great victory and enjoying the pride upon having 'fired the last shot in the Great War,' a sergeant advanced and whispered to one of the staff that unless they withdrew immediately to a place of safety, they would not be allowed to leave the place alive, as the guns of the indignant Canadian soldiers were already trained on them. In less time than it takes to tell the story, Headquarters got into motors and were fleeing for their lives.

It does not seem to be remembered that even Ottawa, neither by government nor Parliament, gave Sir Arthur Currie any official vote of thanks, or any special grant as an evidence of the esteem or appreciation for his services. And this is the only case of the kind in connection with any of the high commanding officers of the War. He was allowed to return to Canada unnoticed by officials of the government or of Parliament and permitted to sink into comparative obscurity in the civilian position as President of McGill University. The official desire to glorify Mons, therefore deserves more than a passing or silent notice. Canadian valour won Mons, but it was by such a shocking useless waste of human life that it is an eternal disgrace to the Headquarters that directed operations. [16]

Reported in virtually ever newpaper from coast to coast, the trial quickly became a *cause célèbre*. Currie was inundated with offers from his old comrades to testify on his behalf, and he also received a share of crank mail. Defeated generals expect and usually receive judgment by court martial; they are judged by their peers – namely, other generals with an equal understanding of the difficulties and risks involved in a military operation. Currie, as far as can be established, was the only successful commander of any British force ever to have his actions adjudicated by a civilian court. He faced, moreover, a legal counsel who was even more critical in his insinuations than the original article had been. Official records were introduced into the proceedings as well as testimony from numerous eye-witnesses and experts. From the casualty records it was finally established that on 11 November 1918 the entire Canadian Corps suffered only one fatal casualty – a fact that cut much of the ground from under the defence.[17]

The trial ended on 1 May. After deliberating for three hours, the jury returned with a verdict in Currie's favour. Although the action against the Port Hope paper was for $50,000, Currie had stated on oath that he did not want the money. Presumably, therefore, he got what he wanted – a verdict of guilty and a token award of $500. After the strain of the trial there followed the exuberance of a victory celebration, much enlivened by cheering McGill students. When the principal returned to Montreal, crowds of people stopped the traffic while the students pulled their triumphant leader through the streets in a coach. The next day, 3 May 1928, the *Montreal Gazette* editorialized on the trial:

It may be said at the bar of public opinion there was never an issue or doubt of any kind as to the absolute propriety of the course pursued by the leader of the Canadian Corps in the concluding action of the war. Sir Arthur Currie was never the kind of man to needlessly expose his troops to danger and possible death, and least of all for the petty purpose of self-glorification. No commander worthy of the name who had passed through those four years of horror and had witnessed so terrible a harvest of death, would have stooped at any time, and certainly not within a few hours of the armistice to such an act ... It was a monstrous accusation, one that found no response in the minds of decent and right-thinking people.

McGill's board of governors demonstrated its 'admiration and affection' for Currie by paying the trial costs plus 'a sufficient margin over these expenses to enable you to take a much needed rest.'[18] The rest was welcome indeed; for the trial had taken its toll. When he was informed that a defence appeal had been launched, Currie collapsed and was discovered unconscious. Later, he confessed that he was ashamed of himself for letting the trial get on his nerves. But, he added, 'for ten years I had suffered from the malicious lie and when I had a chance to fight my defamers so many seemed to think that I should leave it alone – let it die where it was born. They pointed out to me that I could never get a verdict from the jury of farmers. But I had to do it. I wanted the people of Canada to know the Truth.'[19]

Currie never fully recovered from the action for libel. An extended sick leave in Europe provided temporary relief; but within six months of his return he was again under doctor's care. That the last years of his principalship coincided with the Great Depression was no help. Increasing financial pressures and declining student enrolments hit all academic institutions in the first years of the depression, adding to the burden of the principal. Respite from the immediate pressures of McGill's administration was provided in late 1930, when the Canadian prime minister requested Currie to represent the dominion at the opening of the parliament buildings in Delhi.

Travel to India gave Currie time to lift his gaze from the affairs of McGill and to reflect on the world situation. The broader picture, however, provided little comfort. Currie was deeply troubled by what to him appeared an almost desperate international situation. He saw that at the right time self-government for India was essential; but he had little sympathy with Ghandhi's agitation. 'His political demands are insatiable,' Currie recorded.[20] The situation in India, disquieting to be sure, was still less disturbing than events in other areas. Japan's attack on Manchuria was, in Currie's opinion, blatant defiance of the League of Nations. If it had done nothing else, in his view the war had 'proved that no nation can live unto itself alone and that whatever one nation does must influence for good or evil every other nation.'[21] Alas, relatively few people seemed to have learned the lesson, or so it appeared to Currie as he toured the Far East before returning to Canada.

Currie arrived in Montreal in May 1931 after an absence of five months. He was distressed with both world and domestic scenes. Given existing conditions, he believed that the time was ripe for coalition or national government in Canada, and he did not hesitate to say so publicly. His energies, however, were chiefly focused on problems at McGill. Before his trip, the board of govenors had insisted on the appointment of an assistant principal to relieve Currie of some of his routine duties – a thoughtful act; but the new appointee soon accepted the presidency of Dalhousie University. Currie was, therefore, still on his own, struggling to run a large university in the midst of a serious economic depression. Within a few months his health again declined. On 6 November 1933 he collapsed with a seizure and was rushed to the hospital where he lingered until his death at the end of the month. He was buried with full military honours on 5 December 1933, his fifty-eighth birthday.

Tributes and testimonials were received from every corner of the globe. The funeral ceremony was the most elaborate ever held up to that time in Canada. From coast to coast Canadians followed the procession as it was described by the radio announcer of the Canadian Broadcasting Commission. In his official eulogy Sir Robert Borden recorded that Currie had 'won high distinction during the War not for himself alone but also for the Canadian Corps under his command. I was brought into very intimate touch with him during the agony of that conflict and my high regard deepened into sincere affection and warm admiration.'[22] A fellow member of the imperial war cabinet, who had had fewer opportunities than Borden to assess Currie, was perhaps more discerning in his tribute. Jan Smuts observed that Currie was 'simple, shrewd, sane and human to a degree. He had a mind which was eminently practical and obviously harboured no doubts. He was sure of himself, of the cause for which he stood and its inevitable ultimate success. He was proud of his officers and men, and very proud of his country.'[23] At the time of the funeral Borden was recovering from influenza. In the confidential memorandum he wrote on Currie, the last paragraph ended ambiguously. The funeral ceremonial, Borden recorded, 'was perhaps more elaborate than at any state or military funeral in the past history of Canada. Neither Sir John A. Macdonald nor Sir Wilfrid Laurier received such a tribute. The future historian will have to judge whether Currie's service was comparable with theirs.'[24] Such a judgment is impossible, and asking the question reveals more about Sir Robert Borden than it does of Sir Arthur Currie. Currie's service has to be judged by looking at his record of command during the war. By any standard that record is remarkable.

Currie began with no special advantages and a number of liabilities. He had considerable experience in the Canadian militia, to be sure, but this had hardly prepared him for the grim reality of the trenches. Moreover, he began the war with a desperate and foolish act – one that could have led to his disgrace and possibly to his arrest. He was incredibly lucky that his abuse of regiment funds was never exposed publicly. For the next three years the act haunted him. While he was facing his most serious military decisions, it was on the horizon of his mind. The extent to which Currie's judgments about his political masters were directly or indirectly influenced by the fallout from the 50th Regiment scandal can never be neatly measured. But it is certain that his action in 1914 did influence his perception of others and others' perceptions of him.[25]

Currie was to fight the war as a member of a 'colonial' contingent, one that was dogged by excessive political intrigue. This fact was not a liability in terms of his dealing with British military superiors with whom he seemed at greater ease than with Canadian politicians, particularly during the first three years of the war. Any colonial commander had a more difficult task than his British counterpart, simply because he was invariably required to report to two masters.

The First World War marked an important step in the development of Canada as a nation and in the creation of a sense of Canadian nationalism. Many would see Currie as playing a critical role in this development, especially in his attempt to have the Canadian Corps reunited in the spring of 1918. General W.H.S. Macklin, from the perspective of a Second World War, wrote that Currie's 'best contribution to victory' was his 'successful fight to get his corps reunited after the bungling GHQ had split it into fragments after the German offensive of 1918. Before Currie could turn around he found himself with a Corps HQ and no corps. All his divisions having been filched away to prop up the tottering British front. He put up a terrific fight to get them back, and by July he had succeeded, and this paid off in the masterly performance of the Corps from August 8th at Amiens to November 11th at Mons. The Corps was by far the most powerful single formation on the Western Front in that drive.'[26] John A. Swettenham has compared Currie's attempt to reunite the Canadian Corps in 1918 with General A.G.L. McNaughton's fight to have the Canadian Army reunited in the Second World War.[27] It is dangerous, however, to draw simple nationalistic conclusions from the actions and arguments of either man. Currie was motivated solely by his desire to use effectively the fighting machine that he commanded.

Currie had inherited from General Byng an efficient organization, which he never ceased honing and refining. Currie possessed what Lord Wavell called 'le sens du practicable ... a really sound knowledge of the "mechanism of war." '[28] He had an instinctive understanding for topography, movement, supply, training, and organization, and a flair for spotting and placing on his staff other men whose knowledge of these things equalled or excelled his own. As a corps commander, Currie had little influence on the strategy of the war. He never hesitated to make suggestions about where an attack should be made, but he never questioned the assumption that the main effort of the war had to be made on the Western Front. For him, this was an obvious reality. The conditions on the Western Front could not be changed; therefore, they had to be overcome. Currie's four years in France represented a continual struggle to overcome the obstacles of trench warfare, and he was determined that these difficulties must be overcome with an absolute minimum loss of life.

A more charismatic man, perhaps, would have worried less about casualties. Currie was certainly not charismatic so far as the majority of his soldiers were concerned. His shyness and reticence and his inability to be effective before large groups meant that he would never have the love of his soldiers, though he certainly maintained their respect. The loyalty of his staff to their commander, however, was intense. J.E.B. Seeley, who for a time commanded the Canadian Cavalry Brigade, observed that Currie held 'an almost fanatical hatred of unnecessary casualties ... Of all the men that I knew in nearly four years on the Western Front, I think Currie was the man who took the most care of the lives of his troops. Moreover, again and again he nearly brought his career to an end by bluntly refusing to do things which he was certain would result in great loss of life without compensating advantages.'[29] Currie's fanaticism regarding casualties did not reduce his effectiveness as a commander. He knew that some casualties were inevitable, and providing the tactical returns were sufficiently high, he was not squeamish. He had risked his own life on more than one occasion and was usually in favour of a bold plan if the risks were reduced to a minimum. But the risks, the imponderables, always had to be minimal before Currie was satisfied.

The casualties of the First World War, including the Canadian casualties, were the great price the world paid for the human frailty that led to war. Currie's greatest contribution to Canada was his reduction of the Canadian side of this grim equation.

Notes

CHAPTER 1 Before the war

1 Public Archives of Canada (cited hereafter as P.A.C.), Currie Papers (cited hereafter as C.P.), Memorandum, n.d.
2 Hugh M. *Urquhart, Arthur Currie: A Biography of a Great Canadian* (Toronto, 1950), p. xv.
3 *Ibid.*, p. 11.
4 Robert Craig Brown and Desmond Morton, 'The Embarrassing Apotheosis of a "Great Canadian": Sir Arthur Currie's Personal Crisis in 1917,' *Canadian Historical Review*, LX (March 1979), pp. 41–64.
5 Urquhart, *Arthur Currie*. All details of Currie's early life come from Urquhart, unless otherwise indicated. Hereafter, only direct quotations from Urquhart are cited in notes.
6 F.H. Underhill, 'Canada and the Last War,' in Chester Martin, ed., *Canada in Peace and War* (Toronto, 1941), pp. 135–6.
7 P.A.C., Borden Papers, vol. 361, Currie to Matson, 29 September 1914.
8 Margaret A. Ormsby, *British Columbia: A History* (Vancouver, 1958), pp. 341–3.
9 *Ibid.*, pp. 354–5.
10 Urquhart, *Arthur Currie*, p. 18.
11 See Desmond Morton, *Ministers and Generals: Politics and the Canadian Militia* (Toronto, 1970); *The Canadian General: Sir William Otter* (Toronto, 1974). Brown and Morton, 'Apotheosis.'
12 W.H. Ames, 'The Military Education of Officers of the Auxilliary Forces,' *Selected Papers from the Transactions of the Canadian Military Institute, 1903* (Welland, Ont., 1904), p. 60.
13 Urquhart, *Arthur Currie*, p. 27.

14 A.F. Duguid, *Official History of the Canadian Forces in the Great War 1914–1919* (Ottawa, 1938), Appendix 6.

15 *Ibid.*

16 Henry Borden, ed., *Robert Laird Borden: His Memoirs* (Toronto, 1938), I, pp. 457ff.

17 Duguid, *Official History*, p. 3.

18 Urquhart, *Arthur Currie*, p. 25.

19 Brown and Morton, 'Apotheosis,' p. 48.

20 *Daily Colonist*, 21 November 1913.

21 *Ibid.*, 22 November 1913.

22 *Ibid.*, 3 January 1914.

23 *Ibid.*, 22 November 1913.

24 *Ibid.*

25 P.A.C., R.G. 24, vol. 5871, file HQ 7-52-10, Currie to Moore, Taggart, 11 December 1913.

26 *Ibid.*, Moore, Taggart to Forsyth, 7 May 1916. Ross to Moore, Taggart, 10 September 1915.

27 P.A.C. Borden Papers, vol. 361, Currie to Matson 29 September 1914.

28 *Ibid.*

29 *Ibid.* Brown and Morton, 'Apotheosis,' p. 52.

30 P.A.C., Borden Papers, Currie to Matson, 29 September 1914.

31 Brown and Morton, 'Apotheosis,' p. 52.

32 P.A.C., Borden Papers, Currie to Matson, 29 September 1914.

33 Brown and Morton, 'Apotheosis,' p. 50.

34 P.A.C., Borden Papers, Currie to Matson, 29 September 1913.

35 Interview, General A.G.L. McNaughton with author, 27 March 1963.

36 *King's Regulations and Orders for the Militia, 1910,* para 639, 630c.

37 *Militia List,* September 1914, pp. 45-6.

CHAPTER 2 Preparation for war

1 G.W.L. Nicholson, *Canadian Expeditionary Force, 1914–1919* (Ottawa, 1962), pp. 17–18.

2 *Ibid.*, p.14.

3 Canada, *Debates House of Commons*, 26 January 1916, p. 292. Hughes continued: 'The word was wired to every officer commanding a unit in any part of Canada to buckle on his harness and get busy. The consequence was that in a very short time we had the boys on the way for the first contingent, whereas it would have taken several weeks to have got the word around through ordinary channels.'

4 Duguid, *Official History*, pp. 63–5, 148.

5 P.A.C., C.P. Currie Diary, September 1914.

6 *Ibid.* Urquhart, *Arthur Currie*, p. 38.

7 Duguid, *Official History*, Appendix III. Ronald Haycock, 'Early Canadian Weapons Acquisition:–That Damned Ross Rifle,' *Canadian Defence Quarterly*, 14 (December, 1984), pp. 48–57. For the impact of British small arms changes see Shelford Bidwell and Dominick Graham, *Fire-Power: British Army Weapons and Theories of War 1904–1945* (London, 1982).

8 *Ibid.*

9 Duguid, *Official History*, p. 78.

10 C.L. Flick, *Just What Happened: A Diary of the Mobilization of the Canadian Militia, 1914* (London, 1917), p. 7.

11 Duguid, *Official History*, pp. 145–6. The MacAdam shovel-shield was patented by Hughes's female secretary. It was supposed to serve as an entrenching tool, when fitted with a handle; without the handle it was to serve as a bullet-proof shield when stuck in the ground in front of a prone rifleman. Twenty-five thousand shovel-shields were sent overseas with the first contingent, apparently without benefit of user-trials. In the field the instrument had two main deficiencies: it would not dig and was wholly inadequate as a shield. When it was withdrawn from the Canadians, Hughes was furious and cabled his special representative in England: 'You must hold a tight hand on all that improper work over there. Promptly cancel order for English entrenching tools. See General Alderson and if necessary Earl Kitchener but I will not permit this improper interference. British entrenching tool absolutely useless for any purpose' (p. 219).

12 Borden, *Memoirs*, I, p. 457–63.

13 Duguid, *Official History*, p. 48.

14 *Ibid.*, pp. 62–5.

15 *Ibid*, p. 91.

16 *Ibid*, pp. 63–5. J.A. Swettenham, *To Seize the Victory: The Canadian Corps in World War I* (Toronto, 1965), p. 35.

17 Duguid, *Official History*, p. 88.

18 Canada, *Debates, House of Commons*, 16 January 1916, p. 302.

19 J.A. Currie, *The Red Watch: With the First Canadian Division in Flanders* (Toronto, 1916), p. 43.

20 Duguid, *Official History*, pp. 62–97.

21 P.A.C., C.P., Currie Diary, September 1914.

22 Duguid, *Official History*, Appendix 85.

23 P.A.C., Borden Papers, Currie to Matson, 29 September 1914.

24 Duguid, *Official History*, p. 53.

25 Will R. Bird, *Ghosts Have Warm Hands* (Toronto, 1968), p. 30.

26 P.A.C., Borden Papers, Currie to Matson, 29 September 1914.
27 *Ibid.*
28 Flick, *Just What Happened,* p. 26.
29 Urquhart, *Arthur Currie,* p. 28.
30 Currie's frequent use of the profane vernacular was substantiated by General McNaughton. See note by Mr E. Pye in Canadian Armed Forces Historical Section, Cardex 000.9 (D106).
31 Major-General W.H.S. Macklin to author, 10 June 1962.
32 Lloyd George, *Memoirs,* p. 3384. The editor of Haig's diary confirms this opinion. Robert Blake, ed., *The Private Papers of Douglas Haig, 1914–1919: Being Selections from the Private Diary and Correspondence of Field Marshal the Earl Haig of Bemersyde K.G., G.C.B., O.M., etc.* (London, 1952), p. 27.
33 Cited in Urquhart, *Arthur Currie.*
34 P.A.C., Borden Papers, 'Memorandum respecting the late Sir Arthur Currie,' 13 August 1934.
35 Urquhart, *Arthur Currie,* p. 51. Flick, *Just What Happened,* p. 24.
36 Donald A. Smith, *At the Forks of the Grand* (Paris, Ontario, 1956), p. 294.
37 P.A.C., C.P., Currie to Duguid, n.d.
38 Anonymous, *Unknown Soldiers by One of Them* (New York, 1959), p. 19.
39 Duguid, *Official History,* p. 27.
40 *Ibid.,* p. 98.
41 Lord Beaverbrook (then Sir Max Aitken) thought that during mobilization the Canadian administration rose to an emergency with 'effort that has never been surpassed in military history.' Though he was wrong on the success of the effort, Beaverbrook's words are a more apt description than he probably realized. *Canada in Flanders* (London, 1916), I, p. 2.
42 Nicholson, *CEF,* p. 109.
43 Philip Magnus, *Kitchener: Portrait of an Imperialist* (London, 1958), p. 291. See also pp. 253, 279. A more balanced view of Kitchener by George H. Cassar, *Kitchener: Architect of Victory* (London, 1977), p. 198, confirms Kitchener's dislike of civilian control of the Territorial Army.
44 Borden, *Memoirs,* p. 436.
45 Duguid, *Official History,* p. 65.
46 *Ibid.,* p. 119.
47 Nicholson, *CEF,* p. 34.
48 Urquhart, *Arthur Currie,* p. 50.
49 *Unknown Soldiers,* p. 16.
50 Theodore Ropp, *War in the Modern World,* p. 219.
51 Bidwell and Graham, *Fire Power.*
52 Major-General J.F.C. Fuller, *Generalship: Its Diseases and Their Cure: A Study of the Personal Factor in Command* (Harrisburg, PA, 1936), p. 55.

53 Anthony John Trythol, *Boney Fuller: Soldier Strategist and Writer 1878–1966* (New Brunswick, NJ, 1977), p. 33.

54 Duguid, *Official History*, p. 148. This issue illustrated not only the willingness of Canadians to follow the lead of the British but foggy thinking on the part of the War Office as well. The changes from four to eight to four company battalions in the Canadian forces followed British suggestions, and at one stage the War Office toyed with the idea of having all colonial forces on an eight-company organization, while the British regular and territorial forces would have only four companies.

55 Cited in Urquhart, *Arthur Currie*, p. 48

56 P.A.C., C.P. Currie Diary. Duguid, p. 136. On one occasion, the 4th of December, many units had their files blown away and a unit paymaster lost the treasury notes for a pay parade when a sudden gale blew down the tents.

57 Duguid, *Official History*, p. 135.

58 *Ibid.*, p. 123.

59 *Ibid.*, p. 142.

60 P.A.C., C.P. Currie Diary.

61 P.A.C., Creelman Papers, Diary, 19 December 1914.

62 Duguid, *Official History*, p. 149, Appendices 85, 842.

63 P.A.C., C.P. Currie Diary, 10 February 1915.

64 *Unknown Soldiers*, p. 19.

CHAPTER 3 Brigade commander

1 P.A.C., C.P. Currie Diary, 10–20 February 1915

2 Reproduced in Duguid, *Official History*, Appendix 262.

3 P.A.C., C.P. Diary, 26 February 1915. 'Operation Order No. 2,' 28 February 1915.

4 'Operation Order No. 5,' 9 March 1915, Appendix to W.D., G.S. 1st Cdn. Div.

5 Nicholson, *CEF*, p. 51.

6 Quoted in Duguid, *Official History*, p. 192.

7 Nicholson, *CEF*, p. 53.

8 *Ibid.*

9 R.H. Mottram, 'A Personal Record,' p. 45, in *Three Personal Records of the War* (London, 1929).

10 Cited in Duguid, *Official History*, Appendix II, p. 86.

11 Field Marshal Viscount Montgomery of Alamein, *A History of Warfare* (London, 1968), p. 478.

12 Duguid, *Official History*, p. 203.

13 Cyril Falls, *The Great War* (New York, 1971), p. 103.

14 'Report on Conditions of Trenches,' 21 April 1915 (Duguid, *Official History*, Appendix 334).

15 Duguid, *Official History*, Appendix 330a.

16 *Ibid.*, p. 209.

17 These were (1) Battle of Gravenstafel Ridge, 22–23 April; (2) Battle of St Julien, 24 April–4 May; (3) Battle of Frezenberg Ridge, 5–13 May; (4) Battle of Bulwaerd Ridge, 24–25 May, Cmd. (1138), 1921, p. 14.

18 Erich von Falkenhayn, *General Headquarters 1914–1916 and Its Critical Decisions* (London, 1919), pp. 65, 84.

19 B.H. Liddell Hart, *The Real War* (New York, 1930), p. 130.

20 B.H. Liddell Hart, *A History of the World War 1914–1918* (London, 1938), p. 247.

21 Alan Clark, *The Donkeys* (London, 1961), p. 78.

22 Duguid, *Official History,* p. 214. An artillery officer serving with Currie recorded in his diary that 'something peculiar is in the air and we can smell it coming.' P.A.C., Creelman Papers, diary.

23 P.A.C., C.P. Currie Diary, 15 April 1915.

24 Duguid, *Official History,* pp. 212–13.

25 Nicholson, *CEF,* p. 58.

26 James E. Edmonds, *A Short History of World War I* (London, 1951), p. 92.

27 3rd Brigade Field Message, N.M. 743, 22 April 1915, Appendix to W.D. 3rd Cdn. Inf. Bde. April 1915.

28 2nd Bde. Field Message, B.M. 742, 22 April 1915, Appendix to W.D. 2nd Cdn. Inf. Bde., April 1915.

29 Field Message G.795, V Corps to Second Army, 22 April 1915, Appendix to W.D., G.S. 1st Cdn. Div., April 1915.

30 Field Messages, Y.501, 3rd Bde. to 1st Div., 23 April 1915; G.A.Q. 21, 1st Div. to 1st Bde., 23 April 1915; Appendix to W.D., G.S., 1st Cdn. Div., April 1915.

31 Duguid, *Official History,* p. 288.

32 *Ibid.*

33 Field Message, B.M. 4, 2nd Bde. to 1st Div., 29 April 1915, Appendix to W.D. 2nd Cdn. Inf. Bde., April 1915.

34 At 6:30 a.m. Currie reported to divisional headquarters that telephone communication with his battalions was broken. Field Message, B.M.6, 24 April 1915, Appendix to W.D., 2nd Cdn. Inf. Bde., April 1915.

35 Unnumbered Field Message, 2nd Bde. to 85th Bde., 24 April 1915, Appendix to *ibid.*

36 Urquhart, *Arthur Currie,* p. 72, quoting letter from Currie.

37 P.A.C., C.P. Currie to Duguid, n.d., p. 11.

38 See Field Message quoted in Urquhart, *Arthur Currie,* p. 82.

39 Urquhart, *Arthur Currie,* p. 83.

40 P.A.C., C.P. Currie to Duguid, n.d., p. 11.

41 *Ibid.*, pp. 9–10.

42 This statement is an oversimplification of a very complicated situation. In fact Brigadier Bush first agreed to attack as soon as his second battalion arrived and he went
to hurry them along. When the battalion arrived shortly afterwards without Bush,
the battalion commander refused to move without their brigadier, and so Currie
went to get him, only to find that Bush in the meantime had received new orders
which prevented him from moving his troops.

43 Urquhart, *Arthur Currie*, p. 91, Duguid, *Official History*, pp. 321–2.

44 Duguid, *Official History*, p. 322.

45 Lieutenant-Colonel Kemmis-Betty was one of the relatively few professional
soldiers to come overseas with the First Canadian Contingent. A graduate of staff
college, he had been extremely helpful to Currie.

46 Duguid, *Official History*, pp. 326, 335.

47 *Ibid.*, p. 335.

48 Cited in Urquhart, *Arthur Curruie*, p. 97.

49 Duguid, *Official History*, p. 357.

50 Nicholson, *CEF*, p. 82.

51 P.A.C., C.P. Currie Diary, 6 May 1915.

52 Duguid, *Official History*, p. 407.

53 *Ibid.*, p. 421. The casualties for the entire Canadian Division in this period were over
6,000.

54 *Ibid.*, p. 225.

55 Ropp, *War in the Modern World*, p. 246.

56 Map of Festubert, Appendix 28 to W.D., G.S. 1st Cdn. Div., May 1915. Duguid,
Official History, p. 463.

57 Field Message, B.M.148, 20 May 1915, reproduced Duguid, *Official History*, Appendix 722.

58 Nicholson, *CEF*, p. 102.

59 Duguid, *Official History*, p. 502.

60 Nicholson, *CEF*, p. 108.

61 Lord Moran, *Anatomy of Courage* (London, 1966) p. 58.

62 P.A.C., C.P. Currie Diary, 5–12 June 1915.

63 Nicholson, *CEF*, pp.109–14. C.E.W. Bean, *The Story of Anzac from 14 May 1915
to the Evacuation of the Gallipoli Peninsula* (Sydney, 1943), p. 117.

64 P.A.C., Perley Papers, Perley to Borden, 11 June 1915.

65 *Ibid.*, 22 June 1915. Kitchener to Perley 24 June 1915. Alderson had also recommended Currie as the best prospective division Commander, P.A.C., C.P. Alderson to Currie, 11 August 1915.

66 P.A.C., C.P. Currie Diary, 11 August 1915.

67 Letter, Ropp to Leighton, 21 January 1961.

68 Nicholson, *CEF*, pp. 75–6.

69 Duguid, *Official History,* Appendix III, p. 87.
70 Urquhart, *Arthur Currie,* p. 107. Quoting missing letter from Currie.

CHAPTER 4 Division commander

1 Montgomery, *A History of Warfare* (London, 1968), p. 21.
2 Duguid, *Official History,* Appendices 851, 226.
3 Interview, General A.G.L. McNaughton, 27 March 1963.
4 Canadian Corps Intelligence Reports, 1915.
5 The divisional staff normally consisted of eleven officers and included an assistant adjutant and quartermaster general and his deputy; the commanders of divisional artillery and engineers; and four personal aids for the division commander. *Report of The Ministry of Overseas Military Forces of Canada 1918* (London, 1919), p. 291.
6 W.W. Murray, *The History of the 2nd Canadian Battalion (East Ontario Regiment) Canadian Expeditionary Force in the Great War 1914–1918* (Ottawa, 1947), pp. 75–6.
7 Duguid, *Official History,* Appendix 91.
8 Quoted in Urquhart, *Arthur Currie,* pp. 108–9.
9 Duguid, *Official History,* p. 542. Hughes became a K.C.B. in August 1915. While he was opposed in general to giving British officers positions in the Canadian forces, Hughes would make his own British appointments.
10 P.A.C., Perley Papers, Hughes to Aitken, 29 November 1915. Considerable confusion exists regarding Beaverbrook's (Aitken became Baron Beaverbrook in 1916) position and the extent of his authority. In January 1915 he was authorized to undertake the work 'connected with records generally appertaining to the Canadian Overseas Expedition Forces and particularly the reporting of all casualties occurring therein' (P.C. 29, 6 January 1915). In September 1915 he became the 'General Representative for Canada at the front' (G.O. 117, 23 September 1915). But Beaverbrook usually called himself the 'Canadian Eye-Witness.'
11 P.A.C., Borden Papers, Hughes to Aitken, 30 November 1915.
12 Quoted in Urquhart, *Arthur Currie,* p. 118.
13 P.A.C., C.P. Alderson to Currie, 11 July 1917.
14 P.A.C., C.P. Currie Diary, 13 October–19 November 1915.
15 Interview, General A.G.L. McNaughton, 27 March 1963.
16 Montgomery, *A History of Warfare,* p. 23.
17 The Rt Hon. J.E.B. Seely, *Adventure* (London, 1930), p. 235.
18 Nicholson, p. *CEF,* 142.
19 P.A.C., C.P. Currie Diary, 11 April 1916.

20 Nicholson, *CEF*, pp. 137–44.
21 *Ibid.*, p. 145.
22 The quotation is from a transcript of Haig's original diary held by the Canadian Army Historical Section and does not appear in Blake's published version.
23 Blake, *Haig's Papers*, p. 140.
24 *Ibid.* While it is true that Sir Robert Borden adopted this view later, there is no evidence in the Borden or Beaverbrook papers that he had communicated such a wish to Aitken by 23 April 1916.
25 Lord Beaverbrook later told Sam Hughes's son Garnet that Haig had made the proposal to remove Alderson and that he (Beaverbrook) had at once submitted the suggestion to Sir Robert Borden (Beaverbrook Papers, Beaverbrook to Garnet Hughes, 22 January 1934). Sir Max, however, did not inform Borden directly. He wired to Sam Hughes that the 'loss of Turner and Ketchen would nominally affect the Second Division and must be followed by many resignations.' P.A.C., Borden Papers, Aitken to Hughes, 26 April 1916. See also Nicholson, *CEF*, p. 147, n. 57.
26 W.A. Griesbach, 'Lieutenant General Sir Edwin Alderson, K.C.B., A Brave Commander who was sacrificed to the Ross Rifle,' *Khaki Call* (February 1929).
27 Beaverbrook Papers, Beaverbrook to Garnet Hughes, 27 January 1934.
28 Beaverbrook Papers, Beaverbrook to Sam Hughes, 10 May 1916.
29 Nicholson, *CEF*, p. 147. Italics added.
30 Alderson to Gwatkin, 6 February 1916, reproduced in Duguid, *Official History,* Appendix III, p. 95.
31 *Ibid.*, pp. 95–6.
32 P.A.C., Carson File 4-5-13B, Turner to Carson, 4 May 1916, and Kietchen to Carson, 5 May 1916.
33 See Jeffery Williams, *Byng of Vimy: General and Governor General* (London, 1983).
34 Brig.-Gen. Sir James E. Edmonds, *Military Operations France and Belgium 1916 to July 1. The Somme* (London, 1932), p. 241.
35 J.H. Boraston, ed., *Sir Douglas Haig's Despatches December 1915–April 1919* (London, 1919), p. 20.
36 *Ibid*, p. 19.
37 See, for example, Brian Gardiner, *The Big Push: A Portrait of the Battle of the Somme* (New York, 1963), p. 157.
38 Liddell Hart, *History of the World War*, p. 331.
39 Edmonds, *Short History*, pp. 195–6.
40 Falls, *The Great War*, p. 107.
41 Gardiner, *The Big Push*, p. 33.
42 John Keegan, *The Face of Battle* (London, 1976). John Ellis, *Eye-Deep in Hell* (London, 1976). Denis Winter, *Death's Men: Soldiers of the Great War* (London, 1978).

43 Nicholson, *CEF*, p. 176.
44 P.A.C., Canadian War Records Office File 214, folder 6, Army Order S.G. 66/43, 10 October 1916.
45 P.A.C., C.P. Currie to Canadian Corps, 16 October 1916.
46 *Ibid.*
47 Sam Hughes took a somewhat different view and ascribed any confusion to the ignorance or weakness of his colleagues. In March 1917 he described the situation that had existed in the autumn of 1916 as 'one hell on earth with Borden a weakling, and White [the minister of finance] a mental epileptic, and Perley an intriguing nonentity' (Hughes to Garnet Hughes, Canadian Armed Forces Historical Section File 990.009 (D.8)). See Morton, *A Peculiar Kind of Politics: Canada's Overseas Ministry in the First World War* (Toronto, 1982).
48 Canadian Armed Forces Historical Section, A.M.J. Hyatt, 'Notes on Administration – First World War. Canadian Representative at the Front.' Nicholson, *CEF*, p. 205.
49 D. Vince, 'The Overseas Military Council and the Resignation of Sir Sam Hughes,' *Canadian Historical Review*, XXI (March 1950), pp. 1–24. Nicholson, *CEF*, pp. 201–12.
50 Nicholson, *CEF*, p. 210.
51 It was equally welcome in Canada, where Borden's colleagues had been urging the replacement of Hughes since the beginning of 1915. W.S. Wallace, *The Memoirs of the Rt Hon. Sir George Foster* (Toronto, 1933), pp. 177–8.
52 P.A.C., Creelman Papers, diary 19 November 1916, p. 77. Somewhat later the same writer observed that 'with Sam out of the way, promotion is likely to be according to seniority and ability, which is all that anyone can ask for,' *ibid.*, 8 December 1916, p. 78.
53 Nicholson, *CEF*, p. 211.
54 Allistair Horne, *The Price of Glory: Verdun 1916* (New York, 1961), p. 327.
55 Bidwell and Graham, *Fire Power*, pp. 94–130.
56 P.A.C., C.P. 'Notes on French Attacks North-East of Verdun in October and December 1916,' p. I
57 *Ibid.*, p. III.
58 *Ibid.*
59 *Ibid.*, p. VI.
60 *Ibid.*, p. III.
61 *Ibid.*, p. V.
62 *Ibid.*, p. IX.
63 *Ibid.*, p. VII.
64 *Ibid.*, p. VIII.
65 Bidwell and Graham, *Fire Power*, p. 115.

66 R.C. Sherriff, 'The English Public Schools in the War,' George A. Panichas, ed., *Promise of Greatness: The War of 1914–1918* (London, 1968), pp. 142–3.

67 P.A.C., C.P. 'Notes on French Attacks,' p. XV.

68 Seely, *Adventure,* p. 226.

69 During the winter months a number of trench raids were made. The purpose of these raids was to raise morale. According to Urquhart, Currie was 'by no means keen on this policy.' Although Byng urged Currie to make raids, Currie argued that his division's morale was excellent and that he was 'conserving its strength ... for the battle ahead,' Urquhart, *Arthur Currie,* pp. 145–6.

70 A.F. Duguid, 'Canadians in Battle, 1915–1918,' *Canadian Historical Association Report,* 1935, p. 42.

71 Duguid, 'The Significance of Vimy,' unpublished manuscript in P.A.C., Duguid Papers. This manuscript formed the basis for Duguid's 1936 article, 'Canada on Vimy Ridge,' in the *Canada Year Book.*

72 Nicholson, *CEF,* p. 250.

73 Duguid, 'The Significance of Vimy', p. 3.

74 Nicholson, *CEF,* pp. 248–50.

75 *Ibid.,* pp. 252–8.

CHAPTER 5 Corps commander

1 Cited in Urquhart, *Arthur Currie,* p. 146.

2 Richard M. Watt, *Dare Call It Treason* (New York, 1963), p. 173.

3 Blake, *Haig's Papers,* p. 225.

4 P.A.C., Perley Papers, Perley to War Office, 12 June 1917.

5 *Ibid.,* Perley to Borden, 9 June 1917.

6 *Ibid.*

7 *Ibid.,* Borden to Perley, 13 June 1917.

8 P.A.C., Borden Papers, Macdonnell to Borden, 14 December 1934.

9 Beaverbrook Papers, Hughes to Aitken, 28 May 1916.

10 P.A.C., C.P. Currie Diary, 10 June 1917.

11 P.A.C., Perley Papers, Perley to Borden, 15 June 1917.

12 P.A.C., C.P. Currie to McGillicudy, n.d.

13 Currie Diary, cited in Urquhart, *Arthur Currie,* p. 163.

14 Morton, *Peculiar Politics,* p. 122.

15 P.A.C., Perley Papers, Borden to Perley, 13 June 1917.

16 Morton, *Peculiar Politics,* p. 234, n. 58.

17 *Ibid.,* p. 122.

18 P.A.C., C.P. Currie to McGillicudy, n.d.

19 Urquhart, *Arthur Currie,* p. 164.
20 *Ibid.*
21 Swettenham, *To Seize the Victory,* p. 174.
22 P.A.C., Borden Papers, vol. 72, file 10-8-7, Currie to Perley, 4 August 1917.
23 Morton, *Peculiar Politics,* p. 124.
24 *Ibid.*
25 *Ibid.,* p. 122.
26 *Ibid.,* p. 121, Urquhart, *Arthur Currie,* p. 164.
27 Urquhart, *Arthur Currie,* p. 165.
28 P.A.C., C.P. Currie to Forsythe, 25 June 1917.
29 P.A.C., Borden Papers, vol. 361, Matson to Borden, 28 October 1914.
30 Brown and Morton, 'Apotheosis.'
31 Morton, *Peculiar Politics,* p. 123.
32 P.A.C., Perley Papers, Perley to Borden, 21 July 1917.
33 *Ibid.,* Borden to Perley, 18 July 1917. Urquhart papers, Currie to Forsyth, 25 June 1917; J.H.P. to D.W. Oliver, 17 June 1930.
34 Brown and Morton, 'Apotheosis,' p. 61.
35 *Ibid.*
36 Morton, *Peculiar Politics,* p. 123.
37 *Ibid.,* p. 124.
38 P.A.C., First Army Order, G.S., 658/1(a), 7 July 1917. Appendix I/I to W.D., G.S., Cdn. Corps., July 1917. First Army Order, 137, 10 July 1917, Appendix I/2.
39 P.A.C., C.P. Currie Diary, 10 July 1917.
40 Letter, Dominick Graham to author, June 1986.
41 P.A.C., First Army Order, G.W. 658/13(a), 13 July 1917, Appendix I/I.
42 P.A.C., Cdn. Corps Operation Order 139, 17 July 1917. Appendix II/10 to W.D., G.S., Cdn. Corps, July 1917.
43 For a detailed account of the battle, see Nicholson, *CEF,* p. 297.
44 P.A.C., C.P. Currie Diary, 18 August 1917. German accounts later revealed that five German divisions were engaged by the Canadians at Hill 70. Nicholson, *CEF,* p. 292n.
45 Von Kuhl, *Der Weltkrieg 1917–1918,* ii, p. 123, quoted in Nicholson, *CEF,* p. 297.
46 Currie estimated Canadian casualties at 8,000 in the period between 15 and 23 August, while he thought German losses to be between 25,000 and 30,000. P.A.C., C.P. Currie to Underhill, 17 September 1920. A later postwar calculation put the Canadian losses at 10,746 to the months of July and August. Duguid, *The Canadian Forces in the Great War* (Ottawa, 1946), p. 6.
47 W.S. Churchill, *The World Crisis* (New York, 1929), IV, p. 1177.
48 John Terraine, *Douglas Haig: The Educated Soldier* (London, 1963), p. 337; *The Road to Passchendaele: The Flanders Offensive of 1917: A Study in Inevitability*

(London, 1977). Brig.-Gen. Sir James E. Edmonds, *Military Operations France and Belgium: 1917, June 7–November 10. Messines and Third Ypres (Passchendaele)* (London, 1948), pp. 177–9.

49 Haig's intelligence chief, Brigadier-General Charteris, claimed that it was the wettest August for thirty years. Terraine, *Douglas Haig,* p. 348.

50 Nicholson, *CEF,* p. 308.

51 P.A.C., 2nd Army Operation Order No. 4, 1 September 1917, Appendix XXI to Military Operations: 1917 June-November 10.

52 Terraine, *Douglas Haig,* p. 334; *The Road to Passchendaele,* p. 203.

53 C.E. Calwell, *Field Marshal Sir Henry Wilson* (London, 1927), II, p. 14.

54 Churchill, *World Crisis,* p. 818.

55 Leon Wolff, *In Flanders Fields* (New York, 1958), pp. 157–8.

56 *Ibid.*

57 Edmonds, *Military Operations France and Belgium: 1917, June 7–November 10,* pp. 325–6.

58 *Ibid.,* p. 327.

59 *Mein Kriegstagebuch,* II, p. 271, cited in Falls, *The Great War.*

60 P.A.C., C.P. Currie Diary, 3–6 October 1917.

61 P.A.C., C.P. Currie to Paterson, 8 March 1920.

62 P.A.C., C.P. Currie to Underhill, 17 September 1920.

63 *Ibid.,* Currie to Livesay, 26 January 1933, Blake, *Haig's Papers,* p. 257.

64 Nicholson, *CEF,* p. 312.

65 *Ibid.,* Currie to Beattie, 8 February 1929.

66 C.B.C., 'In Flanders Fields,' program 10, p. 2.

67 *Ibid.*

68 Nicholson, *CEF,* p. 313.

69 Urquhart, *Arthur Currie,* p. 175.

70 P.A.C., Morrison Papers, 'Operations of the Canadian Corps during October 1917,' p. 2.

71 Nicholson, *CEF,* p. 313.

72 Terraine, *Douglas Haig,* p. 369.

73 Nicholson, *CEF,* p. 313.

74 Terraine, *Douglas Haig,* p. 369.

75 A.G.L. McNaughton, 'The Development of Artillery in the Great War,' *Canadian Defence Quarterly,* VI, No.2 (January 1929), pp. 162–8.

76 P.A.C., C.P., Currie to Underhill, 17 September 1920.

77 Seely, *Adventure,* p. 272.

78 P.A.C., Cdn. Corps to Second Army, 'Passchendaele–Causes of Success and Failure,' 20 November 1917, Appendix to W.D., G.S., Cdn. Corps, November 1917.

79 Nicholson, *CEF,* p. 314.

80 Churchill, *World Crisis*, p. 821.
81 Nicholson, *CEF*, p. 320.
82 P.A.C., 'Instructions for Offensive No. 2,' 20 October 1917, Appendix to W.D., G.S., 3rd Cdn. Div., October 1917. Nicholson, *CEF*, p. 318.
83 Nicholson, *CEF*, p. 319.
84 *Ibid.*, p. 323.
85 *Ibid.*, p. 324.
86 W.A. Steel. 'Wireless Telegraphy in the Canadian Corps in France,' *Canadian Defence Quarterly*, July 1930, p. 462.
87 Leon Wolff claims that the Canadians attacked 'in a typical cold rain' (p. 22), but on questions of weather Nicholson's account is invariably accurate. 'The attack was launched under a clear sky that later became cloudy but shed no heavy rain' (p. 324).
88 *Ibid.*
89 *Ibid.*, p. 325.
90 Terraine, *Douglas Haig*, p. 345.
91 Nicholson, *CEF*, p. 326.
92 Wolff, *Flanders Fields*, p. 229.
93 Jay Luvaas, 'The First British Official Historians,' *Military Affairs*, XXVI (Summer, 1962), p. 56.
94 Wolff, *Flanders Fields*, p. 241.
95 Terraine, *Douglas Haig*, p. 337.
96 Wolff, *Flanders Fields*, p. 233.
97 Edmonds, *Military Operations France and Belgium: 1917, June 7–November 10*, p. 361.
98 Nicholson, *CEF*, pp. 329–30.
99 Hanson, W. Baldwin, *World War I* (New York, 1962), p. 103.
100 Falls, *The Great War*, p. 304.
101 C.B.C., 'In Flanders Fields,' program 14, p. 11.
102 *Ibid.*, p. 12.
103 Lloyd George, *Memoirs*, VI, pp. 3422–3.
104 Edmonds, *Short History*, p. 35.
105 C.E.W. Bean, *Anzac to Amiens: A Shorter History of the Australian Fighting Services in the First World War* (Canberra, 1952), p. 458.
106 Lloyd George, *Memoirs*, VI, pp. 3423–4.
107 Lloyd George substantiates the case, especially in regard to Monash, who was 'the most resourceful general in the whole of the British Army,' but he implies that the same would have been true for any number of other civilian soldiers, including Currie. Of Monash he flatly states that 'Professional soldiers would hardly be expected to advertise the fact that the greatest strategist in the army was a civilian when war began and that they were being surpassed by a man who had not received of their advantages in training and teaching' (*ibid.*, pp. 3524, 3382).

108 The establishment of the permanent force at the outbreak of war called for only 247 officers in the entire dominion. Director Canadian Army Historical Section to Author, 15 February 1962.

109 Major-General H. Essame, who fought the battle of Passchendaele as a subaltern, claims that by the end of July 1917, when his battalion entered the Passchendaele fight, there were only thirty of the original 1,025 members of his battalion surviving. 'Second Lieutenants Unless Otherwise Stated,' *Military Review,* XLIV (May 1964), p. 91. Unfortunately the figures for a really meaningful comparison with Canadian battalions do not exist, but a comparison of percentages is at least suggestive. If Essame's figures are correct, his battalion, which he indicates had had a typical casualty record, suffered approximately 97 per cent casualties to its original complement. Its total casualties, of course, would be much higher, because many reinforcements had been killed or wounded. In comparison, the total Canadian casualty record by the end of July 1917, which can be calculated very roughly from the total number of soldiers sent to France (244,898) and the total number of casualties (the total of monthly strengths in France minus the total sent to France, i.e., $2,159,845 - 244,898 = 1,908,947$), was approximately 87 per cent. Though these figures are subject to challenge, they do suggest that a substantially higher proportion of original officers and men survived 1915 and 1916 in the Canadian forces than in the British Army.

110 P.A.C., C.P. Currie to Nelson, 9 December 1925.

111 H.G. Wells, *Outline of History,* quoted in Wolff, *Flanders Fields,* p. 239.

112 One example of this sort of issue was the Canadian preference for collar harness rather than British general-issue breast harness for draught horses. Canadian teamsters came to think that British generals were fools for not knowing that horses could pull better in a collar. What the men overlooked was that the breast harness was cheaper, easily adjusted to any horse, and more readily repaired than the more sophisticated collar, which had to be fitted to each horse. Other men became dedicated to a general 'because he spoke to me at once,' or raged that 'he never returned my salute.'

113 P.A.C., Papineau Papers, T.M. Papineau to B. Fox, 5 August 1915.

114 P.A.C., C.P. Currie to Beattie, 8 February 1920.

115 *Ibid.*

116 *Ibid.,* Currie to Livesay, 24 October 1919.

CHAPTER 6 A new doctrine

1 P.A.C., C.P., Currie to McGreer, n.d., Currie Diary, 22 November 1917.

2 Nicholson, *CEF,* p. 221.

3 *Debates, House of Commons, 1917,* II, p. 1597.

4 P.A.C., Rowell Papers, Vol. 3, Currie to Rowell, 28 June 1917.

5 P.A.C., Perley Papers. Vol. 9, Borden to Perley, 18 June 1917.
6 *Debates, House of Commons, 1917*, III, p. 2770.
7 A.M.J. Hyatt, 'Sir Arthur Currie and Conscription: A Soldier's View,' *Canadian Historical Review*, L (September 1969), pp. 295–6.
8 P.A.C., C.P., Currie to Creelman, 30 November 1917. It is interesting that Currie's views in the autumn of 1917 were almost identical to those that J.F.C. Fuller expressed in 1935. 'The fact was,' wrote Fuller, 'that from the start of the War the Government had suffered from cold feet. It did not so much fear the enemy as its electors. It kept them blind to the true facts and established the strictest censorship more for political than for military reasons.' *The Army in My Time* (London, 1935), p. 146.
9 P.A.C., C.P., Currie to Perley, 3 December 1917.
10 P.A.C., C.P., Currie Diary, 4 December 1917.
11 *Ibid.*, Currie to Perley, 10 December 1917.
12 *Ibid.*
13 Borden, *Memoirs*, II, pp. 859, 971. See also, P.A.C., Turner Papers, Vol. 7, 'Memorandum for Sir Edward Kemp,' by Walter Gow, 26 October 1918; Turner to Kemp, 4 November 1918.
14 P.A.C., Turner Papers, Vol. 8, Currie to Perley, 4 August 1917.
15 P.A.C., C.P., Currie to Daly, 26 October 1918; Currie to Fraser, 7 December 1918; Currie to McGillicudy, n.d.
16 P.A.C., Turner papers, Vol. 8, Turner to Kemp, 3 April 1918; C.P., Supreme Court of Ontario, transcript.
17 Since practically none of Simm's papers has survived, the evidence for this interpretation is nearly all inferential. But the inferences are pointed and are confirmed by the testimony of contemporaries, particularly General McNaughton and the Hon. Allistair Fraser. McNaughton Interview. Letter, Fraser to Author, 5 July 1962. See also, P.A.C., C.P., Currie Diary, 10 June 1917; Currie to Fraser, 7 December 1918; Fraser to Currie, 9 September 1921. Turner papers, Currie to Perley, 4 August 1917. The fact that Currie always disliked Beaverbrook has already been mentioned. The latter's work at the War Records Office merely intensified Currie's sentiments. In October 1918 Currie observed that 'the absolute rot put out by the Canadian War Records is astounding.' P.A.C., C.P., Currie to Daly, 26 October 1918. Part of this antipathy is perhaps explained by the attitude which J.F.C. Fuller claims all soldiers shared towards war correspondents. 'The panegyrics of the newspaper correspondents ... nauseate him (the soldier) more than they flatter him ... This sensation-mongering class was despised by the soldier.' *The Army in My Time*, p. 141.
18 *Canadian Annual Review, 1917*, p. 521. See also, L.G. Thomas, *The Liberal Party in Alberta: A History of Politics in the Province of Alberta 1905–1921* (Toronto, 1959), pp. 179–82.
19 Edmonds, *Short History*, pp. 276–7.
20 Morton, *Peculiar Politics*, p. 139.

21 Quoted in Edmonds, *Short History,* pp. 276–7.
22 P.A.C., C.P., Currie to Daly, 16 October 1918.
23 Historical Section Files, McNaughton to Nicholson, 15 April 1961.
24 Edmonds, *Military Operations, 1918,* I, p. 50–5.
25 The War Office had consistently pressed to have the 5th Division sent to France. The decision that it should remain in England and assume the role of home defence was a compromise between this view and the attitude of the Canadian Overseas Headquarters, which felt that five divisions in France could not be kept up to strength. See, Nicholson, *CEF,* p. 231.
26 P.A.C., C.P., Currie to Loomis, 27 January 1918.
27 P.A.C., C.P., Currie to McGillicudy, n.d.
28 Cyril Falls, *A Hundred Years of War 1850–1950* (New York, 1962), pp. 238–9. P.M.H. Lucas, *L'Evolution des Idées tactiques en France et en Allemagne pendant la guerre de 1914–1918* (Paris, 1932), pp. 215–23.
29 Terraine, *Douglas Haig,* pp. 448–9.
30 Lucas, *L'Evolution des Idées tactiques,* pp. 299–300.
31 P.A.C., C.P., Currie to Nelson, 9 December 1925.
32 P.A.C., C.P., Currie to Loomis, 27 January 1918.
33 P.A.C., C.P., Currie to McGillicudy, n.d.
34 P.A.C., C.P., Currie to Loomis, 27 January 1918.
35 *Ibid.*
36 P.A.C., C.P., Currie Diary, 5 February 1918.
37 P.A.C., C.P., Currie to Minister O.M.F.C., 7 February 1918.
38 *Ibid.*
39 *Ibid.*
40 General E.L.M. Burns, a Second World War Canadian commander, argues that unnecessarily increasing staffs impairs tactical efficiency. In the Second World War, according to Burns, 'considerations of national prestige were the most important among the reasons for the creation' of a Canadian army. He states that the Canadian formations in the later war were probably better trained that those in the First War, but according to the testimony of 'allies and enemies ... the Canadian Corps of World War I was unsurpassed in the Allied Armies for efficiency. The Canadian Army in World War II was not relatively better.' *Manpower in the Canadian Army 1939–1945* (Toronto, 1956), pp. 26, 28, 33.
41 P.A.C., C.P., Currie to Minister, 7 February 1918.
42 P.A.C., Argyll House Files, 0–210–33. P.A.C., C.P., 'Organisation of the Canadian Corps in the Field,' n.d.
43 *Ibid.*
44 G.S. Hutchinson, *Machine Guns, Their History and Tactical Employment* (London, 1938), pp. 314–15. Nicholson, *CEF,* p. 383.
45 *Ibid.,* p. 363.

46 Hanson Baldwin, *World War I* (New York, 1962), p. 141.

47 Terraine, *Douglas Haig*, p. 414.

48 Baldwin, *World War I*, p. 146.

49 A.W. Currie, 'Interim Report on Operations 1918,' in *Report of the Minister Overseas Military Forces of Canada, 1918*, p. 112.

50 McNaughton Interview, 27 March 1963.

51 Currie, *Report*, p. 112.

52 P.A.C., Kemp Papers, Currie to Lawrence, 27 March 1918.

53 P.A.C., Kemp Papers, Kemp to Derby, 19 March 1918.

54 This revelation came some three months after the event, when the Canadian minister of militia – according to Haig a 'well-meaning but second-rate' individual – visited Haig's headquarters. When Mewburn mentioned the desire of the Canadians to fight under the Canadian Corps, Haig exhibited one of his rare outbursts of temper. He informed Mewburn that the 'British army alone and unaided by Canadian troops withstood the first terrific blow made by 80 German Divisions,' and noted that when he was through, Mewburn had become a 'changed individual.' Blake, *Haig's Papers*, p. 319.

55 P.A.C., C.P., Currie Diary, 11 April 1918.

56 *Ibid.*

57 On the first day of March Currie recorded: 'We are holding a 10 mile front with two divisions – altogether too much but owing to lack of men in the British Army it cannot be helped. I am told we have 430,000 men in Mesopotamia, what a splendid place for a reserve!' *Ibid.*, 31 March 1918.

58 *Ibid.*, 14 April 1918.

59 Blake, *Haig's Papers*, pp. 303–4.

60 Lord Beaverbrook, *Men and Power, 1917–1918* (London, 1956), p. xvii.

61 B.H. Liddell Hart, *Reputations, Ten Years After* (Boston, 1928), p. 290.

62 Blake, *Haig's Papers*, p. 290.

63 'Douglas Haig's Diary,' *Canadian Army Journal*, III (July, 1953), p. 108.

64 Borden, *Memoirs*, II, p. 77.

65 P.A.C., Kemp Papers, Milner to Kemp, 6 May 1918.

66 J.H. Boraston, *Sir Douglas Haig's Dispatches* (London, 1919), p. 110.

67 P.A.C., Borden Papers, Secret Memorandum, 15 June 1918.

68 P.A.C., C.P., Currie to Borden, 26 November 1918.

69 P.A.C., Borden Papers, Secret Memorandum, 15 June 1918.

CHAPTER 7 The last phase

1 Dorothy McMurray, 'Only Grandfathers Wore Beards' (n.p., Canadian War Museum Library), p. 7.

2 Wilfred Benton Kerr, *Arms and the Maple Leaf: Memories of Canada's Corps 1918* (Seaforth, Ont., 1943), p. 28. See also Wilfred Benton Kerr, *Shrieks and Crashes Being Memories of Canada's Corps 1917* (Toronto, 1929), pp. 40–1.

3 Urquhart, *Arthur Currie*, p. 223.

4 Kerr, *Arms and the Maple Leaf*, p. 28.

5 C.B.C., 'In Flanders Fields,' program 11, p. 15.

6 *Ibid.*, p. 12.

7 *Ibid.*, p. 13.

8 Kerr, *Arms and the Maple Leaf*, p. 45.

9 G.S. Hutchinson, *Machine Guns* (London, 1938), pp. 314–15. H.T. Logan and M.R. Levy, 'History of the Canadian Machine Gun Corps, C.E.F.' (August 1919), manuscript in three volumes held by Canadian Army Historical Section, I, pp. 15–16.

10 P.A.C., C.P., Currie to McGillicudy, n.d.

11 H.F.H. Hertzberg, 'The Re-organization of the Engineering Troops of a Canadian Division–Great War, 1914–1918,' *Canadian Defence Quarterly*, I (July, 1924), p. 41.

12 The units disbanded included four pioneer battalions and two tunnelling companies.

13 P.A.C., C.P., Currie to McGillicudy, n.d.

14 Currie, *Report*, pp. 122–3.

15 *Ibid.*, p. 124.

16 *Ibid.*

17 *Ibid.*, pp. 123–4.

18 *Ibid.*

19 S.F. Wise, *Canadian Airmen and the First World War: The Official History of the Royal Canadian Air Force* (Toronto, 1980), p. 596.

20 P.A.C., Urquhart Papers, Currie to Turner, 3 November 1917.

21 P.A.C., C.P., Currie to W.G. Morden, 4 May 1918.

22 Hertzberg, 'Reorganisation of the Engineering Troops,' pp. 41ff.

23 Currie, *Report*, p. 124.

24 For a sample of views on Monash see Lloyd George, *Memoirs*, VI, pp. 3368, 3382. B.H. Liddell Hart, *Through the Fog of War* (New York, 1938), pp. 147–8. Sir Frederick Maurice, *The Life of General Lord Rawlinson of Trent* (London, 1928), pp. 217, 220. W.L. Morton, *The Kingdom of Canada* (Toronto, 1963), p. 422. Terraine, *Douglas Haig*, pp. 448–50.

25 Cited in Terraine, *Douglas Haig*, pp. 448–9.

26 Falls, *The Great War*, p. 373, states quite flatly that 'the main blow was to be struck by the Canadian Corps,' while Nicholson, *CEF*, p. 395, states that 'To the Canadian Corps fell the responsibility of striking the main blow on the Fourth Army's right.' Technically Nicholson's account is accurate, but since

the Australian attack is barely mentioned in his statement, one gets the impression that the Canadian effort was considerably more important. The relevant operation orders for the attack, attached to W.D., G.S., Cdn. Corps, July and August 1918, indicate that the interpretation given above – the main effort was by British Fourth Army, that is, by both the Australian and the Canadian Corps – is correct. This is also the interpretation found in the Australian official history. C.E.W. Bean, *The A.I.F. in France, 1918*, VI (Sydney, 1942), pp. 483–90.

27 E. von Ludendorff, *My War Memories* (London, 1919), II p. 679.

28 Currie, *Report*, p. 127.

29 Bean, *A.I.F. in France*, VI, p. 484.

30 *Ibid.*, p. 485. V. pp. 25–32.

31 Terraine, *Douglas Haig*, p. 454. According to Bean, 'the average infantry strength of the Australian divisions of July 31 (1918) was 10,561. That of the 46 active British divisions in France was 9,389; that of the Canadian Divisions 12, 777.' *A.I.F. in France*, VI, p. 484n.

32 A.R.M. Lower, *Colony to Nation*, p. 456. D.G. Creighton, *Dominion of the North* (Boston, 1944), p. 451.

33 Bean, *A.I.F. in France*, VI, p. 464. Cf. Maurice, *The Life of Rawlinson*, p. 224.

34 Currie, *Report*, p. 129. W.A. Steel, 'Wireless in the Canadian Corps in France,' *Canadian Defence Quarterly*, VI (October, 1930), p. 84.

35 Nicholson, *CEF*, p. 389.

36 P.A.C., C.P., Corps Commander's Log, 8–14 August 1919.

37 Ludendorff, *My War Memories*, II, p.679.

38 Currie, *Report*, p. 28.

39 W.W. Murray, *The History of the 2nd Canadian Battalion in the Great War 1914–1919* (Ottawa, 1947), p. 256.

40 P.A.C., 'L.C. Instructions No. 2,' 4 August 1918. Appendix II–72 to W.D., G.S., Cdn. Corps, August 1918.

41 Cited in Terraine, *Douglas Haig*, p. 359.

42 Currie, *Report*, p. 138.

43 Falls, *The Great War*, p. 375.

44 Currie, *Report*. p. 138.

45 *Ibid.*, p. 139. Between 8 and 13 August the 4th Tank Brigade attached to the Canadian Corps lost ninety-nine fighting tanks, eighty from enemy fire and nineteen from breakdowns. Nicholson, *CEF*, pp. 420–1.

46 P.A.C., C.P., Currie to Fourth Army, 13 August 1918.

47 Terraine, *Douglas Haig*, p. 459.

48 Bean, *A.I.F. in France*, VI, p. 716.

49 P.A.C., 'Special Order of Corps Commander to Canadian Corps,' 13 August 1918. Appendix to W.D., G.S., Cdn. Corps, August 1918.

50 Falls, *The Great War,* p. 373.
51 McNaughton Interview.
52 Arthur Lower, *Colony to Nation* (Toronto, 1957), p. 460.
53 Monash, *Australian Victories in France in 1918* (New York, n.d.) p. 141.
54 Nicholson, *CEF,* pp. 419, 460.
55 Currie, *Report,* p. 184.
56 Liddell Hart, *History of the World War,* p. 567.
57 Essame, 'Second Lieutenants Unless Otherwise Stated,' p. 92.
58 *Ibid.*
59 Kerr, *Arms and the Maple Leaf,* p. 29.
60 C.B.C., 'Flander's Fields,' no. 11, p. 13.
61 *Ibid.*
62 *Ibid.*
63 Currie, *Report,* p. 47.
64 McNaughton Interview.
65 Hutchinson, *Machine Guns,* p. 224.
66 P.A.C., C.P., Currie Diary, 24–28 August 1918.
67 Hutchinson, *Machine Guns,* p. 175.
68 Sir Andrew Macphail, *Official History of the Canadian Forces in the Great War 1914–1919; The Medical Services* (Ottawa, 1925), p. 387. A.E. Snell, *The C.A.M.C. With the Canadian Corps During the Last Hundred Days of the Great War* (Ottawa, 1924), p. 207.
69 Currie, *Report,* p. 174.
70 P.A.C., C.P., Currie Diary, 20 October 1918.
71 *Ibid.,* 1 November 1918.
72 P.A.C., 4th Cdn. Div. Report on Valenciennes, Appendix 30, 'Report on Operations October 27th to November 2nd, 1918 – 50th Canadian Battalion.'
73 P.A.C., C.P., Currie to Daly, 26 October 1918.
74 Desmond Morton, 'Kicking and Complaining: Demobilization Riots in the Canadian Expeditionary Force, 1918–19,' *Canadian Historical Review,* LXI (September 1980), p. 335.
75 *Ibid.,* p. 336. P.A.C., C.P., Currie to Kemp, 6 November 1918.
76 P.A.C., C.P., Currie to Kemp, 6 November 1918. Currie Diary, 6 November 1918. Currie to R.H. Macklin, 4 October 1918.
77 P. von Hindenburg, *Out of My Life* (London, 1920), p. 430. Ludendorff, *My War Memories,* II, p. 723.
78 P.A.C., W.D., P.P.C.L.I., R.C.R., 11 November 1918.
79 P.A.C., Appendix II-33 to W.D., G.S., Cdn. Corps, November 1918, Message Log, Corps Commander, 11 November 1918.
80 Borden, *Memoirs,* II, p. 865.
81 P.A.C., C.P., Currie Diary, 11 November 1918.

CHAPTER 8 Inspector-general

1 *Debates, House of Commons,* 4 March 1919.
2 P.A.C., C.P., Currie Diary, 1 December 1918.
3 Morton, 'Kicking and Complaining,' p. 337.
4 C.B.C., 'In Flanders Fields,' program 16, p. 21.
5 P.A.C., C.P., Currie Diary, 26 November, 1 December 1918.
6 C.B.C., 'In Flanders Fields,' program 16, p. 21.
7 Morton, 'Kicking and Complaining,' p. 339.
8 P.A.C., Kemp Papers, Currie to Kemp, 23 November 1918.
9 Morton, 'Kicking and Complaining,' p. 344.
10 *Ibid.,* p. 343.
11 Currie, *Report,* p. 194.
12 P.A.C., C.P., Currie Diary, 1 January 1919.
13 Nicholson, *CEF,* p. 531.
14 P.A.C., C.P., Currie Diary, 1 and 3 January 1919.
15 *Ibid.,* 12 February 1919.
16 Terraine, *Douglas Haig,* p. 364 *n.*
17 *Ibid.*
18 P.A.C., C.P., Currie to Fraser, 7 December 1918.
19 Currie's correspondent was Alistair Fraser, who subsequently became lieutenant-governor of Nova Scotia. In 1917 and 1918 Fraser had been Currie's aide-de-camp. Unfortunately the letters from Currie to Kemp and Rowell could not be found in the Public Archives.
20 *Debates, House of Commons,* 4 March 1919.
21 *Ibid.,* 14 March 1919.
22 Colonel Urquhart gives a very different impression, which is difficult to believe in view of Currie's correspondence about Turner.
23 P.A.C., C.P., Currie to Fraser, 7 December 1919.
24 P.A.C., Turner Papers, Turner to Kemp, 3 April 1919.
25 *Debates, House of Commons,* 7 July 1919.
26 P.A.C., C.P., Currie to Sclater, 29 June 1920.
27 P.A.C., C.P., Currie Diary, 10 July 1919.
28 Cited in Urquhart, *Arthur Currie,* p. 284.
29 *Debates, House of Commons,* 29 September 1919.
30 *Ibid.*
31 Roger Graham, *Arthur Meighen, A Biography: The Door of Opportunity,* Vol. 1 (Toronto, 1960), p. 273.
32 P.A.C., C.P., Currie to Farmar, 5 January 1920.
33 P.A.C., C.P., Currie to Dyer, 2 January 1920.

34 Quoted in Urquhart, *Arthur Currie,* p. 284.
35 *Ibid.*
36 P.A.C., C.P., Currie to Farmar, 5 January 1920.
37 *Ibid.*
38 *Ibid.*
39 P.A.C., C.P., Currie to Fraser, 31 August 1920, Currie to Winslow, 5 May 1920.
40 P.A.C., C.P., Currie to MacBrien, 13 December 1919.
41 *Ibid.*
42 *Ibid.,* 12 April 1920.
43 P.A.C., C.P., Currie to Meighen, 5 August 1920, Currie to Guthrie, 5 August 1920.
44 P.A.C., C.P., Currie to Webber 19 January 1920.
45 Beaverbrook Library, Lloyd George Papers, Churchill to Lloyd George.
46 P.A.C., Borden Papers, 'Memorandum Respecting the late Sir Arthur Currie,' 13 August 1934.
47 Urquhart, *Arthur Currie,* pp. 282–3.
48 P.A.C., C.P., Currie to Paterson, 24 February 1920.
49 P.A.C., C.P., Currie to Radcliffe, 6 July 1920.
50 McNaughton Interview, Urquhart, *Arthur Currie,* p. 284.
51 P.A.C., C.P., Currie to Urquhart, 7 June 1920.

CHAPTER 9 The old soldier

1 The Currie papers at the Public Archives and at McGill contain many such letters.
2 P.A.C., C.P., Currie to Clowes and Sons, 31 July 1922. See also, Currie to Hyde, 27 July 1921 and Currie to Brutinel, 10 June 1925.
3 *Ibid.,* Currie to Watson, 11 December 1920.
4 Roger Graham, *Arthur Meighen, A Biography: and Fortune Fled* (Toronto, 1963), II, p. 265.
5 P.A.C., Borden Papers, 'Memo re General Currie's Remarks to the delegates to the Tax Conference and Civil Servants Research Institute of Canada, September 11th, 1924.'
6 P.A.C., C.P., Currie to Richardson, 6 January 1924.
7 *Ibid.,* Currie to King, 1 September 1923.
8 Cited in R.C. Featherstonhaugh, *McGill University at War, 1914–1918, 1918–1945* (Montreal, 1947).
9 Hugh MacLennan, ed., *McGill: The Story of a University* (London, 1960), p. 100.
10 Interviews with ex-McGill students. See also, Sir Andrew Macphail, 'Sir Arthur Currie: The Value of a Degree,' *Queen's Quarterly,* XLI (Spring, 1934), pp. 1–19.

11 Urquhart, *Arthur Currie,* pp. 299–349.
12 *Evening Guide,* Port Hope, Ontario, 13 June 1937.
13 Macphail, 'Sir Arthur Currie,' pp. 1–19.
14 W.T.R. Preston, *My Generation of Politics and Politicians* (Toronto, 1927). See Morton, *Peculiar Politics,* pp. 139–41, 147–8.
15 For a more detailed account of the Currie trial see Swettenham, *To Seize The Victory.*
16 *Evening Guide,* 13 June 1927.
17 Swettenham, *To Seize the Victory,* p. 18. P.A.C., C.P., trial transcript. See also C.B. Topp, 'The Cease Fire at Mons November 11, 1918,' The *Legionary,* 43 (November 1968), pp. 8–10.
18 Quoted in Urquhart, *Arthur Currie,* p. 321.
19 *Ibid.*
20 *Ibid.,* p. 330.
21 *Ibid.*
22 P.A.C., Borden Papers, 'Memorandum respecting the late Sir Arthur Currie,' n.d.
23 Quoted in Urquhart, p. 326.
24 P.A.C., Borden Papers, 'Memorandum respecting the late Sir Arthur Currie,' n.d.
25 See Brown and Morton, 'Apotheosis.' See also Morton, *Peculiar Politics.*
26 General W.H.S. Macklin to author, 10 June 1962.
27 See Sweetenham, *To Seize the Victory,* and *McNaughton* (Toronto, 1968–9).
28 Cited in Ropp, *War in the Modern World,* p. 14.
29 Seeley, *Adventure,* p. 226.

Bibliographic note

Greater bibliographical detail can be obtained by consulting footnotes. Those interested in reading further on any aspect of Canadian military history now have an invaluable tool available in Owen Cooke, *The Canadian Military Experience 1867–1983: A Bibliography* (Ottawa, 1984). The best general histories are G.F.G. Stanley, *Canada's Soldiers: 1604–1954: A Military History of an Unmilitary People* (Toronto, 1954); and Desmond Morton, *Canada and War: A Military and Political History* (Toronto, 1981).

For the First World War one should begin with the official histories. Colonel G.W.L. Nicholson, *Canadian Expeditionary Force, 1914–1919: Official History of the Canadian Army in the First World War* (Ottawa, 1962) is the most comprehensive of these. Colonel A.F. Duguid, *Official History of the Canadian Forces in the Great War, 1914–1919* (Ottawa, 1938), Vol. I, covers a very short time period in great detail. Sir Andrew MacPhail's account, *Official History of the Canadian Forces in the Great War, 1914–1919: The Medical Services* (Ottawa, 1925), though opinionated, cannot be ignored. The most important background book on the war is Desmond Morton, *A Peculiar Kind of Politics: Canada's Overseas Ministry in the First World War* (Toronto, 1982). By far the best tactical study is Shelford Bidwell and Dominick Graham, *Fire Power: British Army Weapons and Theories of War 1904–1945* (London, 1982).

Works on Currie are few. Both Hugh M. Urquhart, *Arthur Currie: A Biography of a Great Canadian* (Toronto, 1950) and Daniel G. Dancocks, *Sir Arthur Currie: A Biography* (Toronto, 1985), obscure Currie's weaknesses.

Other works in which Currie figures prominently are John Swettenham, *To Seize the Victory: the Canadian Corps in Word War I* (Toronto, 1965); D.J. Goodspeed, *The Road Past Vimy: The Canadian Corps, 1914–1918* (Toronto, 1969); Herbert Wood, *Vimy* (Toronto, 1967); D.E. Macintyre, *Canada at Vimy* (Toronto, 1967). Currie wrote the section on the operations of the Last Hundred Days in *Report of the Ministry: Overseas Military Forces of Canada, 1918* (London, 1919). Two biographies on other men contain much about Currie: John Swettenham, *McNaughton* (Toronto, 1968-9); and Jeffery Williams, *Byng of Vimy: General and Governor General* (London, 1983).

Much can be learned from memoirs, though there are fewer Canadian accounts than might be expected. The following are particularly useful: Will R. Bird, *Ghosts Have Warm Hands* (Toronto, 1968); C.L. Flick, *Just What Happened: A Diary of the Mobilization of the Canadian Militia, 1914* (London, 1917); E.L.M. Burns, *General Mud: Memoirs of Two World Wars* (Toronto, 1970); Anonymous, *Unknown Soldiers, by One of Them* (New York, 1959).

Index